WITHDRAWN

HUMBLER FAITH,
BIGGER GOD

HUMBLER FAITH, BIGGER GOD

Finding a Story to Live By

SAMUEL WELLS

WILLIAM B. EERDMANS PUBLISHING COMPANY
GRAND RAPIDS, MICHIGAN

Wm. B. Eerdmans Publishing Co.
4035 Park East Court SE, Grand Rapids, Michigan 49546
www.eerdmans.com

© 2022 Samuel Wells
All rights reserved
Published 2022
Printed in the United States of America

28 27 26 25 24 23 22 1 2 3 4 5 6 7

ISBN 978-0-8028-7931-8

Library of Congress Cataloging-in-Publication Data

Names: Wells, Samuel, 1965– author.
Title: Humbler faith, bigger God : finding a story to live by / Samuel Wells.
Description: Grand Rapids, Michigan : William B. Eerdmans Publishing Company, [2022] | Summary: "A reframing of Christianity that portrays traditional belief and the response of skepticism as two rival stories and offers a third story that incorporates doubts and failures into a renewed understanding of Christian faith"—Provided by publisher.
Identifiers: LCCN 2021041070 | ISBN 9780802879318
Subjects: LCSH: Apologetics. | Christianity—Controversial literature. | Storytelling—Religious aspects—Christianity. | BISAC: RELIGION / Christian Theology / Apologetics | RELIGION / Christian Theology / General
Classification: LCC BT1103 .W45 2022 | DDC 239—dc23
LC record available at https://lccn.loc.gov/2021041070

For Lola and Harry

CONTENTS

PREFACE

I'M A PREACHER BEFORE I'M A WRITER. I'm grateful to James Ernest and David Bratt for watching a recording of my Easter Sunday 2020 sermon at St. Martin-in-the-Fields and seeing in it the embryo of a book, and then abiding as I pondered carefully how that could come to pass. I'm especially thankful for Ruth Taunt, who's made these chapters a personal pilgrimage and has, through comment and conversation, put me in touch with how deeply these questions matter. I'm grateful too to Steph Wells, who helped me identify what the book was really about. I'm glad for conversations with Octavia Stocker, without which one topic in particular would never have surfaced; with Frances Stratton, who was especially helpful with articulating the ten key questions; with Gabriella Noble, who added finishing touches; and with Karl Travis, who urged me on as he counted the days. Ray Barfield, Stanley Hauerwas, and Maureen Knudsen Langdoc have been cherished conversation partners throughout; the kind who say, "The manuscript's fine, but you can't publish it if you use that single word here and that phrase there." John Inge and Farley Lord kindly took time to read every word and make helpful, insightful, and encouraging comments: such readers' scrutiny is a precious gift to any writer.

I can't imagine this book outside of three contexts with which I'll always associate it. The first is the company of Jo, Laurie, and Steph

Wells, who contrived to make the desert of the pandemic bloom, and with whom I found blessing, peace, and space to think and write when all around was tense, troubled, and tearful. The book was born in the first lockdown, on long sunny spring days when the positives of the disruption still kept pace with the tragedy. It became a lifeline later in the year when the skies were granite gray and the mood was darker still.

The second context is the emerging Being With course, imagined with my colleague Sally Hitchiner. Devising, delivering, and developing the course together, and sharing training and participation with a cloud of witnesses in London, the United Kingdom, and across the world, made questions of faith more central to my ministry in 2020 than perhaps at any other time, and provided the practice to which writing this book offered the theory. I am grateful to everyone involved in this process for giving me so many experiences of grace.

The third context was of the extraordinary colleagues, congregation, and community with which I have been blessed at St. Martin-in-the-Fields. I believe in the church because of the solidarity, improvisation, resilience, and goodness I have witnessed—never more so than in 2020 in this place. I want to be a Christian because I want to keep the company of people like this—people who turn grief into possibility, trial into opportunity, sorrow into dancing. I write of Christianity with confidence because of the dignity I have seen in the face of adversity, the glory I have felt amid hardship, the love I have met despite pain. These people are a better argument for the truth of Christianity than this book could ever be.

Many of the themes in these chapters I've pursued elsewhere. The notion of essence and existence in chapter 1 is developed further in *Walk Humbly*. The relation of Jesus to suffering and evil in chapter 2 is considered in *Hanging by a Thread, A Nazareth Manifesto,* and *A Cross in the Heart of God,* while the distinction between *with* and *for* I consider in many books, originally in *Living without Enemies* and most succinctly in *With.* The notion of improvisation and the five-act play in chapter 3 is discussed at length in *Improvisation*. The intersection of the personal and the political addressed in chapter 4 arises in the US edition of *How Then Shall We Live?* where there is also discussion of LGBT+ issues in the church that expands the treatment in chapter 5. The prospect explored in chapter 6 of a better church arising from past failures is the subject of *A Future That's Bigger Than the Past*. The questions of peace and reconciliation addressed in chapter 7 are the subject of *Love Mercy*. The discussion of other faiths in chapter 8 revisits themes I have explored in *God's Companions* and *Incarnational Mission*. Issues of science and ecology that surface in chapter 9 gain further treatment in *Learning to Dream Again* and *Incarnational Ministry*. And the difficulty of trust, which is the subject of chapter 10, is the leitmotif of *Be Not Afraid*.

In the more likely event that this book leads the reader not to pursue my other publications but to find people who do a better job than me, the four extraordinarily different books that have influenced me the most are as follows. It turned out I began writing this book just after reading Tom Holland's *Dominion: How the Christian Revolution Remade the World* (New York: Basic Books, 2019), and I found Tom's research, argument, and illustration wonderfully compelling as a backdrop to my own project. I first read Stanley Hauerwas's *The Peaceable Kingdom: A Primer in Christian Ethics* thirty years ago. He'd be the last to consider it a book doing what this book sets out to do; but its chapter on Jesus I virtually committed to memory, and it worked on me as a powerful call to faith. The book was important for me because it so clearly recognized what was wrong with Christianity but still offered a constructive, intelligent faith: which is what I'm seeking to do here. It would be hard not to be stirred by David Bentley Hart's *Atheist Delusions: The Christian Revolution and Its Fashionable Enemies* (New Haven: Yale University Press, 2009): its erudition, humor, and polemical agility are second to none. If your concern is the challenge of the so-called New Atheists, it's the best book in the field. You want Hart on your team if you find yourself in an argument.

Finally, Vincent Donovan's *Christianity Rediscovered* (London: SCM, 2001) continues to be, for me, the most inspiring argument available for the practical workability of Christian faith.

The book is dedicated to two friends who've walked with me through many tender moments and great adventures. The kingdom of heaven is made of such as these.

INTRODUCTION

We live our life in stories, but it often takes a clash of stories, or a dramatic event that we can't reconcile with our sense of story, to realize it. Thus the covid-19 pandemic burst into the story the world thought it was in—reshaping that story with much greater attention to mortality, public cooperation, and disruption than almost anyone hitherto thought possible or necessary. And during the pandemic there was a constant struggle for story—an impatient need to feel near the end, a reluctance to recognize that things might get worse before they got better, a desire for heroes and rapid cures. Likewise, the Black Lives Matter movement highlighted that the story of America, of the world, was not, as conventionally told, everyone's story; it was still being told, too often and without censure, as a partial story for some and not others. Meanwhile the climate crisis repeatedly highlighted that the human story, let alone the planet's story, would not automatically continue—at least not without urgent action and a change of heart and lifestyle.

This is a book about stories. It recognizes a time, largely past, but not so long ago, when a story known as Christianity was widely understood, in the West, as a largely unquestioned story, or fundamental part of a cultural story, such that belief in its doctrines and trust in its ways were a normal, unproblematic default, and to call oneself a Christian was to subscribe to a reasonable, plausible, or beneficial structure of authority and morality. It appreciates that a rival story has emerged over the last 250 years, and particularly over the last 60 years, which could broadly be termed secular humanist, and which has changed the template on which trust and conviction rest. This story assumes that to follow a controversial figure from 2,000 years ago, and see him as the focal point for all reality and the face of forever, runs against today's conventional wisdom. Thus Christianity is shorn of its identity as a benign bedrock and now increasingly appears to be many less agreeable things—judgmental, small-minded, absurd, bigoted, foolish, and plain wrong. Just as Christianity once failed to realize it was a story but imagined itself to be normal, sane, and wise, so the rival story has come to consider itself in similar unreflective terms.

I do not lament this change. I believe it's largely good for Christianity. Why? Because many, perhaps most, of the criticisms the rival story levels at Christianity have been accurate, appropriate, and acute; and far more than most people realize, they're made up of arguments that had their origin in Christianity itself. So rather than treat the rival story as hostile and disrespectful, failing to honor Christianity's rightful place in society, I see the rival story as a stimulus to the renewal of Christianity, drawing it closer to its core tenets. This refiner's fire strips away wrong steps and unwise accretions, revealing what Christianity should have been all along: radical, courageous, and vulnerable, yet glorious, thrilling, and true.

This is a book equally for the person who has no background in Christianity, for the person coming from another faith tradition, for the Christian who is struggling with faith, and for a person giving Christianity another chance after disappointment, hurt, or disillusionment. Elsewhere I've talked of five kinds of people: seekers, the lapsed, those of no professed faith, those of other faiths, and the hostile. Each of these terms, with the possible exception of those of no professed faith, assume a story. I cannot hope to do justice to the intricacy of stories of those who read this book. But I hope that those who identify with any of these stories will find themselves respected here. There are plenty of reasons not to be a Christian, and yet I am one. And I believe the way to become one, or to remain one, is not to ignore or dismiss the reasonable and widely held convictions that run counter to Christianity but to work one's way through those convictions, receiving each as a gift of a critical friend, expressing gratitude for the insight and challenge they bring, being honest about where Christianity has gone wrong, and seeking a renewed, gentler, yet even more dynamic faith. The phrase I like to use is, "a humbler faith with a bigger God."

What I've done is taken what I understand to be the ten most substantial arguments against Christianity, turned them into hostile accusations—and then made those the titles of my ten chapters. I did this by talking in depth to people of different ages who find themselves a foot in and a foot out of faith, are sharply aware of the embarrassments of admitting to being involved with the church, are constantly reminded by friends and family members of the faith's perversions and eccentricities, and yet find themselves still drawn to something they welcome help articulating. Rather than start with what I believe Christianity to be and to mean, I've chosen to respond to its cultured despisers, and in the process, address lingering fears and concerns of those who wouldn't know where to put themselves on any spectrum of faith. It's turned out that of the ten chapter titles, five are complaints against God and five are protests about Christians and the church. While this was not by design, it seems an appropriate balance between theology and ethics, the faith and the practice of the faith.

It took me a long time to identify how each chapter was to be structured, but once I'd done so, I realized it was similar to the approach Thomas Aquinas took in his remarkable (and very lengthy) thirteenth-century *Summa theologica*. Thomas derived from the twelfth-century Andalusian Muslim scholar Ibn Rushd (often known as Averroes) a method of argument as follows: he starts with objections, then moves to a counterstatement, quoting established theological authorities, before articulating his own position and finally replying to objections. This rigorous method means he's able to place the traditional, the contrary, and his own position side by side and make the best case for each one. I have simplified Thomas's method: I start with the traditional account, then offer a rival account, before suggesting my own proposal. Readers familiar with my work will recognize the pattern of what in *Improvisation* I describe as overaccepting and regard as the key element in Christian ethics. Thus, when presented with the "offer" of the rival story (and the critique of the traditional story), I don't reject or try to pummel them into submission—but neither do I simply accept them: instead, I treat them as a gift and seek to overaccept them by taking them as stimulus to portray a larger story. In doing so I'm trying to model how Christians may engage both the hostility of critics and the hurt of those the church has let down. I'm seeking to combine the clarity of Aquinas with the tenderness of a pastor-theologian.

Thus each chapter begins with what I call the old, old story: a broadly traditional, orthodox Christianity. It then challenges that faith with the conventional, and plausible, arguments and evidence set against it. I do this because I want to recognize how Christianity has been flawed, not just in the application of its principles but sometimes in its expression of those principles themselves. The chapter then offers space for what I call the rival story—what an educated, rational, contemporary person would generally think. Of course, this story is a generalization, and in some cases I identify more than one rival story. But it's designed to set up a counterargument. I then pause to assess the validity and flaws of this rival story. The third part of each chapter is my opportunity to offer what I call a story to live by. This is my chance to express the territory covered in the first two sections, not in a defensive way that replies to objections one by one, seeking to uphold the old, old story and protect it from all criticism, but as a constructive vision for a renewed Christian faith. The chapter finishes by highlighting where this proposal differs from the traditional Christian and conventional secular positions.

It's possible that the structure proves to be the most helpful aspect of the book. That's because of the way it differs from the two more familiar ways of presenting the Christian faith in a book such as this. The first of these simply sets out the faith from scratch. This makes it very hard to explain why we should move from contemporary wisdom about deep truth and healthy living to a particular set of historical events two thousand years ago: in short, it's very hard to shift from reason to tradition. It also becomes hard to engage with a person's prior experience of Christianity, good, bad, or indifferent. It's an argument from anywhere. Such an argument tends to hide the degree to which it is in fact a particular story—and is likely to antagonize those who identify where that story originates and what it takes for granted, particularly if the reader feels excluded by any of those factors. Most of all, this approach makes it very difficult to disentangle what I call a faith to live by from what I call the old, old story. In areas where the church has manifestly got things wrong for a long time, and sometimes still has them wrong, this approach can't distinguish between what has long been believed and what the author is actually commending. The result is generally to avoid difficult subjects. Which leaves the reader feeling shortchanged.

The alternative familiar approach is a response to critics. But if that response makes no space to articulate a constructive alternative, it falls into the same trap as the "faith from scratch" model. To describe a humbler faith with a bigger God means both to confess the bewilderingly large number of the church's failings and to recognize how the church's articulation of its faith has in some respects failed to comprehend the full wonder of the mystery of God. The point is not to win an argument. It's to demonstrate that the challenges to the old, old story and the assertions of the rival story are in very many respects well founded. This enables each chapter to concentrate on affirming and encouraging and inspiring the reader to more wonderful and more dynamic convictions.

The heart of the book lies with the section in each chapter entitled "A Story to Live By." Much of the material here revisits my own published work. This is inevitable, because what I'm articulating are the conclusions I've reached over a lifetime and the arguments I've propounded across forty previous books. Having said that, it's not true to say this book constitutes an introduction to that straggly collection of publications: it highlights some of my most carefully honed convictions, but this format doesn't provide opportunity to proceed down all the avenues that have occupied my theological inquiries over the years. The style of these sections is deliberately more conversational and playful than that of the preceding sections: after all, I want to communicate that Christianity is about joy.

It will by now be clear that the notion of story plays a big part in the book. The book was written during the covid-19 pandemic, a time when story became extraordinarily important, because at every stage people were searching to understand what story they were in, where it was going, and where they featured in the story. It was concluded during the chaotic days of President Trump's last weeks in power, when it became evident that if you repeat a lie often enough, people will begin to believe it. Donald Trump's genius was to tell a story, invariably one of resentment, and locate his supporters within it. The claim that's crucial to this book is that we all construct our lives around, within, and out of stories—and that's at least as true of those who reject faith as of those who uphold it. The irony underlying my argument is that often those most critical of Christianity derive their reproof from convictions woven so deep into the Christian story that neither they nor those they accuse any longer realize it. The evaluation of respective stories is not so much about digging down to establish which one is based on the sounder facts (because there is no value-free fact that's not already part of a value-laden story); it's about which story enables us to live well.

The first three chapters address what I regard as the three most far-reaching challenges to Christianity: that it's all made up, that its God is a failure, and that its guidebook, the Bible, is unreliable, inaccurate, and sometimes immoral. Responding to these challenges gives me a chance to distinguish between eternal essence and temporal existence, and to identify Jesus as the aperture in the hourglass that connects the two. I take the opportunity to see suffering as a manifestation of the great mystery of death and to highlight the notion of God being with us as transcending our desire for God to be for us and fix our predicament. I move on to suggest ways to appreciate what the Bible is and does, rather than criticize it for not being things it never sets out to be. The next four chapters concern expressions of fury against the church, most of them entirely justified. Here I point out that human failure is not a sign of the falsehood of Christianity but of the need for repentance and for practices of reconciliation. Each of these challenges—on poverty, sexuality, overt oppression, and conflict—demands a renewal of Christianity, and in each case I try to articulate what that renewal might entail. The two subsequent chapters consider remaining "old chestnuts" of the field: other faiths and science. In both areas Christianity has often diminished itself by being overreaching in its claims or ungracious in its lack of humility. These are rival stories that can each stimulate a repristination of Christianity, not its dominance or submission. Finally I recognize that, for all the arguments that swirl around, the questions that matter are not about cerebral belief but about faithful trust, and in the last chapter I make a case for the grounds on which such trust may validly be founded.

The book concludes with a succinct summary of my constructive arguments, framed as a contemporary creed. I don't intend these words to displace what Christians have together confessed for centuries, and I have some misgivings about replacing a story with a series of propositions, but I want to extricate the reader from a mountain of argument and offer something one can, finally, say yes or no to. It doesn't pretend to be comprehensive, any more than the ancient creeds do. But I hope it gets to the heart of things. In it I substitute the word "trust" for the more conventional "believe." I do so because I think trust is the larger half of faith, and if there's one thing that sums up the challenge the church faces today, it's not the ebbing away of belief but the erosion of trust.

Faith in the end isn't a lone journey but a shared experience. So I've appended some materials to assist group discussion should the book prove useful for people to read together.

Those whose theological imaginations have been shaped as mine have— described variously as postliberal or ecclesial, immersed in the rhythms of liturgy, prayer, and pastoral care, seeking to be with the rejected and isolated, looking always to attend to the voices the church has invariably excluded—such people have tended not to write books like this. We've habitually said there's no argument, only example; no apologetics, only rhetoric; no first principles, only the life of a community in midstream; no foundation, only Jesus. I haven't changed my spots. But I'm aware of how such convictions, while humbly held, can appear arrogant or complacent. I'm also mindful that if Christians feel uncomfortable with some ways in which the faith is publicly aired, the only thing to do is to provide an alternative that is closer to their own convictions. Which is what this book seeks to be. The aim is to be inspiring, refreshing, honest, direct, persuasive, and transformative—while also generous, respectful, humble, and not overstated. Some areas remain mysteries, and it does no good to pretend otherwise.

In a recent inquirers' course, a participant pondered an account of Christ's death. The account related to the participant's own experience of being with others and being alone, and God's presence and absence. It concluded with the way Christ's spread-eagled hands are saying, "I have set you as a seal upon my arm, to show you love is stronger than death." Pondering her perplexity about what she'd been told about the cross a decade earlier, and the expansiveness of this new perspective, she broke down in front of the group and said, "Why did no one tell me this before?" This book is written for her, and many like her.

- 1 -

CRUTCH FOR THE DELUDED?

We begin with what we may call a frontal assault on Christianity: the claim that it's a fantasy, entirely invented, flying in the face of the facts of existence; that God is an imaginary friend. In fact, says this sweeping critique, there's nothing really there: it's a figment of the imagination. It's been created to console those who fear that life is meaningless and to encourage any who suspect that life is without purpose. There may be a social or instrumental use for Christianity, and it may have some emotional resonance, but as far as truth claims are concerned, it's basically nonsense.

The Old, Old Story and What's Wrong with It

The Standard Account

A broad account of Christianity might go like this. There was a small nation on the eastern shore of the Mediterranean, which we call Israel. It was made up of twelve tribes, but the northern ten tribes were destroyed in the eighth century BC. Only two tribes remained, based around the city of Jerusalem and its glorious temple. But at the start of the sixth century BC, the remnant of Israel, known as Judah, was destroyed and its ruling class was transported five hundred miles away to Babylon.

In Babylon the exiles reflected profoundly on their history and identity. They wrote down stories of how they had once been in slavery in Egypt and how under Moses they'd been brought to freedom. They recalled accounts of how at Mount Sinai Moses had met the God who had brought Israel out of slavery, and had received a covenant that bound Israel to that God forever. They perceived that that liberating God had also, at the dawn of time, created the world out of nothing. They remembered that after the ways of the world had gone awry, that same God had called the great ancestor Abraham to be the father of the people Israel and to inhabit the promised land. They commemorated the way the covenant with Israel, inaugurated in Abraham and renewed in Moses, was tested during forty years in the wilderness but came to fruition when Joshua entered the promised land and by endeavor and miracle subdued that land (sometimes brutally) and made it Israel's own.

In Babylon the exiles recorded that it was a long time before Israel had a settled pattern of leadership and government, but eventually Saul, and then David, and then Solomon became kings of a united people. After this high point, the kingdom split and departed frequently from the path of the covenant; it was this weakness and shortcoming that led eventually to the nation's destruction and deportation to Babylon. This was the story Israel came to understand in exile. Yet after fifty years of exile, Israel returned to the promised land, rebuilt the temple and city walls, and resumed the life of the covenant. Domination by the Persians was replaced by that of the Greeks and finally the Romans. But the flame of the covenant remained alive.

By the power of the Holy Spirit, a boy called Jesus was born. He was of the line of David and Abraham but was also fully God. He embraced the heritage of Israel but renewed the covenant and opened it up to all humankind. He healed and taught and proclaimed the kingdom of God—a coming era when all would live in the wonder of God's presence and just relations between people would be restored. Jesus came to Jerusalem, in the midst of much hostility, and one night reinterpreted the Jewish Passover meal as the way his followers could experience the liberation he was bringing. But that night he was betrayed by one of his followers, and the next day he was disowned by his people and crucified by the Romans. On the cross Jesus took upon his shoulders the sins not just of Israel, stretching back to Abraham, but of the whole world, tracing back to the first human being. Yet God raised Jesus from the dead, in that action defeating not only sin but also death. Before Jesus departed to heaven, he commissioned his followers to baptize those of all nations and take the news of forgiveness and eternal life to the ends of the earth. Ten days later the Holy Spirit came upon the disciples, and the church began to grow rapidly.

A former opponent of Christianity, Paul of Tarsus, became the leader of the movement to bring the faith to the Mediterranean world. His letters to the new churches spoke of how the grace of God in Christ withstood the judgment due to humankind and of the resultant freedom of the life of the Spirit. Together with the scriptures of Israel, and four accounts of the life, death, and resurrection of Jesus, the Gospels, Paul's letters and those of others came together to form what, by about two hundred years after the birth of Jesus, was called the Bible. The early church struggled with trials and challenges, but in the book of Revelation it recorded its confidence that Christ would return as judge of the tyrants and vindicator of the oppressed.

After three centuries of minority existence and frequent persecution, in the early fourth century Christianity came to be embraced by the Roman emperor and soon by the empire as a whole. Things became more chaotic after the fall of Rome in 451, but Constantinople became the center of Eastern Christendom, whose relations with the Western church eventually broke down. Christianity continued to be spread by monks and missionaries, until by the Middle Ages it was almost unchallenged in Europe, although threatened by Islam on Europe's southern borders. The relationship between government and church was complex and often fraught. In the sixteenth century the Protestant Reformation split the Western church, and varieties of Protestantism, seeking to reassert the authority of the Bible over traditions accrued through the centuries, continued themselves to split, with violent conflict sometimes accompanying differences of faith. Meanwhile the missionary movement advanced and fostered the spread of faith in the Americas, in Africa, and in Asia, yet was invariably accompanied by colonial attitudes and structures.

From the late seventeenth century onward, criticisms increasingly surfaced about the accuracy of the Bible's story, the plausibility of Christianity's account of the natural world, and the culpability of the church's use of power. Nonetheless, until the mid-twentieth century, Christianity largely retained its hold on the imagination of Europe and its colonial or postcolonial spheres of influence. Starting in the late twentieth century there came a great reversal, where believing, or at least belonging, became a minority pursuit in the West, while the preponderance of Christians now came from the two-thirds world, or global South.

For the last two thousand years, the life of faith has remained broadly unchanged. It exists on three levels. First, the church is the gathering of the faithful. Believers share together a sacred meal, recalling Christ's last supper and anticipating the banquet of heaven; they also read the Scriptures, hear interpretation, pray and sing together, yearn for forgiveness, seek reconciliation, and set out to commend the faith to others in word and action. Second, each Christian prays, seeks to be a blessing to neighbor and world in work, strives for growth in faith and holiness through public actions and through relationships, and tries to walk with Christ each day. Third, Christians look for the purpose and presence of the Holy Spirit in the world, through grand events and humble encounters, and pray for the coming of God's kingdom through which all will be transformed into glory.

Challenges to the Standard Account

The contemporary Western secular worldview is materialist. Immanuel Kant's project in works like his 1781 *Critique of Pure Reason* was to save morality from the acids of science—from the suggestion that life has no purpose. Nonetheless, his work discouraged speculation about things we can't see, touch, taste, hear, or smell. Majority opinion has gradually come to concur. This renders the basic structure of Christian faith problematic. It does so because Christianity has almost universally assumed that what is beyond our sense experience is nonetheless real—indeed, more real than we are.

A materialist worldview says that's nonsense. When we close our eyes, envision a conversation partner, or open our hearts to a presence greater than all things, there's actually nothing there. It's a figment of our imaginations, conjured up by our desire for meaning, our fear of being alone, or our instinct to conform to social expectations. "God" is simply a word for the infantilizing insistence that we make ourselves subject to an unseen external force rather than build up resources and resilience within ourselves. Like a child creating a world of her own, talking to patients on an imaginary ward, bossing her toys with an admonishing frown, or pleading with the goblins to release her favorite fairy, our prayers are attempts to structure our world in ways more pliable and rewarding than the unrelenting ordinariness or fragility of regular life. Such things are not necessarily ridiculous. Prayer has its secular equivalents in meditation and mindfulness—quests for depth, peace, and honesty, shorn of a transcendent frame of reference, although sometimes with their origins in Buddhist practice. Liturgy is an ordered sequence of symbolic gestures and resonant words—and is to be found in many human activities, from the order of a law court to the start of a football game to the traditions of an annual general meeting. Many of the things Christians seek to be and to do—as activists, truth tellers, reconcilers, sources of blessing, contributors to a flourishing society—are amply echoed in secular equivalents; the materialist would say no transcendent dimension of reality is needed to underpin such goals and aspirations. That last part's just something Christians have made up.

Why might Christians invent such a make-believe realm of an imaginary heaven and a fantasy deity interacting in unpredictable ways with our space-time existence? Perhaps the biggest reason is fear. Our lives are circumscribed by death. In death we face personal extinction, annihilation, obliteration. This is a terrifying, paralyzing, horrifying prospect. Most of us are not foolish enough to try to resist inevitable mortality by building up hopeless fortifications of possessions, reputation, health, descendants, or other fruitless attempts to outwit the all-consuming prospect of our own demise. But it's understandable that some, finding the future unbearable, construct a system of meaning and purpose that promises to go beyond death and open out a life that never ends. Faith is thus an elaborate system of defiance and denial: denial of the power, finality, and inevitability of death.

Another reason for conceiving the superstructure of deity might be projection. It's very appropriate to separate worthy human motivations, desires, impulses, and convictions from unworthy ones. It's quite understandable that one would seek ways to dismantle the less worthy and uphold the worthy by creating public monuments, festivals, celebrations of the worthy qualities, and private rituals and habits that foster such virtues. It's not a great leap from there to turn those worthy aspirations into an external figure of admiration, veneration, worship, and adoration. There's no human being whose life and character can sustain such acclaim; consequently, that figure has to be elevated to the level of the divine, eternal, permanent, unchanging. This is how a community can create a deity to fly the flag for its highest aims for its own flourishing. Such a deity can then become the focus for a host of other projections—about suffering, safety, fear, mercy, shame, conflict, justice, and prosperity. Faith, in this sense, is the creation of an external, shared idea that can carry the hopes and anxieties of a whole community—and can serve therapeutic and calming purposes, as well as forge common identity, regardless of whether it's actually true.

Alongside these two rationales for the invention of a deity, there's a third, equally plausible and perfectly understandable one: the need to identify a cause of otherwise inexplicable phenomena. When the

Bible was written, people had little idea about other planets, let alone a solar system, or a galaxy—still less the idea that there are one hundred million stars in our galaxy and one hundred million galaxies in the universe. The biblical worldview has simply been superseded by astronomical discoveries in the modern era. Is it credible that there could be no life on any planet besides this one? Is it conceivable that a God could have concern for one minuscule planet when the universe is so colossal? Meanwhile there are fewer and fewer gaps in understanding for a "mysterious-cause" God to fill. The Darwinist account of the origin of species notoriously challenges the creation accounts in Genesis; but this no more than the best known of many areas of knowledge where the scriptural account lags behind contemporary wisdom. God seems an outmoded and clumsy name for a series of things that have more comprehensive modern explanations.

Together these arguments constitute the greatest and most abiding challenge to Christianity: it's all made up. It's a huge, elaborate, overwrought hoax, based on fantasy and fear. Christians are like Dumbo the elephant, clutching a feather whose power was simply a deception to get them to jump. It's time they grew up and found that courage and resilience in themselves. There's no God: deal with it.

A Rival Story, Its Validity and Flaws

A Rival Story

Those who don't subscribe to any notion of the transcendent, and dismiss Christianity on those grounds, don't constitute a unified movement. Some were once believers; some have no professed faith; some subscribe to another faith that rules out transcendence, like some forms of Buddhism; others are explicitly hostile. Here I synthesize a constructive position out of a whole range of positions—some of which, like those of the so-called New Atheists, are largely destructive, but others of which, like Marxism, constitute a fully developed alternative story.

At its most aspirational, this story says that it doesn't abolish wonder, joy, even glory—it simply denies that the universe or anything within it needs something outside or beyond it to explain or cause it. Indeed, some would argue that makes it even more wondrous, because it isn't the sculpture of an unseen force—it's self-generating, self-replenishing, self-sustaining. It takes all the waterfalls, rainbows, and sunsets that move Christians to awe and praise and translates them into reasons to glory in the complexity and subtlety of 14.8 billion years of emerging existence since the big bang.

It's a view that divides phenomena into two kinds: those for which a rational, natural explanation has been found, and those for which a rational, natural explanation will one day be found. It's great to rejoice in and enjoy the natural world, the workings of the human brain, the extent of the universe and the complexity to be found under a microscope, but there's no use in seeking a rationale or ultimate purpose of such things beyond the explanations science can or will give. There is no ultimate noncontingent meaning: everything is connected to everything else and requires no external "hand" to trigger, guide, or fulfill it. Death is as natural as birth; our bodies, animated for a season by a life force, have evolved fundamentally to reproduce; whether they do so or not, they eventually yield to the process of decay, which itself fertilizes endless forms of micro-life that contribute to the circle of existence.

The whole universe is thus a self-contained system, and Earth a largely autonomous system of its own. The kinds of singular, unique events to which Christianity is fundamentally tied simply can't take place within such a system. As the eighteenth-century philosopher G. E. Lessing put it in his 1777 book *On the Proof of the Spirit and the Power*, "Accidental truths of history can never become the proof of necessary truths of reason." Truth lies in what is always, everywhere so, not in what is supposed to have happened once, however arrestingly.

The Validity and Flaws of the Rival Story

This rival story is helpful to Christianity in two ways: it points out the missteps Christianity has often taken in making its claims, and it encourages Christianity to elucidate the nature of faith.

There's no question Christianity has mistaken its claim to perceive the why of creation and assumed that gave it privileged insight into the what and how of existence. Some of the pioneers of scientific discovery were motivated by their desire to understand the breadth and depth of God's ways: for example, in the nineteenth century Gregor Mendel, father of genetics, was an abbot of an order of Augustinian friars. Such people saw no reason that the search for truth should be in tension with the expansion of faith. But whether out of protection of its power, anxiety about its authority, or narrowness of its vision, too frequently the church has seen scientific inquiry as a threat rather than a gift—and provoked aggressive sentiments in its self-made adversaries. While Christianity was the default worldview in the educated West, the church's voice had to be respected and its misgivings entertained. But having misused that voice so frequently, it hardly deserved to keep it. And it has created a situation where many people feel they need to choose between science and faith.

More significant is the nature of faith itself. The problem with the scientific story is not the expanding range of phenomena for which it offers a rational account: this is a blessing to all humankind. The problems are four. First, it tends to deny that it is itself a story. I've deliberately called it a "rival story." This is not a battle of idle story against factual discovery. It's a setting of two stories alongside each other, noting tensions and correspondences. Take the periodic table. It's a brilliant, valuable, and dynamic construction, condensing a great deal of information in comprehensible form. But it's still a construction, a best guess. It's not that all the elements really *exist* on a table. The table is an account—a story. It's a compelling story—but it's still a story. All facts are components of a story. Within that story they may be asserted as indisputable facts. But "indisputability" is really an assertion of the universality of a particular story. Stories are, by their nature, particular: they're told from one point of view. The assertion of universality isn't a claim to truth: it's really a claim to power—a way of saying, "You have to accept my story." The scientific story (assuming it's just one story) is a plausible, compelling story—but it can't step out of the slippery realm of story and reach the high, dry ground of fact. It can only tell a more convincing story.

Second, there is only history; there's no ahistorical truth. When the philosopher said, "Accidental truths of history can never become the proof of necessary truths of reason," he was proclaiming a lot of confidence in necessary truths of reason—perhaps a little too much. But he wasn't in a position to say that accidental truths of history were false. It begs the question, Aren't there only accidental truths of history—are there any other kind? Today the distinction between arbitrary event and solid, reliable time-independent fact isn't as clear as it was once thought to be. Christianity rests on certain unrefuted historical claims: notably the incarnation and resurrection of Jesus. It's true that Christianity has regarded as foundational and nonnegotiable a bunch of other quasi-historical claims about events that now, in the light of historical and scientific research, appear mythological: the six-day creation, most obviously. But the core of Christianity is what uniquely happened in Christ; while Christians struggle to prove it, no one has succeeded in disproving it, either.

Third, reductionism overstates its case. It's one thing to say, "There are rational explanations for most phenomena, and will one day be for all," but it's quite another to say, "The only legitimate discourse is about how things work: questions of why they exist are idle, outside the realm of speculation, and fruitless." Such a claim impoverishes every realm of discourse—even its own. Likewise it's one thing to say, "Questions of ultimate meaning and purpose can never be answered for certain," but it's a rather different thing to say, "The only legitimate field of discourse is about things we can know for certain." The mistake made by this rival story is one of overstatement. It's true that Christianity can't prove that there's a personal being with whom we may converse in prayer, from whom we derive depth and truth, and in whom we find identity and hope. But simply because it can't be proved doesn't mean all such talk is nonsense.

Finally, and summarizing all these arguments, is this insight. Everyone believes in something—if to believe is to place trust and invest meaning despite not being able to rely totally on the object of one's reliance. Believing isn't a weird eccentricity of "people of faith": it's a universal characteristic of everybody. You can't love, plan, anticipate, assume, or trust unless you place confidence in something or someone of whose reliability you can't be certain. And you can't have much of a life if you don't do all these things. What Christians should say to people who profess no faith, of whom some may be hostile to faith, is not "Tell me what you don't believe," because that's not the interesting part; they should wonder, "Tell me what you do believe"—because it's a fantasy and a falsehood to say "Nothing." Then it becomes a different conversation; not the credulous believer against the realistic skeptic, but two people discussing the grounds, durability, beauty, tradition, generativity, and promise of what they respectively trust in but can't prove.

A Story to Live by, and How It Differs from Both Stories

A Story to Live By

What follows is what I as a Christian have come to understand as the heart of the faith in the light of the tradition I've outlined and the challenges I've acknowledged.

There are things that last forever, and there are things that have a limited duration. We are among the latter, and we have had a tendency to assume that these latter are the only things, to assume that the story is about us. But the story is not fundamentally about us, because we come and we go, like all transient things. The story is really about what lasts forever.

What lasts forever is called essence. Essence was sufficient: it needed no other. There was no deficit. It was superabundant. It was in a dimension where time and space are of little or no account. Existence wasn't necessary. Essence was more than enough. Essence is synonymous with forever, and forever and essence are constituted by relationship. It is out of these understandings that we may begin to consider the word "God." "God" is another word for forever; forever is the essence that transcends and evokes existence; and essence is relationship. God is therefore relationship. That relationship is Trinity—three persons in utter relationship. Trinity means three entities, three persons, so in one another that we call them one, but at the same time so with one another that we call them three. Oneness we call union; togetherness (in Latin) we call *com*. Hence communion: the perfect combination of with and in—the condition of the Trinity forever. Thus essence is characterized entirely by relationship—or communion.

So why did essence bring existence out of nothing? It is the great wonder of time and space that essence desired to extend its own perfection of relationship beyond itself; in short, to be with creatures, and invite them to be with one another and with their surroundings. That desire crystallized in one body—the body of one member of the Trinity, the second member in fact, known as Jesus—the body in whom relationship between essence and existence became fully realized. Because of this pure, unnecessary, glorious desire, the universe came into being—began to exist—as the backdrop, the context, for the relationship of God and humankind. There was no hurry: only one thing was predestined, and that was that one day there would be humankind, and one person would be both the epitome of humankind and the heart of God: the body in whom essence and existence would meet.

That's not to say essence, or God, had been absent from existence before that moment. The Holy Spirit had woven its thread through the fabric of the universe all along and been especially close to Earth—tiny backwater of a planet as it may seem—and had found an abiding companion in Israel, a people on whom God's heart was set from ages past. It was natural that, when essence entered existence, it should do so as one of that chosen people, embodying that people's history just as it embodied the heart of God.

For thirty years that utter God, utter human dwelt in obscurity with humankind—thereby demonstrating that essence is characterized fundamentally by being with, rather than fixing problems or unveiling solutions. But for three years that being, Jesus, shared the heart of God in word and gesture, pleading with Israel to rediscover ways to be with God. Eventually, the story took a tragic twist: people had an allergic reaction to the prospect of perfect communion with God, and Jesus was grotesquely and agonizingly executed. Though its perpetrators didn't realize what they were doing, this was an attempt to sever the conjunction between essence and existence: to live without fundamental relationship. Jesus experienced this agony of utter separation as he died.

Was the relationship of essence and existence then to be thwarted, casting existence adrift from its meaning and purpose into a realm of nothingness and emptiness? Here lies perhaps the most significant moment in the whole story. Essence might have had every reason to let existence spiral away to complete alienation. But essence didn't do that. In an act perhaps even more wondrous than the conception of existence in the first place, essence resolved to restore the relationship with existence that existence had sundered. This was resurrection. The fundamental character of essence—relationship—was not going to be lost by rejection or death. It could not be so clumsily contained or curtailed. Resurrection was a demonstration of the ultimate weakness of all that inhibits communion; it was a promise that essence being with existence was no temporary gesture but a forever thing.

And that was perhaps an even greater revelation than anything that had preceded it. For the resurrection of Jesus prefigured God's final purpose for existence: that it should ultimately be drawn back into essence, and that there would be a place in forever for us—for those with whom God had always longed to be in relationship. And that forever would be to enjoy with ourselves, one another, and the creation the indescribable glory of being with one another that characterized the life of the Trinity forever and a day.

See what this story says and doesn't say. Christianity rests on an inner and an outer conviction. The outer is that beyond what lasts for a limited time, there's a something that lasts forever. The inner is that relationship is the heart of it all: the true heart, greatest dynamic, and ultimate future of all things lies in the word "with." Is it so far-fetched to suppose there's something that lasts forever? That there's something that was, 15 billion years ago, before the big bang; that is, uncontaminated by Earth's failings and uncompromised by the relativity of one dimension of the universe to another; and that will be, after the big crunch comes, a good few billion years hence? It's almost more difficult to imagine that there's not. And if there is a forever, is it not plausible to suppose that it's characterized significantly by the most profound experiences a human being can have? And is it so absurd to epitomize those experiences as love—that's to say, relationship in the context of mutuality, durability, desire, communion, and joy? And meanwhile, is it not apt to set that love against the two forces that appear bent on dismantling it: that which discredits it, which we call sin, or evil, and that which decomposes it, which we call death?

At which point we see this ancient yet riveting story of the utter human, utter God, forever in historical shape, confronting on the cross both sin and death—in short, complete alienation; and yet in the resurrection showing that love is stronger than death, essence will not be submerged by existence, poison will not destroy trust. In this story we see both the epic scale of essence and the humble obscurity of existence: it's a once-for-all revelation of the heart of the Trinity and a mundane tale of the factors that dismantle relationship. We can accept, embrace, rejoice in some parts of this story perhaps: that there is a forever; that this forever is an alternative name for God; that forever, when we call it God, is personal, indeed entirely characterized, within and without, by relationship, for there is no God that is not Trinity, that is, perfect, eternal relationship; that this relationship is utterly embodied in Jesus; that Jesus's coming as one among us, which we call incarnation, was the reason for existence in the first place; that this relationship, being with us, or communion, was the purpose of Jesus and is the purpose of existence; that the rejection of this "being with" was the force that crucified Jesus; that the indomitability and unswervability of God being with us was what made the resurrection happen; and that in the resurrection we see God's ultimate desire to bring us and the whole creation into essence, to be with the Trinity forever. We can indeed choose which part to highlight, but the story exists as a whole. And once grasped, it becomes one's identity, purpose, destiny, joy, and . . . essence: one's reason for existence.

All of which accounts for why prayer is the definitive Christian practice. Because prayer is the moment in which we, as a part of existence, open our lives to be suffused by essence. In prayer we recognize that this transitory world is only partly real—if by "real" we mean that which is permanent, and that which has wholly fulfilled its potential. Nothing in existence is permanent, and nothing fulfills its potential. But both qualities apply to essence. Thus essence is real in a way that existence can never be. Prayer is the moment we apprehend this and place our hope, trust, and expectation on that which is truly and ultimately real—at the same time casting aside the desires, actions, and judgments that don't bear scrutiny in the light of essence. Prayer isn't reeling off a list of requests to make our existence more agreeable; it is an action and a commitment to live life in the light of essence—to live God's future now. The words "Thy kingdom come. Thy will be done on earth as it is in heaven" are a plea to suffuse existence with essence.

CHAPTER 1

How This Story Differs from the Rival Story

The rival story often claims not to be a story. But the emergence of reality from a big bang and the origin of species through a process of the survival of the fittest are indisputably narrative in character. By contrast, the story to live by is avowedly a story. What's most significant about it is that it starts in the middle. It starts with the desire of essence to connect to existence—a desire that precedes the inception of existence. The story to live by thus rests on two fundamental claims; we could call them hypotheses. First, there is a realm of essence beyond the realm of existence, and that prior realm is both permanent and more real than existence. Second, essence is utterly constituted by relationship. In other words, relationship is more foundational than materiality or even life itself.

Neither of these two foundations is provable, but neither are they refutable. The story to live by is profoundly affirming of materiality—because the first element in the story, Christ becoming utterly human, is a deeply material statement—but it still proposes materiality as secondary to relationship. Relationship is the nature of the Trinity—and the Trinity could have continued indefinitely, infinitely in mutual relationship, without there ever being an existence. For the story to live by, there is no simple, uncontroversial notion of "God," who is judged either to exist or not to exist. The whole notion of existence is problematic and provisional. Essence is the first notion, and essence is found to be inherently relational. So God is from the beginning relational—there's no question of God's somehow making an adjustment or concession to be with us in Christ: essence is shaped from the outset to be with.

But isn't it all a fantasy—too good to be true? Here we come to the crux. There are perhaps two ways to answer this question. One is, "Which is harder to believe—that everything just appeared in a cause-and-effect sequence without a specific cause, or that there is a dimension, truer and more real than this one, that holds existence within its even greater purpose?" Put like that, it's surely an even balance—and the story to live by is certainly not a preposterous upstart alternative to clear rational logic. The other way to answer is, "Given the roughly even balance of probabilities, which story would you prefer to be in? One in which our spark of imagination and wonder is an impossible possibility amid the prevailing material contingency of life? Or one in which relationship is foundational, and every time we form, establish, restore, and deepen tender, understanding, gentle, humble connection with one another, we imitate and anticipate the way essence seeks to be with existence and glimpse the glory of eternity?"

How This Story Differs from the Old, Old Story

While immediately recognizable to almost every Christian, the story to live by differs from the standard account in one very significant respect. It assumes Christ's coming is an original intention, indeed the very purpose of creation, whereas in the standard account Christ's coming was to rectify the effects of the Fall, in which humankind lost the joys of paradise.

The story to live by takes issue with the standard account because it sees that in the latter story, the most significant event in all history (Christ's birth, life, death, and resurrection) arises out of a deficit. That deficit is sin, death, and evil, and the need, through sacrifice and judgment, to eradicate their effects on humanity and all creation. What this entails is that the means of salvation—death, agony, abandonment, punishment—are in tension with the ends gained, namely, heavenly joy.

By contrast, in the story to live by, Christ's coming arises out of an asset. That asset is the primordial desire of essence to be with, and the corresponding creation of existence in order that essence might have a partner to be with. In this latter story Christ would have come whether or not there was some historical or prehistorical fall from grace. Christ comes out of God's abundance, not out of human scarcity. Just as importantly, the means are consonant with the ends. It is relationship from start to finish. Relationship in Christ is the center, relationship in the Trinity is the beginning, and the sharing of that essential relationship with existence is the end. The final purpose of all things is for God to be with us, and for us to be with ourselves, one another, and the renewed creation. Christ is all of those things—he is with us in the ordinary things of Nazareth, in the causes and projects of Galilee, and most of all in the suffering and agony of Calvary. In the resurrection his being with us prevails over even its most threatening enemies. God becomes utterly and permanently with us not by making a detour into a sacrifice or battle or punishment out of keeping with being with—but instead by being with unto the last. Thus in the resurrection we have seen heaven: God being with us beyond death. Nothing can separate us from such love.

- 2 -

CATALOGUE OF BETRAYALS?

On almost anyone's list of objections to Christian belief, suffering and death come near the top. I've placed them second here because I sense the issues discussed in the first chapter are primary. Suffering poses a twin question: If terrible things happen, is God not powerful enough to stop them—or is God not good enough to care? Suffering is not just about degree—how painful it is; it's also about distribution—whether it's experienced fairly or equally by all people. In both cases it's closely linked to a sense of injustice. As has been said, "If it turns out that there *is* a God, I don't think that he's evil. I think that the worst you can say about him is that basically he's an underachiever."* Suffering thus presents itself as the most egregious of a catalogue of betrayals by which the story of God promises much yet too often fails to deliver.

The Old, Old Story and What's Wrong with It

The Standard Account

Why is the world not perfect, if that was God's intention in creation? The conventional story goes like this. There was an original

* *Love and Death,* directed by Woody Allen, MGM, 1975.

temptation, described vividly in Genesis 2–3. Adam and Eve are given the whole of the garden of Eden to enjoy—a glorious playground of delight. But they fixate on the one thing they're told they can't have: the fruit of the tree of the knowledge of good and evil. In so doing they turn the abundance of God's creation into the scarcity of their own scheming, and transform boundless liberty into constricting incarceration. Thereafter, they still have freedom, but they no longer know what to do with it. This remains the fate of humankind to this day. Sin poisons every relationship, motive, and initiative. It's one thing all humanity has in common. It permeates even communities that have set out to resist it and catches out even individuals who've lived apparently exemplary lives. Meanwhile, no living thing can avoid death—humanity included. Sin and death together constitute the fallout from humankind's original sin.

But the damage done by the Fall isn't limited to its effects on humanity: its ramifications affect all creation. There seems to be an extraordinary cruelty and savagery written into the life cycle of many creatures. In Delia Owens's 2018 novel *Where the Crawdads Sing*, the teenage Kya sits by a lagoon that smells "of life and death at once, an organic jumbling of promise and decay." She watches fireflies "scribbling across the night." She's learned that each species of firefly has its own language. The female flickers the light under her tail, to signal to the male that she's ready to mate. Kya settles down and watches as a female attracts a male of her species this way. But a few minutes later, she sees the female change her code. In no time, a male of a different species hovers above this adaptable female. Suddenly, we're told, "the female firefly reached up, grabbed him with her mouth, and ate him, chewing all six legs and both wings." It hardly makes sense to call this sin: instead, it tends simply to be called biology. Indeed, the novel continues, "Kya knew that judgment had no place here. Evil was not in play, just life pulsing on, even at the expense of some of the players. Biology sees right and wrong as the same colour in different light."*

Yet analogies of sin crop up frequently in life experience: a cancer feeds off the lifeblood of the body it resides in; addiction impels people to do something injurious to their own and others' well-being; a virus multiplies and spreads, doing no good to the species in which it takes root. Moreover, egregious terrible events—tsunamis, hurricanes, earthquakes, plagues, famines—cut a swathe through whole populations or regions, without any sign that those most affected have done anything particular to bring such tragedy upon themselves.

The Bible takes for granted such an understanding of the nonhuman effects of the Fall. But both Scripture and subsequent theological reflection have an impulse to ascribe deeper meaning to events that wreak pain and destruction both collectively (like floods) and individually (like sickness or sudden adversity). Sometimes such events are understood as an act of judgment; most obviously, this was how the exiles in Babylon in the sixth century BC came to understand the fall of Jerusalem, the ruin of the temple, and the dispersal of the people of Judah. Sometimes they're perceived as a test: the book of Job portrays a challenge to discover whether Job would curse God in the face of boundless suffering. Other instances of distress remain inscrutable—and the plight of the innocent sufferer is a regular theme in the psalms, several of which lament the incongruity between the distress of the righteous speaker and the goodness and justice of God.

The conventional place to look for a cause of suffering is in the notion of sin, and the related concept of evil. Whereas suffering is a result of the Fall, sin is the cause of the Fall. Sin is thought of in many ways, but is most simply described as living as if the world were not created, sustained, redeemed, and awaiting final consummation by God. Thus, Adam and Eve forget that God has given them astonishing abundance

* Delia Owens, *Where the Crawdads Sing* (New York: Putnam, 2018), 142–43.

and come to resent their situation. Likewise, a character who disobeys his master in one of Jesus's parables says, "I knew that you were a harsh man, reaping where you did not sow, and gathering where you did not scatter seed" (Matt. 25:24).* Those who sin generally know they are transgressing, but they invariably say to themselves things like "Just this once," "Everybody does it," "It's not as bad as what she does," "No one was really hurt," or "I don't know what possessed me." Sin makes the transition into evil at the point where the notion of transgression disappears and perpetrators convince themselves what they're doing is actually good. This turns a poison into a virulent contagion. Racists surround themselves with those who uphold the plausibility of their perspective: Nazis maintained that ridding the world of Jews was in some way good for the world. Evil of this kind is capable of untold harm. Evil is always a secondary, willed intrusion on an original benevolent grace. It should not exist; there's no logical explanation for it; it has no essence, only existence: which means there can be no such thing as pure evil—it's always adulterated. It's a disease that plagues the world. But there was a world without it, and there will one day be such a world again. Evil will not, in the end, exist.

In some cases Scripture and the tradition suggest an actual personification of evil—the devil, or Satan—and attribute much of the evil (and suffering) in the world to such a figure. There are problems with this notion. One is that when we suppose a heavenly being whose existence predates the Fall, we come close to imagining the permanence of evil. Evil persists, but it's not permanent. Another problem is that an indestructible Satan figure, like a Voldemort (in Harry Potter) or Moriarty (in Sherlock Holmes), who keeps reappearing just when you thought he was done, glamorizes evil and ends up becoming more interesting than God. A third is that such a figure discourages people from taking personal responsibility for mundane

* Unless otherwise indicated, Scripture references come from the New Revised Standard Version.

acts of goodness and courage, in the expectation that all of life should be an animated spiritual battle.

Indeed, there's an argument that it's immoral to find a comprehensive explanation for suffering—because such a rationale might discourage urgent efforts to alleviate it. While suffering is miserable, there's no doubt that it can sometimes bring out the best in people, both in the fortitude of the sufferer and in the care and tirelessness of the one committed to address the anguish of another. Some of the best dimensions of human nature come to light in the face of adversity. Abolish adversity, and they would never come to light. Just as in the body pain can be distressing but usually draws attention to something that needs urgently to be addressed, so adversity in life becomes the opportunity that brings to the fore gifts, talents, and merits that would otherwise have no outlet. In the church as a whole, perhaps less energy has gone into speculating about the causes or purpose of suffering than into attempts to mitigate or cure such suffering, or bring perpetrators to justice.

God's response to sin and evil focuses on the sending, and specifically the death, of Jesus. In Jesus's death we see the convergence of the two strands: first, sin, guilt, and judgment; second, innocence, injustice, and vindication. Several theories are hinted at in Scripture and developed in the tradition about how Jesus's death overcomes sin and death. But what is widely accepted in Christianity is that, in his crucifixion, Jesus bears the sins of the world, and in his resurrection he overcomes death, to which all living things are subject. An analogy is sometimes made between June 6, 1944, the day the Allies landed in Normandy, and May 8, 1945, the day the Second World War in Europe ended. It's said that in Christ's death and resurrection the decisive victory over sin and death has been won, and suffering will therefore not prevail—but the war is not yet over, and sin and death, along with suffering, are thus still very much with us.

However coy the standard account has been about explaining or justifying suffering, it's been unequivocal on one issue: suffering will one day come to an end. Every tear will be dried from every eye; mourning and crying and pain will be no more. The convictions that Christ will one day return, and that injustice and suffering will not finally prevail, are the last word of Christianity on suffering and evil. They are often dismissed as "pie in the sky when you die." They've no doubt been offered inappropriately as a panacea in contexts where a concerted effort to change circumstances would have been more appropriate. Nonetheless, these two convictions are crucial to any conviction of the ultimate justice of God.

Challenges to the Standard Account

We can identify broadly four kinds of suffering. (1) Mischance is stuff that just happens, and we feel so sorry because it could happen to anyone, at any time, and it could have happened to me, and it seems random and unjust, although it happens to everyone in the end. (2) Muddle is when stuff happens, but in truth the sufferer was idle or careless, and could have helped themselves or alleviated the problem, and we feel sorry, but we make a note to learn from their folly. (3) Malice is when stuff happens because of genuine malign intention, whether cruelty (the deliberate infliction of harm) or selfishness (the casual infliction of harm while seeking some other goal). This makes us sorry, but also angry, because it's no accident. Finally there's (4) martyrdom, in which the victim knew suffering or death was likely or even probable but went ahead with their endeavor undaunted, because it was so important it was worth the cost. It usually takes place on the receiving end of malice. It leaves us full of admiration, or sometimes incomprehension.

The oft-cited free-will defense, which asserts that if God is not to dictate events, human beings must be allowed to do as they choose, seriously engages only with muddle. The principal controversy lies instead around mischance and malice. With mischance, the question is, How could God create a universe in which such things could happen—and allow them to happen when they do? With malice, the question is, Is evil outside God's control, or is God content to let it carry on uninhibited?

It's important to identify the theological challenge that suffering represents. It's conventionally represented as a creation issue. Thus the standard question is, How can a good God make a world where such horror can come about? or Why doesn't God intervene to prevent such suffering? This latter question contains a problematic word: "intervene." The word "intervene" presupposes that God is fundamentally distant and disengaged, either unable or unwilling to be present amidst human affairs. But this is a contradiction of Christian conviction—most obviously of the foundational and unambiguous words "In the beginning was the Word, and the Word was with God, and the Word was God. . . . And the Word became flesh and lived among us, and we have seen his glory" (John 1:1, 14). These words change the default assumption about God from distant and disengaged to incarnate, involved, and invested. Words like "intervene" are from the wrong frame of reference. This is not an idle, distant God; it's an already-given-everything and utterly-involved God. There is no world from which God is aloof; there is no life with which God is not intimately enfolded; there is no existence that God has not wholly embraced. Anything else is either Deism (belief in a God who has no engagement in earthly affairs) or docetism (belief that Christ was not truly human and thus, in Christ, God did not really suffer).

The problem doesn't lie with creation. Christianity has never pretended things are as God always intended. The problem lies with Jesus. After all, he was supposed to set everything right. The conventional Christian contention (that Christ was God's response to the Fall, and that his purpose was to reverse or dismantle its effects, releasing humanity from the grip of sin and death) runs into serious difficulty in the face of suffering—especially what I've called mischance and malice. The difficulty is twofold. It could be

1. that the salvation brought by Jesus, though unlimited in extent, being forever, was limited in scope, in that it achieved heavenly bliss but left earthly existence unchanged.

This is the kind of understanding that brings theology into dispute, because it seems immoral to claim the heavenly glory if the collateral damage is such horrendous earthly grief. Moreover, if what Christ achieved was largely or entirely restricted to the ethereal realm, Christians need to recognize and accept that another Nazi Holocaust, or South Asian tsunami, is more than likely in the near or distant future.

Alternatively, it could be

2. that Christ indeed inaugurated a kingdom of peaceable messianic fulfillment, as anticipated by Isaiah 11, but somehow that kingdom is temporarily thwarted by those bent on evil.

If this were so, it's hard to comprehend how Christ ascended to heaven believing he'd completed his work among us, since his work, if it's understood as installing the kingdom, seems to us so manifestly incomplete, and must have seemed even more so to him. Should Christ then come again—either to complete what he started or, as anticipated on the last day, to conclude the story, perhaps because he has judged our human condition to be beyond any less drastic form of redemption? This alternative seems to run profoundly counter to Christian orthodoxy and humble faith, but it's raised by an orthodox conviction of the sufficiency of Christ's coming.

Thus the theological problem is about Christ's first coming and his second. The problem about Christ's first coming is, if Jesus ascended to heaven having completed his work on earth, why is there still evil? The problem about Christ's second coming is, if, in the fullness of time, God will vindicate the oppressed, why does God not do so now? Terrible suffering, whether deriving from mischance or malice, continues to happen after the coming of Christ. When people have interceded and called on the Holy Spirit to make Christ's work tangible, the Holy Spirit seems not to have responded in anything like the degree that they or we might regard as constituting answered prayer. There are three possible theological reasons for this. Christ's death and resurrection are

1. insufficient for addressing such an overwhelming number of desperate situations as people find themselves in;
2. sufficient, but the Holy Spirit is unable to make them tangible in every case, or is unwilling to do so because God's purpose is being worked out more mysteriously and over a much longer time frame than the intercessors want or appreciate; or
3. tangible, but people are looking for them in the wrong place.

Answer (1) leads to the discrediting of Christian convictions, because it acknowledges that God is not sovereign over all things. Answer (2) has been the conventional theological response to notorious events of great suffering, such as the Holocaust. It's a way of reconciling the goodness of God with the continuance of suffering. It's seldom seemed an adequate answer. Any suggestion that "It's all part of the plan" has, after all, to explain what kind of a plan it could possibly be that would make the Holocaust part of it. We will consider answer (3) later in this chapter, when we come to a story to live by.

Turning to Christ's second coming, there's always a balance to be struck in Christian theology between the emphasis given to Christ's first coming and the emphasis given to his second. It's like two equal sides of an equation: the more that's attributed to his first coming, in defeating death, dismantling sin, and destroying evil, the less there remains to be accomplished on the last day. By the same token, the greater the expectation that's focused on the last day, in terms of vindicating the oppressed, inaugurating the kingdom, and dispelling the forces that oppress us, the more the decisive character assigned to Christ's first coming is correspondingly reduced. The one other element in the reckoning is Pentecost. Some accounts explicitly or implicitly give the clothing of the disciples with power an importance comparable or even parallel to Christ's own work, whether in the sense of performing miracles or in the sense of building institutions and society that closely resemble or even advance the kingdom.

All these perspectives have drawbacks. A thoroughgoing emphasis on the sufficiency of Christ's first coming begs the question of why things seem so little improved thereafter. Shifting the weight to ultimate fulfillment both begs the question of why Christ came at all and risks diminishing investment in and commitment to this earthly existence by overplaying hope of the world to come. Resting a decisive role upon Pentecost carries the danger of either trivializing salvation, by restricting it to signs and wonders, or overemphasizing human capacity to fulfill God's purposes.

The answer to why God doesn't just bring history to an end now must be that, in doing so, something would be lost as well as something gained. If this were not so, there could be no explanation for any distinction between the first coming of Christ and the second. Why delay Christ's second coming if there were only gain in its arrival? There is indeed something lost. That something is all the good in the world in the years since the ascension of Jesus. Heaven does not create new life: it restores the life that's already been created, healing the wounds and mending the flaws. But it doesn't take too much imagination to dwell on what would be lost if there were no new life: not just the joy and fulfillment and wonder of bringing new creatures into being but the renewal and replenishment and enrichment of existence. There's no question that the prospects for retrieval of what has been lost in the suffering, neglect, rejection, and oppression of so much of humankind and the wider creation are beyond enumeration; but if heaven is truly everlasting, a point will surely come when the joy of restoration will seem insufficient without the dynamism of new beginnings. That's what's lost in moving from creation to new creation.

A Rival Story, Its Validity and Flaws

A Rival Story

At this point it's important to note that the issues raised in this second chapter are significantly different in character from those explored in our first chapter. "Crutch for the deluded" is an observation of scorn, or perhaps pity, from the self-assured as they observe the credulity of the inadequate. "Catalogue of betrayals," by contrast, is a cry of hurt, and often anger, from those who had looked to God with some degree of hope and been disappointed. Whereas the first evinces confidence that the world is logical and doesn't require external agency, this second manifests the disappointment and bitterness of those who sought solace and didn't find it.

The consequence of that distinction is that there is no articulate rival story to put up against the old, old story; this reason for rejecting Christianity is instead rooted in protest. It's sometimes said that you can't be angry at something you don't believe exists; you can't reject something you never upheld. The discourse around suffering is more lament than argument.

Nonetheless, there's an implied story behind some such debates, and it goes like this. We are entitled to an enjoyable, extensive, rewarding life. That life should, indeed, go on forever—but at least it should include infancy, adolescence, maturity, achievement or parenthood (or both), and late maturity, perhaps also dotage. It should incorporate a breadth of experience, including the opportunity to withstand or overcome adversity. If it ends after all these things have been encountered, it's sad but fair—you can't complain. But if any of these things have been missing, some kind of contract has been broken—and if many or all have been absent, such as in the death of a young child, or in a life that's been severely constrained by poverty or pain, then it's a case of plain injustice.

Who is the perpetrator of this injustice? To return to the four categories set out above, muddle, malice, and martyrdom are comprehensible enough—but what of mischance? The child with leukemia, the unexpected flood, the catastrophic earthquake: Where can the finger point? Here God stands in the dock, accused of heartlessness; if not heartlessness, then impotence; if not impotence, then malevolence. God may have no existence or credibility, but he can still serve as a punching bag for human fury in the face of the cruel, harsh, and merciless twists of the human narrative.

The assumption of this implied story is that if there's going to be existence, if there's going to be life, if there's going to be human life surrounded with the sophistication of intelligence and technology—then this life ought to be happy: and that happiness is defined as the fulfillment of reasonable desires and the absence of pointless pain. Anything else is the result of faulty design or malicious intent. Thus God is, at best, an underachiever.

The Validity and Flaws of the Rival Story

The truth is, no one has a good explanation for the existence of suffering and evil. The appearance of sin after humanity's fall from grace is a story, not a reason. Some sense of God's greater purpose, in training human beings for tasks ahead or subduing one force in order to advance another, more benevolent one, is in danger of portraying God as a heartless manipulator, always playing the long game at the regular expense of those caught in the short game. God's holy inscrutability—ours not to reason why, ours but to do and die—is by definition not even trying to be an explanation. None of the conventional treatments are a genuine justification.

I said earlier that suffering and evil are not a creation problem but a Jesus problem. The rival story demands a modification of that judgment. What the rival story points out is the inadequacy of an account of suffering and evil that locates all the unresolved issues of existence in the story of the Fall. It seems we have alternative understandings, equally unfair. It could be that

a. a cosmic mistake was made early in creation, and all subsequent beings are subject to it.

This lifts the emphasis off the shoulders of individual guilt but fails to explain

- why God allowed this mistake to happen,
- why subsequent people should pay the consequences and share the blame for an error that was not theirs, and
- how such a story fits with our current understanding of how humans came to exist.

Or it could be that

b. the mistake was not primal and definitive but repeated and cumulative; in other words, Genesis 3 describes not an actual event but a pattern of human acting and relating, so common that it is practically universal. This understanding sits better with the second and third objections raised above, but it creates other problems, namely:

    - it more explicitly pins the blame on the creator, as being responsible for a design flaw that is present in every human being, and
    - it highlights that death is integral to the original design and not a malfunction of it, because new life and growth in the absence of death are unsustainable. Death is necessary for plants, animals, and humans to source nutrients and grow.

This analysis reveals that the "problem" is, at root, the fact that things (in existence) don't last forever—and that the seeds of their not-being lie within them as soon as their life begins. In other words, sin and evil are not fundamentally different from death—all three are features of the limited, inhibited, and transitory nature of life. To complain that God allows suffering, evil, and death is therefore to upbraid God for making life (as we know it) at all—rather than going straight to eternal life as we are promised it. But such life, as we have seen, lacks one crucial element—the capacity to create new life: a price we would be unwilling to pay.

But we still ask the question, Why should we not expect life to be happy, and, if happy, comfortable, and, if comfortable, free from pain and suffering? It's a fair expectation, provided it's an aspiration for everyone rather than for just oneself. But it hides a profound flaw. It's founded on the notion of an implied contract: provided we respect the freedom and dignity of others and don't act recklessly or foolishly, we're entitled to a good outcome from the deal. But what deal was that? With whom did we make a deal that we take to be valid on a cosmic scale? If we've ruled out the notion of a transcendent God, there's no party with whom we could sign such a contract.

Which of us chose to be born? At what point did we enter into a deal? On what grounds do we expect better of life than we find it gives us? Here we see that the "problem of suffering and evil," as it's often known, isn't an argument for the nonexistence of God. It isn't a first-order reason for the rejection of Christianity; instead, it's a protest that arises within the veil of faith. It presumes a divine party with whom we have or can come to an arrangement. To say that the divine party is weak, impassive, or cruel is not to say there is no such divine party. This is a moral problem, not a metaphysical one. It seems to be a less-than-ideal kind of deity, rather than a less-than-existent one. Without some notion of God, you still have suffering—but you don't have a "problem of suffering."

A Story to Live by, and How It Differs from Both Stories

A Story to Live By

Finding a story to live by means two things in the case of suffering. It means recognizing that there are some things one can never, finally, comprehend, and it means accepting that there is a partial answer, even if that answer doesn't cover all the emotional territory we want it to. So here I offer the two approaches in turn.

I

Consider, as you lie on your bed, how long it takes you to get to sleep. There's something extraordinarily vulnerable about lying down with your eyes closed not knowing what will happen next. It puts us in touch with our isolation. For those who sleep alone, or feel alone even if another person is asleep beside them, this can be the most terrifying moment of the day. All the busyness, demand, activity, or entertainment of the day is now ruthlessly revealed to be an organized construction to avoid this merciless feeling: of powerlessness, defenselessness, helplessness. All our deepest anxieties in life are crystallized in this moment: however dynamic, accomplished, or abundant our life has been, at this moment, poised between waking and sleeping, we have to renounce it all and feel naked, weak, and empty. It's an experience of standing on the brink of death.

Which makes it ironic that the very thing we long for with every fiber of our body is to go to sleep, to dive deep into the darkness of oblivion, and to be replenished to face the next day. It's ironic because, for most of us, what we fear most about death is that very same thing that each night when we lie down on our bed we long for: namely, oblivion. It's one of the great ironies of life. Our deepest fears are to be utterly alone and to cease to have meaning, and yet every day we urge these conditions on ourselves and become extremely anxious if we can't achieve them. It's the way sleep teaches us one of the most important lessons of life.

When we step back a little and place things on a larger canvas, we face a larger paradox. The paradox comprises three dimensions and a contradiction. The first dimension is this. We exist in a world of myriad complexity, subtlety, intricacy, and wonder. If we simply consider our own bodies, the daily processes of breathing and digesting, moving and thinking, feeling and expressing—all these require astonishing degrees of detailed intention and meticulous execution; and those just name the things we take completely for granted, that happen without us even making a decision to set them in motion. If we look beyond us, we find the world is at least as fearfully and wonderfully made. Take for example water, which comes to us in oceans and raindrops, ice cubes and fountains, crashing waves and hailstorms, steam and paddling pools. There are unfathomable numbers of animals and insects, forms of terrain and vegetation, rocks and landscapes. And if we raise our eyes to the skies, we behold, with greater or lesser understanding, planets, stars, and galaxies—an incomprehensible extent and unfathomable depth of glory and astonishment. That's the first dimension.

The second dimension is our either acute or dim recognition that, behind, beyond, and within all this life and existence, there is some logic, purpose, or intention. At this point I should make it clear that I don't believe in atheism. The reason I don't believe in atheism is that it's almost impossible to argue that there's no logic whatsoever in the universe. That logic is, after all, what all the great ventures of physics are trying to establish, from gravity to relativity. Whatever you arrive at as your most significant organizing principle, whether by scientific deduction, by contemplative reflection, or by interpreting the signs of revelation, that is your God. It's fair to say the so-called New Atheists have a somewhat thin notion of God, but I don't think it's accurate to say they are actually atheists, who believe in no God, even if they say they are. Even if you have very little notion of a discernible purpose, intention, or personal identity, you're inevitably searching for some kind of logic: all of us are, all the time, every time we check the weather forecast or try to work out whether that tumor we're worried about is malignant or benign. That's the second dimension: the logic behind all things.

The third dimension is the realization, sudden or gradual, common or unique, that this logic is more than just a cold or mechanical chain reaction but has purpose, intention, and (this is the crucial step) personality. This personality is by its nature shaped for relationship. For Christians, being shaped for relationship means God is not just always looking to enter into and sustain relationship with us but is also inherently made up of relationship—what we call the Trinity of Father, Son, and Holy Spirit. Thus relationship isn't an afterthought for God—relationship is the very essence of what God is, and thus what eternity is. Jesus is the ultimate and utter proof of these two things—proof that God is shaped to be in relationship with us, and proof that God's inner life consists of relationship.

So these are the three dimensions—the world and universe are immeasurably intricate and beautiful, there is at least some level of logic behind it all, and that logic turns out to be a personal being whose deepest nature is relationship, and whose deepest purpose is to be in relationship with us. And here's the contradiction. We die. Apparently, our breathing stops, our organs shut down, our consciousness ceases, our body begins to decay, and we are finished: no feeling, no awareness, no life, no future, no anything.

See how death is a contradiction of all three dimensions of life I described earlier. No one can explain how a world and a universe that has such complexity and intricacy can collapse into the still, silent, inert form of a dead body. No one can identify the logic behind why all the processes that create the miracle of life are finally thwarted by the absurdity of death. No one can understand why the God who looks, in every moment, to establish or sustain relationship is content to see that relationship come to such a sudden, overwhelming, and permanent end. It seems totally illogical, uncharacteristic, unjust, and incomprehensible.

When we lie on our deathbed, or perhaps, more truthfully, when we lie on our bed at night and for a change don't seek the oblivion of sleep but search the darkness for meaning and hope, this is the conundrum we are wrestling with. How can life end? How can that which brought life into being countenance its obliteration? How can the one who does everything to be in relationship with us tolerate the permanent elimination of that relationship?

These are the questions that dominate the book of Job. Job is usually thought of as a book about suffering, but suffering is really a subset of the problem of death; most people could endure almost any amount of suffering if they were sure that restored relationship and abundant life would duly follow. So the real issue for Job, and for us, is not so much suffering as it is annihilation. The story of Job doesn't claim to be historical but is more like a parable. It begins, "There was once a man in the land of Uz, whose name was Job." In some ways, the book is like a long version of the struggle in Genesis 32 between Jacob and the angel, where Jacob strives all night until finally the angel blesses him. The blessing Job seeks throughout the book is to know that God will not finally abandon him.

In the parable of Job, Satan wagers that Job's loyalty to God only stretches as far as his prosperity, and if Job faces adversity he will turn against God. Consequently, in four disasters Job loses his oxen, sheep, camels, and children; and then his body, his wife, and his friends turn against him. But Satan loses his wager: Job refuses to turn against God. Job does, however, curse the day of his birth. His friends queue up to offer plausible reasons for his plight, largely that Job is being punished for his sins and that he is being stubborn and proud for not recognizing this. But Job dismisses these shallow rationalizations. His complaint is not the suffering itself; it's the way that suffering encapsulates the three dimensions of the paradox I explored a moment ago.

Job says, in a roundabout way, "This just doesn't add up. Here is a magnificent and complex universe; there is surely a logic behind, beneath, and beyond it; and that logic is the purpose of a God who longs to be in relationship with us. How then can there be death, if that death entails annihilation? Annihilation goes against everything else I know about existence." The point is not, as Job's comforters maintain, that humans are punished for their sins; the point is, as Job irrefutably points out, that everyone is headed for annihilation—faithful and fickle alike. Job isn't doubting God's power; he's questioning God's goodness. Job's suffering is unendurable because he has nothing to look forward to. He discerns that God's power is useless if it's not grounded in love.

We and Job have to wait thirty-eight chapters before we get any kind of answer to Job's question, but when God does speak, we and Job don't quite get the answer we long to hear. God's answer is to affirm the mystery of our and the universe's origin and destiny, and to assert that those mysteries lie with God alone. In other words, we are left still clinging to the three dimensions of our quandary, but now knowing that God endorses that paradox and recognizes our struggle. While not offering a clear-cut answer, God's words in effect restore the relationship with Job and thus affirm that our communion with God transcends death. We aren't given a concrete picture of what our lives will be like in eternity, but we are given the one thing we need to know: that our communion with God will abide. It's as if we're offered a choice: choose the material comforts of life, and lose everything forever; or choose communion with God, and all other things will be added unto you. In Job 38, communion with God feels like shouting at each other through a whirlwind; but both parties are hanging on each other's every word, and that's what intimate communion is.

The story of Job is in the Bible. That means two things. It means Job is a parable about Israel, which in exile in Babylon found itself, like Job, having lost everything and wondering if it was going to be annihilated, and if all the good things in its history amounted to no more than a teasing form of torture. But this story being in the Bible also means that the answer to Job's question is, in the end, Jesus. In Jesus we see the story of Job played out in intense form, most of all upon the cross. Jesus's dying words, "Why have you forsaken me?" are a concise summary of the book of Job. They don't get an answer. For those three hours, and for two nights that follow, it seems that God's love and God's power have parted company, and the whole of creation is a pitiless mockery ending in annihilation. But Jesus's resurrection once again unites power and love, and shows us that we will not ultimately be forsaken.

When we lie on our beds at night or our deathbeds facing eternity, we do indeed face the loss of everything. But the witness of Job is that we lose everything—but God. The one thing we don't lose is communion with God. The one and only thing that in the end really matters. The source from which all blessings flow. So, and only so, may we rest in peace.

II

Such is a story that offers a way to separate what we won't ever know from what we do know, and to live both our knowledge and our ignorance. But if we wish to go further, we can explore what we know in more detail and strive to put some logic around it. This is the second approach.

Why was the world created? For what purpose did we come to exist? One deceptively simple reply answers both questions. Because God willed to be *with* us in Christ. Within that answer lies a fundamental conviction—one that sits slightly at odds with the majority strand in Christian theology. The conviction is that *being with* is the character of essence. In other words, not only is *being with* the experience of everlasting life with God; *being with* is also the nature of the Trinity—Father, Son, and Holy Spirit—God's three-in-one self. *Being with* is the nature and purpose of God, and the character both of Christ's first coming in the person of Jesus and of Christ's second coming at the end of all things.

In the Old Testament we can discern two threads of Israel's relationship with God—both of which are highlighted in the face of suffering. The first we could call contractual. This depicts a God who is for Israel. Israel is called to keep its side of the bargain: to worship no other gods, to walk in God's ways; meanwhile God is expected to work for Israel, bringing blessings and security and growth. The second we could call covenantal. This portrays a God who is with Israel. It's not clear, and often a source of anguish, why Israel is in jeopardy or distress. But what matters is that God is with Israel in that distress. If God is with Israel, Israel's outward circumstances or sense of well-being is secondary: what's primary is to understand and experience the God of *with*.

The definitive story in this regard is that given in Daniel 3 of the punishment Nebuchadnezzar of Babylon metes out to the three men who will not worship his golden statue. Nebuchadnezzar has the three men, Shadrach, Meshach, and Abednego, thrown into a fiery furnace. And what happens? The fire does not go out; the three men do not escape the fire; yet the fire does not consume them; and a fourth figure appears in the fire alongside them. The story portrays the experience of Babylon for the Jewish exiles: they do not escape exile, but they meet God in a new way in exile. The God they meet is a God who is principally and definitively *with* rather than *for*. God is not a useful instrument that can give them benefits: God is one whose relationship they seek for itself alone. Somehow the fire of exile is a fire not just for them but for God too.

If we turn to Jesus, we see the same tension between *with* and *for*. It's easy to assume Jesus comes to do a job: to overcome sin and death, to bring Israel's long exile to an end, to offer forgiveness and eternal life. That has been the majority emphasis in theology from the start. But what if Jesus is primarily God being with us rather than God working for us? Consider the shape of Jesus's life. He spent thirty years in Nazareth being with us, sharing our humble existence, before his three years in Galilee working with us, building a movement, and his week in Jerusalem working for us, facing death and being raised. Ninety percent of his incarnate life was *with* rather than *for*.

Then, if we look at the cross, we see the same pattern as in Babylon: Jesus isn't spared the cross. Jesus isn't rescued from the cross. Jesus is with God on the cross. The bonds of the Trinity are stretched to the limit but not broken. The cross is a proclamation that we see that God is with us, however, whatever, wherever, forever. On the cross Jesus cries, "My God, why have you forsaken me?" We're given an insight into the inner relationships of the Trinity. Father, Son, and Holy Spirit are utterly with one another: there is no need of *for*. But at this central moment in history, Jesus has to choose between being with us and being with the Father, and he chooses to be with us. Meanwhile the Father has to choose between insisting that Jesus be with him or letting Jesus be with us, and he chooses to let Jesus be with us, even to death. It's impossible fully to appreciate or express the depth or significance of these choices.

As Jesus dies, apparently forsaken, all seems lost: the Trinity is broken asunder. It's the ultimate act of *with*, utterly embodying God's demonstrated purpose never to be except to be with us. Yet the resurrection shows that God being with God in the Trinity and God being with us in Christ and the Holy Spirit are two ultimately indestructible bonds. This is why Christ's death and resurrection constitute the epicenter of the Christian faith.

But it also constitutes the Christian response to suffering. Let's return to our earlier question. If Jesus had completed his work on earth, why is there still evil? If we return to the distinction between essence, which lasts forever, and existence, which lasts for a limited time, we begin to see an answer. In forever, the realm of essence, there is no suffering, sin, evil, or death. There is complete *with*. Suffering, sin, evil, and death name the ways *with* is, in existence, inhibited or incomplete. Suffering isolates us so we cannot share the experience of *with*. It takes us to a place where others can't reach us—where we are terribly alone. Sin names the habits and patterns of relating that separate us from God and one another; that dismantle, diminish, or poison such relationship, persuading us falsely that there is something better or more attractive than *with*, that relationship can be used rather than enjoyed. Evil is sin transformed from a lapse into a program, from a wrong move to a whole enterprise founded on pernicious principles: those principles being ones that destroy relationship and obliterate *with*. Death is the condition of being utterly without everything—without life, relationship, existence—and thus utterly without *with*.

So these malign forces are still at large after Jesus's ascension because, while they are features that do not characterize essence, they do characterize existence. The expectation of Jesus's early disciples was that Jesus's second coming would come hot on the heels of his first—in other words, that essence would displace existence. But instead we are given Pentecost—the bestowal of the Holy Spirit to give us the tools we need to address suffering, sin, evil, and death as long as existence abides. We lament and bewail our existence; what we are doing is wishing Jesus's first coming were more like his second coming. But if the disciples' expectation had come to pass, history would have ended, and we seldom enumerate the losses this would entail: we only aspire to the gains. The only conclusion we can draw from the "delay" of Jesus's second coming is that the losses of bringing history to an end are greater than the gains.

We may consequently need to set aside the language of victory when talking about Jesus's cross and resurrection, and replace it with revelation. Jesus, on the cross, demonstrates the utter *with*-ness of God, the presence of essence amidst existence, even when surrounded by all the forces that bedevil existence and attack *with*-ness—suffering, sin, evil, and death. In so doing he reveals what essence promises—forgiveness of sin, abolition of evil, the end of isolation and suffering, and being with God in a way that transcends death. And Jesus, in his resurrection, demonstrates the eternal *with-ness* of God and God's purpose to restore what the prophet Joel calls "the years the swarming locust has eaten"—all that sin and suffering have tarnished—and portrays what it means for death no longer to be a barrier to being with one another, the creation, and God. Together, Jesus's death and separation display *with* by showing how nothing can separate us from God.

And this, finally, yields the answer to our question. If Jesus ascended to heaven having completed his work on earth, why is there still evil? The answer is, because Jesus's work on earth was not straightaway to destroy death, dismantle sin, or dispel evil; neither was it to rescue souls for heavenly bliss that they might temporally escape bleak earth and eternally evade excruciating hell. It was to display the purpose of God ultimately to bring us into essence—a kingdom beyond suffering, death, sin, and evil—and to demonstrate conclusively the original design of God to be with us always, most especially in our moments of distress and isolation. Jesus ascended into heaven when he had demonstrated the former—the promise of the kingdom—in his resurrection, and the latter—the will never to be separated from us—in his crucifixion.

How This Story Differs from the Rival Story

What this story, in both its versions, exposes in the rival story is an assumption that if there is a God, the job of that God is to fix human problems, ameliorate existence, and arrange benefits. The rival story is, perhaps inevitably, a human-centered story where, by common effort, individual endeavor, and a fair wind, we can rise above our challenges and achieve nobility, dignity, freedom, and peace. Suffering and evil hamper and beset this story, but in some cases people individually or collectively can overcome such cruel and pointless trials.

The story to live by is a very different story. It maintains that the heart of all things is relationship. If there is hardship and yet there is still relationship, it is well with our soul. By contrast, if there is prosperity but no relationship, there is no reason to rejoice. Thus God is fundamentally not a means to secure comforts but one in whom we find everlasting and inexpressible relationship. An ancient prayer puts it succinctly. "God of time and eternity, if I love thee for hope of heaven, then deny me heaven; if I love thee for fear of hell, then give me hell; but if I love thee for thyself alone, then give me thyself alone." The "problem of suffering" assumes that God's role is to bring health and flourishing—and if God fails to do that, God is malign or weak. But what if God's role is to be with us always, in person in Jesus, in myriad ways through the Holy Spirit, and forever in heaven? God is not an instrument we discard if it malfunctions. God is the essence of all things who astonishingly chooses to be with us even in desperate hardship—and even, in the crucified Christ, in indescribable agony. That doesn't make suffering go away. But it turns God's engagement with suffering from a reason for rejection into a reason for worship.

How This Story Differs from the Old, Old Story

The story to live by fears that it's not just the rival story that tends to instrumentalize God. The old, old story is prone to the same tendency. The center of the story to live by isn't our human problem—the sin we perpetrate and the suffering we endure. The center of the story is Jesus. Christ's incarnation was at the heart of God's purposes in creation—indeed, it was the reason for creation—and is far from a secondary action of God in response to the setback of sin and death. God's life is, from the outset, ordered to be in relationship with us. The gospel is not that God responded to our sin by diverting from other duties to fit in a sacrificial intervention on earth to justify and sanctify us; the gospel is that being with us is written into the nature of God, and Christ's coming fully embodied what was always God's purpose.

Christian theology has too often been captivated by the notion of *for*, to the detriment of the truer reality of *with*. By this I mean that it invariably perceives Christ as working or being for us—fixing our infirmities, dying for us, rising for us—rather than focusing on the more lasting gift of his working with or ultimately being with us. In the penultimate chapter of the book of Revelation, we read that God is among us—God will dwell with us; we will be God's peoples, and God will be with us. God will wipe every tear from our eyes. Death will be no more; mourning and crying and pain will be no more, for the first things will have passed away (Rev. 21:3–4). In the coming of the kingdom, once the tears have been wiped away, there'll be nothing left for God to do for us. We shall fully be God's companions. The relationship will be the utter embodiment of *with*. Thus *with* is not only the *goal* of salvation; it's also the *method* of salvation. *God is with us* through the very worst of life and in the very separation of death—in, through, and beyond. The theology of *with* insists that the method and goal of God in creation, incarnation, and salvation are the same.

It's important not to miss the significance of equating the form of salvation with its content—or, to put it another way, making the way Jesus restores us entirely consistent with the restored life to which he calls us. The Christ we see on the cross bears all things, believes all things, hopes all things, endures all things—and demonstrates a love that never ends. The cross is not a sacrifice that appeases God's righteous wrath or a conquest that defeats our last enemy. It's a vision of a God whose purpose is to be with us more intimately, more permanently, more comprehensively than we can imagine; and is so committed to be so, that Christ is willing to endure even crucifixion to embody the ultimate commitment to be with. Meanwhile, what traditional theology calls the "benefits of Christ's passion"—forgiveness and eternal life—are both aspects of *being with*. Forgiveness removes the guilt and bitterness that inhibit being with God, one another, and ourselves; eternal life represents being with God and the renewed creation forever. The point is that the Jesus we see on the cross and the Jesus with whom we spend eternity are consistent in character: profoundly with us, not fixing our infirmities but sharing our condition, without waver, without limit, without end.

- 3 -

FAIRY TALE FOR THE INFANTILE?

CHRISTIANITY ASSUMES THAT GOD'S presence, character, and purpose are revealed in a number of ways, but definitively in the Bible. For some, the whole idea of revelation is a stumbling block. For others, the Bible itself seems flawed in multiple ways. Its presentation of God is sometimes belligerent and at other times angry or small-minded; its characters behave in countless less-than-commendable ways; its claim to historicity is in places unlikely and in other places questionable; and overall, it's a sprawling collection of sixty-six books that seems to contain internal inconsistencies and unreliable convictions. How could one trust one's existence to such a flaky foundation?

The Old, Old Story and What's Wrong with It

The Standard Account

The standard account is that God wrote the Bible, so we should believe that the Bible is true. A modified version of this account is that humans recorded the words of the Bible by the inspiration of the Holy Spirit, and if there are inconsistencies or inaccuracies in the Bible (for example, in the different accounts of precisely which words Jesus spoke from the cross, or who were the first witnesses to his resurrection), these are attributable to fallible humans inscribing timeless truth.

There have been attempts to secure the reliability of the Bible in the historical narrative that it relates. For example, many have sought, in archaeology, verification of the events described in the Old Testament. Meanwhile, attempts to unearth evidence for a huge movement of water that coincided with the parting of the Red Sea, or for an appearance of a star to coincide with the journey of the Magi, are legion. It is no small fact that there are around 5,800 early copies of the Greek New Testament in existence, almost three times as many as any other ancient manuscript in its original language. The figures described—Herod, Pontius Pilate, Felix—are historical people, independently attested in other contemporary documents.

More substantially, it is argued that the Bible points to Jesus, and Jesus points to the Bible. Thus, as Paul suggests in 2 Corinthians 1:20, all the promises of God find their yes in Christ. Jesus fulfills the expectation frequently articulated in the Old Testament for a Messiah to restore God's favor and deliver Israel from its oppressors—and also, more controversially, to open out God's promises to the gentiles. Jesus also inhabits all the roles by which Israel designated its leaders: he is prophet, priest, and king. He is Adam, Noah, Abraham, and Moses combined. In return, Jesus affirms the authority of the Old Testament. At his ascension in Luke 24:44 he says, "'These are my words that I spoke to you while I was still with you—that everything written about me in the law of Moses, the prophets, and the psalms must be fulfilled." In his Sermon on the Mount in Matthew 5:17–18 Jesus asserts, "Do not think that I have come to abolish the law or the prophets; I have come not to abolish but to fulfill. For truly I tell you, until heaven and earth pass away, not one letter, not one stroke of a letter, will pass from the law until all is accomplished."

If the question is asked, how are we to trust the Jesus who attests to the Bible's credibility and authority, the answer given by the old, old story is that Jesus rose from the dead. One who does such a thing is a figure unique in history, and his doing so, in apparent fulfillment of repeated predictions that he would do so, makes all his other statements and actions trustworthy. If we ask how we can accept that Jesus rose from the dead, given that our evidence is found in the Bible, the conventional answer is that there is no other way to account for the astonishing turnaround in his disciples' behavior—from dispirited depression to invigorated and courageous proclamation. These were eyewitnesses of the events described, and eyewitnesses were those who for the most part wrote the New Testament, giving their testimony extra authority. The Bible, despite its length, never claims to be comprehensive; but it does claim to be conclusive, notably in the original conclusion to John's Gospel at John 20:30–31: "Now Jesus did many other signs in the presence of his disciples, which are not written in this book. But these are written so that you may come to believe that Jesus is the Messiah, the Son of God, and that through believing you may have life in his name."

Challenges to the Standard Account

The Bible poses a number of problems, most of which began to surface in the seventeenth, eighteenth, and nineteenth centuries, with the emergence of various kinds of criticism. Five immediately arise.

First, the Bible comes from a worldview alien to the twenty-first century. The first two chapters of Genesis describe two creation stories, both of which have no connection with what geologists, astronomers, and biologists are now confident constituted the beginnings of the universe, the world, life, and humankind. Throughout the biblical narrative, portents in the skies are frequently attributed to God's action, and characters often have encounters with God, meetings with divine surrogates, or disclosures of God's will. Miracles happen. What today might be diagnosed as physical or mental illness is often spoken of as punishment or possession. The action takes place in a narrow corner of the world, seldom departing beyond a remarkably small geographical region, and characters seem unaware of the extent of the globe, let alone the enormity of the universe.

Second, the Bible describes extraordinary events that are hard to verify historically. Was there a figure called Abraham who was called by God to a promised land? Did a man called Moses lead his people through the Red Sea between reared-up walls of water? Did that same Moses climb Mount Sinai and receive the Ten Commandments on two tablets of stone? Did the prophet Elijah really rise up through the skies on a chariot of fire? Did three men at the behest of a Babylonian king truly go into a fiery furnace and emerge unscathed? These stories play vital roles in the Old Testament but are indigestible to many a contemporary reader. Even more significantly, how can we trust a story that suggests Jesus was conceived without the conjoining of female egg and male sperm in the time-honored way? What are we to make of his string of miracles, including raising the dead? How could he ascend to heaven if humans can't ascend and heaven isn't above the clouds? And most of all, did he himself rise from the grave on the third day as the Gospels attest? The whole thing collapses under modern scrutiny and is therefore at best a myth.

Third, the Bible portrays a God that falls short of contemporary expectations of divine character, and seems to endorse activity that offers a poor example to those seeking to walk the way of righteousness. The Lord is described as "a God merciful and gracious, slow to anger, and abounding in steadfast love and faithfulness" (Exod. 34:6). But that same God appears to exhibit plenty of anger and bring about a good deal of smiting and slaughter; not least in the Israelites' settlement of the land of Canaan, which, as the story attests, was already occupied by local tribes that required forcible removal. And God's will seems to be exercised through some dubious characters, notably the trickster, liar, and cheat Jacob, who dupes his twin brother out of his inheritance and runs away from the consequences, and the compromised murderer David, who sends into the heat of battle the husband of the woman he's kidnapped and raped. Meanwhile, the oppression of women and the merciless treatment of enemies are among many moral habits that sit painfully with the contemporary reader.

Fourth, to the more combative, the Bible is filled with fabrications, excuses, and schemes posing as revelation. The Old Testament is in great part the response of a beleaguered people who found themselves in exile in Babylon and were searching for hope. They recorded these stories to try to construct meaning and purpose about how they came to be in exile and how they could find conviction to envisage that somehow they might return home. More acutely, it is sometimes maintained, the New Testament is the response of Jesus's companions, locked in denial about the fact of his gruesome demise and seeking to find energy and imagination to go on with life and trust his teaching and example. Some would say Paul captured the Jesus story and turned it into his own account of redemption. Others would argue that Jesus anticipated an imminent end of the world, and the fact that he seems to have been wrong about this expectation renders doubtful the credibility of his other statements. More provocatively, some would say the writings affirmed as part of the New Testament rigorously excluded documents that portrayed Jesus rather differently, and carried no account of resurrection. Those looking to smell a rat have found a host of gaps in the floorboards to pursue.

Fifth, and perhaps most conclusively, the Bible is just a story. In fact, it isn't just a story—it's poetry, law, lament, history, parable, letter, satire, and much else. But the power of the phrase lies not in the word "story" but in the word "just." It's a phrase that feels the Bible is not enough. It's not convincing enough, not comprehensive enough, not compelling enough, not certain enough. How can a single story, albeit one told across generations and centuries and interlaced with other kinds of literature, go to the heart of everything? It's such a clumsy, fragile, partial, ignorant document. There's so much that we know that it doesn't know. Enjoy it for what it is—a fascinating historical artifact, a remarkable collection of ancient reflections on life, truth, and history—but it is not a trustworthy guide to here or hereafter.

A Rival Story, Its Validity and Flaws

A Rival Story

The world today is full of assertion, rebuttal, counterassertion, speculation, opinion, denial, fact checking, and skepticism. In academic circles, arguments need to be evidence-based, peer-reviewed, scrutinized for plagiarism, and attested as making a contribution to the field. In the newsroom, agencies to different degrees hold to a sense of integrity about how information is derived and verified. Those who tread a boundary between fact and fiction are viewed with some suspicion as clouding the one and betraying the other. The idea that a story could claim to be the story of everything, and have a morally and conceptually binding effect on vast numbers of people, would generally be seen as fanciful.

The story this world upholds is that there is no overarching story. There are facts, which, once verified, become the building blocks for plausible narratives, which become more convincing once further hard evidence is gathered around them. There's propaganda, marketing, and opinion, which tell a one-sided story no doubt full of interest but seldom trespassing near the truth. And then there are all kinds of fiction, from the myth to the fairy story, sometimes profound, often idle—but surely not valid for basing your life upon. Stories are always partly falsifications. What this rival story seldom acknowledges is that it itself is a story. That's to say, it's not a truly foundational account that goes to the very roots of every earthly phenomenon and looks guilelessly in the face every shade of influence or distortion. It makes its own assumptions and is subject to the particularities of its own social location, just like any account. It may tend to be inhospitable to any other account: hence its description of other accounts as stories and its reluctance to describe its own account as a story. But in practice it usually has the humility to recognize how much it doesn't know, and thus to respect other stories as legitimate in their own sphere—even if it claims complete authority in its own sphere, which it not surprisingly regards as the only sphere that matters.

By the estimation of this story, the story the Bible tells is irrelevant or negligible. That's because the Bible concerns themes like destiny, vocation, providence, incarnation, resurrection, hope, and faith—themes that have no solid foothold in its own story. It's an alien vocabulary and conceptual field. Such a list contains things that can't happen (resurrection), concepts that lie beyond the scope of any rational account (destiny), or items that are simply impossible to quantify (hope). The Bible also describes qualities like courage, love, loyalty, fear, solidarity, and sacrifice. These the rival story can comprehend and often admire; the Scriptures thus become one source among many sources of inspiration that illuminate values after which many in the world strive. By contrast, the egregious actions of God and human beings that pepper some books of the Bible only confirm that this is at heart an alien document from another world.

The Validity and Flaws of the Rival Story

The authority of Scripture was especially asserted during the Reformation as a way of countering what were perceived as the unwarranted accretions of church tradition that characterized Catholicism at the time. But it has sometimes become too grand and sweeping a claim. Most of the objections to the old, old story set out above are very reasonable. There's no use defending, for example, the creation accounts at the beginning of Genesis as reliable historically or scientifically. To do so is to impose a set of assumptions alien to the era in which the accounts were written. But that doesn't mean those accounts are nonsense. In chapter 2 I described how the story of Adam and Eve identified the heart of sin as substituting human scarcity for God's abundance. That's what the second creation story is about. And that insight is as true as it ever was. Likewise, when the Israelites in the wilderness ignore God's injunction not to collect two days' worth of manna the day before the Sabbath, the fundamental issue isn't about whether God rains food down from heaven or not. The point is that Israel had got into the habit of trusting more in its own devices than in its relationship with God. And that tendency is, again, as active as ever.

That's not to say historicity is unimportant. The resurrection of Jesus is the foundational historical event for Christianity: if it could somehow be proved not to have happened, Christianity in any conventional form would be profoundly compromised—perhaps thoroughly undermined. Likewise, the incarnation of Jesus is vital to the Christian faith, albeit almost impossible historically to discredit or verify. It's not entirely clear whether the virgin birth is indispensable for the doctrine of the incarnation. But again, the point of the virgin birth is to say that Jesus is God's new beginning—perhaps the real beginning of all things. Matthew's Gospel makes that clear when it uses the Greek word "genesis" to say "The genesis [usually translated 'birth'] of Jesus the Messiah took place in this way" (Matt. 1:18). As for the exodus, it's hard to disentangle exactly what happened from the account in Exodus 14–15, which is often said to have been drawn together from two or three originally separate documents. There have even been suggestions that the whole story was a myth created by tribes who never left Canaan and lived there without ever sojourning in Egypt. It seems that something profound and remarkable that constituted escape from bondage did happen, although whether it was a meteorological event is another matter.

Some criticisms display a curious naïveté—for example, about what the writers of the Bible knew. When it's maintained that the Gospels, and Jesus, are untrustworthy because Jesus was anticipating an imminent end of the world that didn't come, the very information being used to criticize the Gospels comes from within the Gospels themselves. The gospel writers knew the end of the world hadn't come. We have no Jesus except the Jesus given to us by the early church. The idea that Paul constructed a radically different message is likewise drawn from information only available in the New Testament. The Bible didn't fall in one piece from heaven; its contents were hotly debated, and the likelihood is that the books themselves, especially the Gospels, marinated for years in communities that pondered each word and sieved each sentence for whether it was true to the Jesus they'd known.

The real question is about how authority works in the Bible. Here there are broadly three answers. The simplest answer is to perceive the significance of the events the Bible describes—looking "behind the text." The Bible may be a fallible account, but what matters are the events the Bible describes, not the Bible's description of them. The most abrasive answer is to rest authority on the very words of the Bible itself— the authority is "in the text." This allows for no slip of the pen, and commits itself to upholding the text's historicity when it might seem shaky and asserting its moral probity when words or actions may seem far from admirable. Scripture so understood may be modified by such other authorities as tradition and reason, but when it stands alone (as many denominations claim it does), it constitutes a claim that is frequently almost impossible (and, I would say, unnecessary) to defend. The subtlest answer and, I would suggest, the most sustainable, is to locate authority "in front of the text"—that is, in the ways the Scriptures are heard and in the actions that result from that hearing. This is an understanding that the Holy Spirit works through faithful reading and performance more than through inspired (or infallible) writing. The search for infallibility is seen as a false quest as soon as one recognizes that the Bible is an invitation to a relationship, and that far from infallible, all relationships are subject to misunderstanding, setbacks, reappraisals, and refined perceptions.

My contention in the way this book is structured is that we don't get to choose between story and fact. There is only story. Every arrangement of facts is an implied or explicit story. "Fact" is the name for the parts of the story we regard as foundational. Story is the way we find meaning, purpose, connection, and significance. If Christianity is rejected, it can't be on the grounds that it's "just a story"; nor on the grounds that its story includes some elements that sound implausible or can't be verified. The simple question, "Did it happen?" is not a synonym for "Is it true?" Few if any historical events are self-defining, detached from context. "Story" is an elaborate and nuanced word for context. If Christianity is rejected, it has to be on the grounds that this story is based on inadequate and inaccurate understandings of humanity and yields unrealizable or unconscionable forms of life among those who adhere to it. That's how one tells if a story is true.

A Story to Live by, and How It Differs from Both Stories

A Story to Live By

I'm going to take the story to live by in three stages. First, how are we to read the Bible? The best way to discuss the Bible is not to debate its significance in the abstract but to take a relatively obscure passage and see how it works in Scripture and faith. Second, how does our own context shape our reading of the Bible? Here I take a foundational passage of Scripture and seek to demonstrate how it's meant to subvert our lives today. Third, how do we live the Bible? Here I briefly introduce two concepts that I have found transformational in appreciating the way the Bible changes lives.

I

Here is a proposal for how we might consider the story the Bible tells us. Let's reflect on the account of Jacob sojourning in Haran with his uncle Laban in Genesis 29–31. It's an obscure story. Jacob cheats his brother Esau and flees. He comes to Haran, and cozies up to his cousin Rachel. Jacob serves Laban seven years for Rachel. Overnight, Laban substitutes Leah for Rachel. Jacob is eventually given Rachel, but only at the cost of another seven years' labor. Leah, the unloved sister, has several sons; Rachel envies her sister, and each sister offers Jacob her handmaid. Both handmaids have sons too, before at last Rachel has a son, Joseph. Jacob loses patience with Laban and escapes with his whole household back to Canaan. Before leaving, Rachel steals her father's household gods, without telling Jacob. Laban chases his departed family and, after a week, catches up with them. Laban searches everywhere for the household gods, but Rachel sticks the household gods up her skirts, and then tricks her father by telling him she's menstruating, so she can't move. Then Jacob completely loses it, and berates Laban because of all the deceit, manipulation, and exploitation he's suffered at Laban's expense. Finally Laban and Jacob make their peace, leaving Jacob, after twenty years of silent enmity, to face his unfinished business with his brother Esau.

What do we do with this story? If we take the Bible as a moral handbook, not a lot. The treatment of women is pretty appalling. The treatment of servants is even worse. There's no suggestion of consent. Jacob and Laban connive, cheat, and steal like two pesky jackals, and this is just within the family; who knows what they're like with strangers. Jacob engages a vendetta against his brother and his father-in-law simultaneously, while his wives constantly jockey for status.

One thing that *is* going on is a narrative of the neighboring tribes with whom Israel later came to struggle. It's a story written hundreds of years later, helping Israel come to understand its special status, the origins of its often-hostile neighbors, and the grounds for their hostility. Jacob's name is changed to Israel. His struggles prefigure Israel's later antagonisms. The story presents the Edomites as descendants of Esau, and thus inheritors of a rivalry that goes back to Rebekah's womb. Likewise, the Aramaeans are descendants of Laban.

What we mustn't miss is the surfeit of infectious humor and biting irony. The description of how Rachel tricks her father by shoving the household gods up her skirts and then pretending she can't move because of her period, not only makes a pantomime fool out of Laban but ridicules the whole notion of household gods. Jacob thinking he's spent the night with Rachel, then waking up to find it's Leah, is worthy of a scene from the bawdiest Restoration comedy. Above all, the story portrays Jacob, the trickster who supplanted his own brother, getting his comeuppance when Laban won't let him snatch the younger daughter ahead of her older sister. We have to imagine these stories being told around the fireside among the folktales of Israel. We shouldn't be surprised by elements that owe more to farce and comedy than to solemn instruction.

So why *do* we read the Bible, given that it's saturated with dubious dealings, compromised characters, endemic enmities, and rambunctious ribaldry? We read it for two reasons—which are just as evident in this obscure and puzzling story as in the New Testament stories of Jesus or letters of Paul.

The first reason is that it shows us who we are. We trust the Bible not because all the "begats" can be historically verified or because every miracle has been medically attested or because someone found a scroll in a cave that dated back to biblical times. We trust the Bible because it knows exactly who we are. We're people who get into lifelong rivalries with our siblings; whose success or otherwise in having children causes envy, anxiety, self-doubt, and pride; who are perpetually manipulated by our in-laws; who play childish tricks on our parents; who take absurd pleasure in getting one over on our neighbors; who think it's okay when we subvert the rules but are infuriated when someone dupes us in return. We're the ones who search the past for explanations for why we're in trouble, who storm off without saying good-bye when we've been taken advantage of one time too many, who end up making face-saving agreements with people we shouted unrepeatable things at. The point is not whether the stories are precisely historical—it's whether they're real. And this story of Jacob and Laban and Rachel and Leah is plenty real, as well as being hilarious and close to the bone.

The second reason why we read the Bible is that it shows us who God is. No one comes out of the Jacob story very well. That's not the point. The point is that God is wholly invested in people who don't come out of stories very well. This isn't a story about how Jacob believed in God. This is a story about how God believed in Jacob. That's the difference between morality and theology. Morality's about us living well with each other in the light of who we've seen God to be. Theology's about recognizing how badly we live with each other, and discovering how God invests in us anyway. The Bible does not teach that we should be good and kind, and if we are, God will keep us safe and well and make us rich and happy, and beyond death will give us harps and clouds and blonde curly hair. The Bible proclaims that we can deceive, betray, manipulate, flee; be hypocritical, envious, hostile, self-righteous; act foolishly, selfishly, craftily, and deceptively—and God will still say, "You can't stop me folding every one of your flawed actions into a story of hope and healing." As Joseph tells his brothers at the end of Genesis, "You meant it for evil; God meant it for good."

But these two reasons are only the background to the true reason we read the Bible. We read the Bible because it shows us how who we are and who God is become fused in one being—Jesus Christ. Here are two mistakes we easily make about Jesus. One is to forget he's fully human. That's why we have the Bible, to show us what full humanity really means. The other is to forget he's fully God. That's why we have the Bible—to meet Jesus, and to discover, more deeply and more truly every day, who Jesus is. The Bible isn't a moral handbook. A moral handbook would be a way of living a good life without coming face-to-face with our humanity and face-to-face with God.

We read a story like that of Jacob, Rachel, Leah, and Laban because it shows us the wondrous ways of God, interlaced with the feckless ways of people who love, labor, loot, and lie. It hints at a grand story, but it's actually a rollicking tale spiced with humor and satire. It leaves us with two questions—questions that bring us to our knees in worship. First, does God want to take flesh as a human being, if this is what people are really like? Second, does that mean—does that really, truly, astonishingly mean—there could even be a place in this story for me?

II

I next want to take a second story, this a much-better-known one, and consider not only how to think about the Bible but also how the whole notion of the Christian story is shaped. There's been a major change in Western culture in the last sixty years: being a Christian is no longer a normal thing to be, and going to church is no longer a conventional thing to do. Christianity's claim to truth hasn't become any less valid, but those who uphold that claim have fewer companions, and their convictions are no longer surrounded by extensive social supports, but are increasingly exposed to the chill winds of indifference, skepticism, and even hostility. It's not surprising that for many, that erosion of Christianity's social confidence becomes internalized, especially when voiced by spouse, parent, sibling, colleague, or friend, and those who sit in church do so with a whispering voice, saying, "Why are you here? What connection is there between worship and reality?"

This is the experience of a collective crisis of faith. To explore what it involves, and what to do about it, I want to reflect on perhaps the most significant story in the whole of the Old Testament, the account in Exodus 14 of the parting of the Red Sea and the liberation of the Israelites. I believe in this story lies everything that's become problematic about being a Christian in our day—but also everything that offers promise of hope and joy.

The crossing of the Red Sea is the foundational story of the Old Testament because it brings together the three things the Old

Testament is essentially about. It's a new creation story—just as in Genesis chapter 1, God brings dry land out of chaos, God makes a kind of birth experience of the waters breaking and a new people coming into being, God speaks and things happen, and the result is new life. It's a story of liberation: God wants Israel to be free, sees Israel's plight in slavery to the pharaoh, creates a path to freedom, and destroys the powers of oppression. And it's a portrayal of covenant: God cares for Israel, God is sovereign over the natural environment, and Israel in turn responds through the obedience of Moses and the active participation of the people. Creation, liberation, and covenant—it's the whole of the Old Testament crystallized in a dozen verses.

At this point we need to pause and recognize how for Western readers, once this whole theological canvas fitted onto our culture and society as comfortably as a jacket slips onto a person's back and arms and shoulders. I'm going to describe the country I know best, the United Kingdom—but a similar story fits the United States and most countries of the West. This theological canvas fitted philosophically because Britain saw itself as the new Israel, which had inherited the status of God's favorite nation, and had a role to play in civilizing the world and bringing order, peace, and justice like a new but better Roman Empire. It was taken for granted that God was all-powerful, and that the parting of the oceans was all of a piece with creating them in the first place. It fitted morally because Britain, whose citizens insisted that they "never, never, never shall be slaves" (while until 1807 actively enslaving others), was a guardian of justice and freedom throughout the world and saw itself as a kind of collective Moses figure, achieving astonishing things through its industrial revolution that rolled back the tide of ignorance and inefficiency and laying down laws that commanded the loyalty of peoples the world over. And it fitted culturally because Britain's leaders were regarded with a degree of deference that assumed they had a divine right to advance the benevolent hand of British authority, which included fostering the expansion and flourishing of the church as justification and guarantee of righteousness.

But over the last 150 years that set of assumptions, by which the crossing of the Red Sea was taken to be a story about Britain that affirmed its place in the cosmos, in the world, and in the social hierarchy—a package underwritten by Bible, church, and God—has come under three kinds of assault. It's come under historical assault because scientists and philosophers have said, "The kind of Charlton Heston–style rearing up of the waves can't happen. This is the most dramatic of a host of biblical miracles that just don't sit alongside a modern worldview. This story was probably created by tribes in Canaan as a myth of origins to explain their distinctive identity and strong sense of unique calling." It's come under moral assault because critics have said, "What kind of a God is this who chooses a favorite people, exercises extensive violence to rescue them, and mercilessly leaves the Egyptians strewn across the shore? If God has this ability to control wind and waves and cares about the plight of the oppressed, how about doing a better job with steering tornadoes away from population centers and delivering innocent citizens from the hands of marauding and murderous terrorists?" And it's come under a more subtle cultural assault because activists have said, "If Britain is a postcolonial power that retains a seat on the Security Council, surely it's a self-serving misreading of the story to characterize us as the powerless Israelites; wouldn't it be more accurate to say we Western powers are more like the Egyptians in this story, and a true fulfillment of the story's promises would leave us and our geopolitical hegemony strewn across the shore."

This historical, moral, and cultural critique amounts to a formidable assault, and it's what has dismantled the church's sense of ease, confidence, and entitlement in British society, and in many others. For many people, the church's historical, moral, and cultural authority is significantly compromised. Christians have responded to this onslaught in three ways—a bad way, an inadequate way, and a good way. The bad way is simply to shout louder, to claim the privileges and status of the past as entitlements, to employ nostalgic notions of being a Christian country, to use influence, manipulation, or force to make things as much as possible like they used to be. Such actions make the problem far worse than it would otherwise be.

The inadequate way is largely to give up on the outward trappings of Christianity and to retreat to an interior realm of spirituality and mood music and untroubling benevolence. The trouble with this is that the crossing of the Red Sea is an intensely political, conflictual, and public story. Creation, liberation, and covenant aren't interior experiences in the Old Testament—they're about society, slavery, escape, social change, and struggle. Assuming that the Red Sea story simply endorsed British colonialism was doubtless distorted and mistaken, but turning the story into the stimulus for interior equilibrium renders the Old Testament meaningless.

So what is the better way? If Christians in the West respond to the cultural revolution that I have described without defensiveness and with a healthy dose of humility, I believe they'll recognize that this revolution has made them able to read the account of the crossing of the Red Sea with fresh eyes. No longer will they read the story—and Christianity in general—as affirming their social standing, their favored place in the world, or any sense of entitlement. Instead they will take the following lessons from this story, which we can perceive as five acts of a drama.

In act 1, God's fundamental purpose, beginning with *creation*, is to be in relationship with us not just personally but collectively. God will not rest, and creation will not be fulfilled, until this desire for full, profound, and universal relationship comes to pass. Every time we form or restore relationships of this kind, especially in the face of adversity or hostility, we are imitating God's signal purpose. In creation, God the Holy Trinity, essence in perfect relationship, the epitome of being with, brings forth existence. Each creature finds its fulfillment in being with the rest of creation and with God. Everything exists to enjoy and be enjoyed: every relationship in which one partner is used is a relationship ripe to grow into one in which both partners truly enjoy one another. Enjoyment is the activity of essence. Use is the transitory method of existence. But there's a scar on the demeanor of creation, which in this story is characterized by Pharaoh. Use treads down enjoyment. Abundance turns to scarcity. The quality of togetherness is strained—and in this story, that's embodied in the institution of slavery. Being with becomes unusual, neglected, out of reach. Sabbath is eroded. Trust is destroyed. God's commitment to be with us turns from being the most natural thing in the world into an achievement to be sought after, longed for, reached only through sacrifice.

In act 2, in order to make such relationships of trust, commitment, and reconciliation, we need to experience a significant degree of freedom. God wills to liberate us not because we should be allowed to do whatever we like but because we exercise freedom most fully by forming and restoring fruitful relationships. This is what the Old Testament calls *covenant*. God's fundamental purpose to be with us in Christ is anticipated in the covenant relationship between God and Israel. When God meets Moses in the burning bush, God says, "I have observed the misery of my people." When Moses says, "Who am I that I should go to Pharaoh?" God says, "I will be with you" (Exod. 3:7, 11–12). Likewise, when Israel is in exile in Babylon, God announces, "I have called you by name, you are mine. When you pass through the waters, I will be with you . . . , [for] you are precious in my sight, and honored, and I love you" (Isa. 43:1–2, 4). The issue is always whether Israel will let the relationship lapse into a contract, instrumentalizing God as a mechanism for gaining blessing, victory, and prosperity (a "working-for" arrangement), or whether Israel will let the relationship blossom into a true covenant (or "being with") in which Israel will fulfill its calling to be the way God blesses all the nations.

In act 3, *Christ* models what it means for God to seek relationship with us, what it entails to bear the cost of our hostility, and what it involves to restore relationship through forgiveness, reconciliation, and healing. The early Christians saw the crossing of the Red Sea as the prototype of resurrection, and they embodied its deliverance in the sacrament of baptism. Jesus's coming, life, death, and resurrection constitute the central event of the story the Bible tells. Everything in the story prepares for it or derives from it. We see what humanity is like and what God is like; this prepares us to apprehend what Jesus, fully human, fully divine, could be like. On a grand scale, Jesus's story is one of nervous kings, vacillating governors, movements in the heavens, earthquakes, a census, a star. On a personal level, his story is one of unexpected pregnancy, loyalty of and betrayal by friends, doubt, trust, courage, wonder, reunion. It centers on how the cosmic and intimate converge in cross and resurrection.

Of these three things that we learn from the biblical story, the third—the coming of Jesus—puts flesh on the first two. Echoing act 2, Jesus is Israel in one person, the epitome of what Israel is called to be—the full presence of humanity before God, and the full presence of God before humanity. He is the new Adam, the new Noah, the new Abraham, the new Moses, the new David, the new Jonah, and the new Esther. But echoing act 1, Jesus is the new creation. His birth is a new genesis. His resurrection is a new creation.

In act 4, the *church* is given the stories of Scripture and the counsel of the Holy Spirit constantly to relocate itself in the places and among the people where this balance of liberation and covenant is taking place. Sometimes it gets things terribly wrong and realizes that it has turned into the oppressive Egyptians. Sometimes it gets things right and has the exhilarating experience of feeling protected by God's power and of being close to God's glory and being alive in freedom and hope. The coming of the Holy Spirit at Pentecost is the first event of act 4. The most important things have already happened, most especially in act 3. The character of God revealed there will not change. And yet in act 4 the Holy Spirit continues to make Christ present—not only in the honored practices of baptism and Eucharist, prayer and Scripture reading, but also in the face of the oppressed, movements for justice, and steps along the path of reconciliation. Sometimes the church acts as salt—invisible in society, yet adding vital flavor. Sometimes it acts as light—visible, vulnerable, seeking truth, beauty, and goodness. One insight disclosed by living in act 4 is that it is better to fail in a cause that will finally succeed than to succeed in a cause that will finally fail. Act 5 is coming, however badly wrong the church often gets things—and it's coming not as a reward for the church's faithfulness but as a gift arising from God's.

Then finally the church looks forward to the day when, like Israel in this story, it rejoices in act 5 on another shore, with dancing and singing and love and laughter and wonder and joy, with all the powers that oppress it in disarray, and with God very present and close and forever and true. This is *consummation*—the final taking-back of existence into essence. Consummation means that being with, hampered since creation, definitively embodied, in a costly way, in Jesus, will finally be made possible for everyone—with God, with themselves, with one another, and with the new creation. Inhibitors to that *with*—fear, oppression, violence, guilt, bitterness, anxiety, hardship—will be dismantled, redeemed, and healed, so that being with may be all in all.

Earlier I said the crossing of the Red Sea was the Old Testament in a dozen verses. In fact, it's more than that. What I've just described is the whole of Christianity in five acts, like a great drama. There's creation, covenant, Christ, church, and finally consummation. And every single one of those great dimensions of God's story is present in embryo in a dozen verses of the book of Exodus. So this story isn't just the whole Old Testament; it's the whole Bible, the whole of everything, the entire story of God and us.

And here's the point. For centuries Christians of privilege clung to this story, and others like it, to justify their standing in the world. For the last 150 years that hegemony has come under wave upon wave of criticism, which has depleted the church's confidence, just as it has created in many people a crisis of individual faith. But the truth is, most of that criticism was fully justified—and, here's the great irony, that criticism was in the spirit of the original story. On the other side of that formidable challenge lies a deeper understanding of the exodus, of the church, and of God. Once Christians let go (and only once they let go) of their certainty that this story has to enhance their security, status, and strength, they can begin to discover that this story reveals to them the purpose of existence, the nature of their struggle, and the heart of God.

III

Having established the shape of the Bible as a five-act play, with Jesus as the central act, it still remains to explicate how the Bible becomes a story to live by. Here we do well to employ the practice and terminology of theatrical improvisation. Contrary to common misunderstandings, improvisation is not about being clever, spontaneous, or original. It's about being so steeped in a tradition that you learn to take the right things for granted. It's about the formation of habits such that you don't even realize what you're doing is a "moral" action: it's simply the obvious thing to do. Improvisation is a practice by which actors come so to trust one another that they allow a story to emerge among them.

This clarifies the role of the Bible. The Bible is not a script Christians learn and perform. It's a training school that trains and exercises the habits and practices of the church. Improvisation describes the ways Christians formed in good habits trust themselves to embody their tradition in new and challenging circumstances. This is precisely what the church is about.

Two narrative practices of improvisation stand out. One is overaccepting. When an actor says no, or refuses to accept the premise of what's being said or done by others, it's known as a block. When an actor says yes and inhabits the implied story proposed by others' words or actions, it's called accepting. An anxious, inhibited notion of Christian existence would assume a constant suspicious tendency to block new developments and threatening plot twists. But blocking assumes a level of power; sometimes it's almost impossible to block a new cultural movement (information technology, social media). Yet supine acceptance seems to threaten the church with loss of identity. It turns out there's a third way. And it turns out that third way is to be found across the Bible story.

Overaccepting means fitting the smaller story of what's in front of you into the larger story of God—the five-act play. The most obvious example is the cross. Jesus doesn't block the cross—he doesn't escape; neither does he accept the cross—passively yielding to his fate. Instead, he overaccepts the cross. In his resurrection he takes the rejection, cruelty, and death into himself and makes them part of a greater story. On an even grander level, God does not block Israel's faltering embodiment of the covenant; neither does God simply accept it: in Jesus God overaccepts the covenant and opens it out to the whole world. Once spotted, this move can be discovered everywhere in the Bible. At the feeding of the five thousand, Jesus doesn't block the loaves and fish as inadequate; nor does he accept them: he overaccepts them and makes them part of the turning of scarcity into abundance. In the Old Testament, God neither blocks nor accepts Joseph's brothers' betrayal of him; instead, what the brothers had meant for evil, God turns to good by overaccepting their rejection of Joseph and making it part of the way Jacob's family goes down to Egypt and is saved from famine.

The second key improvisatory practice is reincorporation. At the end of a Dickens novel or Shakespeare comedy, the characters reassemble on stage, and unresolved antagonisms or misunderstandings are reintroduced and addressed. This is an image of what Jesus calls the kingdom of God. In the kingdom, the neglected, lost, and rejected reappear as a gift. Jesus's ministry reassembles the outcast, the scorned, and the discarded and embraces each as a person with a role to play in God's future. This is a dramatic process of reincorporation. At the end of the feeding of the five thousand story, just cited, the disciples collect up twelve baskets of leftover food—an act of reincorporating that anticipates the way, in God's kingdom, nothing is wasted. It portrays the way act 5 is made up of the discarded elements of act 4. Jesus's words "The stone that the builders rejected has become the cornerstone" (Matt. 21:42; see also Ps. 118:22) outline the way his own reincorporation after rejection by his people heralds manifold forms of subsequent reincorporation of those thought to be outside God's promises. When we read parts of the Bible that jar, offend, or grate with our aspiration of God's kingdom, we are expressing a longing for the reincorporation of all that is sad, grievous, or unjust.

Improvisation is not making the story up. It's being so immersed in the story the Bible tells that one can anticipate the kind of thing God would do. It's being so surrounded, not just by the companions of the present, but by the host of saints and more complex scriptural figures that one can locate a pressing crisis in the context of the shape of the story the Bible tells. It's about freedom, but freedom within an embracing narrative. It's not about replicating a bygone past; it's about enjoying being part of an emerging future, whose key qualities have already been disclosed. It's about recognizing that there's no human desire greater than the need to find our place in the story.

How This Story Differs from the Rival Story

The rival story—to the extent that it acknowledges it is indeed a story—differs from the five-act play in one simple respect. It believes we are living in a one-act play. We live; we die: that's it. There is no other sphere (what I've described as essence); there is no collective future (what I've described as consummation). There's just now. Everything must be experienced, achieved, fulfilled, and completed in this one act. If anything is irreparably damaged (the climate, for example), there's no redress—it's utterly lost. The pressure that puts on individuals to encapsulate in their transitory existence all that this world can offer is immense. Life becomes one of unavoidable disappointment, catastrophic deprivation, and furious demand. Patience becomes indulgent or absurd. All must come to fruition now.

It's worth noting that Israel believed it was in a three-act play: creation-Israel-Messiah. It was surprised to find that Jesus neither assumed political authority nor drew down the curtain on history. So, in addition to thinking you're in a one-act play, it's possible to misjudge which act you're in. Those captivated by fervor to improve or save the world may easily take us to be in act 3, where our generation is crucial, or act 5, where we have to make everything perfect. Likewise, the self-made person is, by definition, in act 1. No historical antecedents are required.

The word "baptism" sums up the difference between the story to live by and the rival story. Baptism is quite simply the way people transition from a one-act play to a five-act play. Baptism takes the Christian from a one-act play to a five-act play. In baptism, Christians move from trying to make meaning and purpose for themselves to receiving the heritage of faith and the hope of glory. They change from dreading their fate to anticipating their destiny. For this is the effect of God's story: it transforms fate into destiny.

How This Story Differs from the Old, Old Story

The old, old story, no less than the rival story, is sometimes reluctant to recognize that it is indeed a story. This is sometimes, understandably, out of a fear of being discounted as a fable from the distant, unsophisticated past. But it's also out of a desire to render truth as a series of propositions. Most succinctly, these have been articulated as the following: we were created good; we lost that goodness; Christ restored it, at the cost of his life; and if we believe we shall share glory with him. However abbreviated, these four propositions constitute the Christian faith for many people. They're obviously in tension with the story to live by that I've outlined in these first three chapters. But the point here is, however much they sound like propositions, they need to keep the same sequence, otherwise they become incoherent: in other words, they constitute a story. The five-act play may have some tensions with this story—most significantly, it doesn't give the Fall a whole act; it insists on Jesus coming at the center of the story, rather than near the end; and it does give consummation a whole act. But in general, it offers a story in which most Christians would recognize their faith.

One real difference is what I describe above in my treatment of the account of Jacob, Rachel, Leah, and Laban in Haran. In the elemental four-step creation-fall-redemption-glory narrative noted above, there's little or no place for Israel. The Old Testament is principally a source of prophecies of what's to come in Jesus. It has little validity of its own. Israel is notable mostly for its failures, which made Christ's coming necessary. This is the context I seek to set right above by delving into the heart of the story, its role in Israel's self-understanding and its remorseless humor. The Old Testament is too quickly overlooked by those who seek to find in the Bible a moral handbook but who, on discovering the rawness of human and divine character, look away.

But the principal difference of the story to live by from the old, old story is the practice of improvisation. Improvisation is designed to honor the ways the Bible is regarded as authoritative while making that authority dynamic rather than static. It accepts many of the criticisms of the standard account, noted above, leaving aside some that are overstated or indulgently belligerent. But it offers a way to enjoy the Bible as the invitation to a living tradition—rather than fierce adherence to a dead document. In the end, Bible and community are inseparable: the one critiques and renews the other. The church historian Jaroslav Pelikan, in a 1983 lecture "The Vindication of Tradition," called Christianity "not the dead faith of the living, but the living faith of the dead." Improvisation offers a practice by which that ancient faith can become a story to live by today.

\- 4 -

DRUG FOR THE POOR?

"We have used the Bible as if it were a mere special constable's handbook, an opium dose for keeping beasts of burden patient while they are overloaded."* So said Charles Kingsley, reflecting on the Chartist movement in the England of the 1840s. Earlier the same decade, Karl Marx wrote, "Religion is the sigh of the oppressed creature, the heart of a heartless world, and the soul of soulless conditions. It is the opium of the people." The criticism of Christianity in this chapter is succinctly contained in Kingsley's words, made combative by Marx: the promise of heavenly reward has been manipulated by the powerful to enforce earthly servitude and extend earthly submission. Christianity, whatever its historical origins or plausibility structure, has been hijacked as a form of social control.

The Old, Old Story and What's Wrong with It

The Standard Account

The New Testament has broadly four approaches to poverty. The first is the adoption of voluntary poverty. Jesus says to the rich man, with

* Charles Kingsley, "Letters to Chartists II," in *Politics for the People,* ed F. D. Maurice and John Malcolm (London: John W. Parker, 1848), 58.

love, "Go, sell what you own, and give the money to the poor, and you will have treasure in heaven; then come, follow me" (Mark 10:21). Jesus says, "Foxes have holes, and birds of the air have nests; but the Son of Man has nowhere to lay his head" (Luke 9:58). And Paul says of Jesus, "Though he was rich, yet for your sakes he became poor, so that by his poverty you might become rich" (2 Cor. 8:9). Thus poverty is a faithful way to follow the one who was himself poor.

The second approach is to share in such a way that no one need be poor. In the new community made possible after the Holy Spirit's coming at Pentecost, we're told, "All who believed were together and had all things in common; they would sell their possessions and goods and distribute the proceeds to all, as any had need. . . . There was not a needy person among them, for as many as owned lands or houses sold them and brought the proceeds of what was sold" (Acts 2:44–45; 4:34). This is a vision of a classless society. In the Gospels, when Jesus says, "You always have the poor with you" (John 12:8), he means "you will always be with the poor." And Jesus is indeed always thronged by the poor; the Greek word for crowd is mentioned thirty-seven times in Mark's Gospel's sixteen short chapters. Jesus is the poor. Meanwhile Jesus said, "It is easier for a camel to go through the eye of a needle than for someone who is rich to enter the kingdom of God" (Mark 10:25; Matt. 19:24; Luke 18:25).

The third is to see in the poor a way of encountering Jesus. The central experience of this comes in being with the poor in their moments of greatest distress. In a parable, Jesus describes how some people fail to recognize him in the form in which he has come to them: "I was hungry and you gave me food, I was thirsty and you gave me something to drink, I was a stranger and you welcomed me, I was naked and you gave me clothing, I was sick and you took care of me, I was in prison and you visited me" (Matt. 25:35–36). People face judgment according to whether they did or did not do such things: "Just as you did it to one of the least of these who are members of my family, you did it to me" (v. 40).

The fourth approach to poverty is to see in Jesus the embodiment of the long-awaited jubilee—a time when social justice is enacted and debts are canceled. This transformation, outlined in Leviticus 25, is described as due every fiftieth year. Mary sings in similar terms when she anticipates the work of her as-yet-unborn son:

> "He has brought down the powerful from their
> thrones,
> and lifted up the lowly;
> he has filled the hungry with good things,
> and sent the rich away empty."
>
> (Luke 1:52–53)

Jesus himself inhabits this tradition when in his childhood synagogue at Nazareth he quotes from Isaiah:

> "'The Spirit of the Lord is upon me,
> because he has anointed me to bring good news to
> the poor.
> He has sent me to proclaim release to the captives
> and recovery of sight to the blind,
> to let the oppressed go free,
> to proclaim the year of the Lord's favor.' . . .
> Today this scripture has been fulfilled in your hearing."
>
> (Luke 4:18–19, 21)

Meanwhile, in his feedings and healings Jesus meets the most disadvantaged people of his time at their point of greatest need.

A combination of these four perspectives turned the early church into a remarkable organization around the Mediterranean. The conventional Roman household was patriarchal. The father of the house had rights over all its members, women, children, and slaves, to use as he wished. Thus a community that treated women and slaves with dignity, respect, and honor was bound to be transformational. Meanwhile, those who weren't part of a Roman household were vulnerable to poverty. A community that saw such people not as sources of contagion but as angels sent to bless them was bound to inspire loyalty and love.

These are the foundations of how the early church engaged with poverty: relational and not transactional, seeing what people can bring and not just judging what they lack, and expecting to meet the face of Christ in them. It has not always been so; but that is how it was supposed to be.

Challenges to the Standard Account

For all its noble foundations, the church has for most of its history had a more complex relationship with poverty. We could trace this history in four stages.

From the moment the emperor Constantine adopted Christianity and began to make it the faith of the Roman Empire, the church entered into a bargain with economic and political power from which it has seldom released itself. Among the magnificent mosaics of Ravenna, in Italy, lies a depiction of the sixth-century emperor Justinian that portrays him in visual language corresponding to Jesus. The rivalry that in John 20 has Thomas describing the risen Jesus as "My Lord and my God!" (a contemporary title for the emperor), now has Christ and the emperor fused in one person. The faith that was once persecuted now becomes the ideology of the state. Opulence, once seen as an insult to the poor, who display the face of Christ, now becomes a celebration of God's endorsement of the regime. Such instrumentalization of Christianity to justify the powerful has been exacerbated by a tendency toward pietism; when faith is considered wholly or primarily an inner, private disposition, rather than a public identity, directing attention to the wonder of another world, rather than the realities of this one, the wealthy can commune in their hearts with God and encourage the poor to do the same, leaving material inequality unchanged.

The second dimension goes beyond fostering unjust economic relations within the church's surrounding culture. The practice of imperialism grew from the time of Columbus in the late fifteenth century to its height in the nineteenth century. The slogan "Christianity, commerce, civilization" captures the way a paternalistic understanding of evangelism partnered with a rapacious economic imperative and an unquestioned sense of social superiority. The irony of how this played out is perfectly captured by a line in Chinua Achebe's 1958 novel *Things Fall Apart*, often quoted by Desmond Tutu: "When the missionaries came to Africa they had the Bible, and we had the land. They said 'Let us pray.' We closed our eyes. When we opened them, we had the Bible, and they had the land." Becoming Christians did not seem to have made people equals. Far from liberating local populations, Christianity became part of an imperial project of acquiring raw materials and opening up new markets for manufactured goods.

Festering within the imperial project lay the practice of slavery. Between 1730 and 1745, Bristol was the leading slave port in the world. In the course of the eighteenth century, around 500,000 slaves provided the profitable goods in the triangular trade between Bristol, West Africa, and the West Indies. When slavery was abolished in the British Empire in 1833, Henry Philpotts, bishop of Exeter, received the sum of £12,729 (£1.5 million today) in compensation for the emancipation of 665 slaves held on plantations in Jamaica. Slavery became the foundation of an entire social system in the American South, where, at the outbreak of the Civil War in 1861, 3.5 million, out of the 9 million living in the nine seceding states, were enslaved. Slavery was defended as something the Old Testament patriarchs practiced, Jesus didn't criticize, and Paul assumed; as having brought people from a benighted culture and exposed them to the gospel; as an appropriate treatment of an inferior race, who lived under the curse of Ham (Gen. 9:25) or the punishment of Cain (Gen. 4:12).

Come the era of industrialization, and the class antagonisms that arose from it, a consistent story emerges of churches fearing disorder, being well connected among the ruling classes, supporting the owners of farm and factory, and calling upon the masses to keep their place. For example, at the 1819 Peterloo massacre in Manchester, in which local magistrates ordered a charge by the yeomanry on a crowd gathered to call for parliamentary representation, resulting in fifteen deaths and six hundred injuries, two of the magistrates were Anglican clergy; prior to the massacre, those same magistrates fomented tension by employing spies and provocateurs. The notorious third verse of Cecil Frances Alexander's 1848 hymn epitomizes this perspective: "The rich man in his castle, The poor man at his gate, God made them high and lowly, And ordered their estate."

To the present day, wealthy elites have frequently used Christianity to validate inequality, blame the poor for poverty, emphasize the need for social order, insist faith is a private matter, and regard wealth as God's blessing. It's hardly surprising that many have consequently come to perceive Christianity as a conspiracy and a lie.

A Rival Story, Its Validity and Flaws

A Rival Story

There are two kinds of rival stories in relation to poverty. The louder of the two arises from convictions rooted in Marxism that see life as fundamentally conflictual and perceive those in society who hold the puppet strings employing every available form of ideology to manipulate the masses. Marxists maintain that consciousness determines the way we interpret our experience. Ideology infiltrates this consciousness, never more so than when bourgeois ideology shapes the understandings of a whole society.

In a capitalist system, the owners of factories, machines, and capital produce both goods and profit, while workers sell their labor for a wage. Producing commodities, selling labor, and amassing capital are social conventions; they become normalized and are largely unquestioned. What makes them so isn't just their universality; it's the subtle perversion of ideology that underwrites them. Christianity is just such an ideology—not just in its encouragement to accept one's earthly condition but more significantly in two connected assertions: that social change comes about fundamentally through conversion and amendment of life (leaving structural oppression unchecked), and that those so converted can confidently look forward to an eternal bliss that will enormously outweigh any current distress. It's this latter prospect of bliss that constitutes the "opium" that's perceived to dull the critical faculties of the proletariat in Marx's celebrated quotation.

The second kind of rival story is less combative but is also skeptical about the role of Christianity in bringing about a just society. The contractarian tradition, and notably its most prominent contemporary proponent, John Rawls, is resolutely individualist. Justice is the contract each citizen makes with the state to hand over a degree of freedom in order to gain secure access to goods of one's own choosing. It's a process of give and take, governed by rational self-interest. Thus justice is a wise thing to pursue for others, because in due course those others may be induced to pursue it for you. Christianity is a problem for this contractarian approach because it's seen as insufficiently rational: it has nonnegotiable convictions and partial loyalties that sometimes run counter to an individual's perceived well-being—and thus inhibit the whole society's process of generating affluence and stability. Poverty is the result of influential groups being unwilling to buy into the common project. From this point of view, all would be well if Christianity remained an idle set of harmless convictions; when it seeks to shape a social vision, it weakens cohesion and confuses people's appropriate sense of enlightened self-interest.

The Validity and Flaws of the Rival Story

There's no question powerful elites have often used Christianity to coerce subjugated peoples into obedience and complicity, when in fact they were perpetrating injustice and oppression. The virtue of humility has been misused to mean servility and docility, and the prospect of heavenly bliss has been manipulated as a panacea for miserable conditions on earth. The way clergy were active in the 1819 Peterloo massacre in Manchester is a suitable example of the ways the church in many countries has allied itself with wealth and status and adopted a paternalistic, rather than a transformational, approach to poverty and disenfranchisement.

And yet in almost every area where the church has fallen so badly short, it can also be found to have been in the vanguard of change and renewal. Where there have been classes in subservience to one's betters and clergy collaborating with forces of coercion, there have also been radical leveling movements and endless charitable work among the destitute and forsaken. Perhaps most illustrative is the question of slavery. There's no denying that scriptural texts were widely employed to justify the practice of slavery. But at the same time, a person such as the sixteenth-century friar and bishop Bartolomé de Las Casas could argue that, if the church intended to enslave the people of South America, it should not be baptizing them; and a man like Benjamin Lay, the diminutive eighteenth-century Quaker, could campaign in Barbados and Philadelphia against a practice at the time almost universally regarded as a fact of life. Christians were not especially responsible for introducing slavery, but the campaign for the abolition of slavery would have been unrecognizable—and unsuccessful—without them. Likewise, contractarians could be frustrated with a movement such as Christianity that had such a particular view of human flourishing; but many figures such as Abraham Kuyper in the Netherlands and William Beveridge and William Temple in the United Kingdom had social proposals that shaped society as powerfully and beneficially as any political theory. In short, the promise of eternal life for those who believed was indeed often used as a call for quiescence in this life, but it was also an inspiration to those who sought to make this world more nearly resemble the life to come.

The chief flaw in the rival story is that the fact that Christianity doesn't always live up to its principles does not invalidate those principles; the failure of Christians to live faithfully to their story over many centuries doesn't mean that story is not true; to highlight occasions when Christianity has been misused to support false ideologies is not to prove Christianity false.

A poignant example of this comes in the figure of Dutty Boukman, a voodoo priest who played a major role in the slave revolt that triggered the Haitian revolution of 1791. Speaking of the French colonial rulers, he said these words:

> The Good Lord who created the sun which gives us light from above, who rouses the sea and makes the thunder roar—listen well, all of you—this god, hidden in the clouds, watches us. He sees all that the white people do. The god of the white people demands from them crimes; our god asks for good deeds. But this god who is so good demands vengeance! He will direct our hands; he will aid us. Throw away the image of the god of the whites who thirsts for our tears, and listen to the voice of liberty which speaks in the hearts of all of us.*

The colonialists regarded Boukman as an agent of the devil, but they maintained that their god supported slavery and oppression. Was the rejection of their rule really the rejection of Christianity, or a grotesque caricature of Christianity? From today's perspective, Dutty Boukman looks closer to Christianity than they were.

A Story to Live by, and How It Differs from Both Stories

A Story to Live By

The issues outlined in this chapter constitute, not a falsification of Christianity, but its distortion in two ways. The first is to assume that

* Arlene B. Tickner and David L. Blaney, *Claiming the International* (London: Routledge, 2013), 147.

Christianity is "personal," in a sense that excludes the political; this corresponds to a notion of the "spiritual" that sets it above and beyond the physical. The second, closely related, distortion is to insist that faith is about the eternal destiny of the soul rather than the present condition of the body; that it concerns a future hope and not a present reality.

Both distortions begin with genuine Christian convictions: the problem is that they emphasize those respective convictions to the exclusion of other, equally important convictions. Thus Christianity is indeed personal. It is a thing most wonderful that the essence of all things invests not only in existence but also in my own existence, and seeks connection not just with the universe in general but also with me in particular. But that isn't a reason to suppose the essence of all things is thereby uninterested in the relations creatures in existence have with one another, particularly relations that impoverish or diminish one party at the expense of another. Likewise, faith is indeed about the future. It is most wonderful to know that essence does not simply want to share our existence in Christ but also intends ultimately to draw us into essence forever. But that isn't a reason to underplay the significance of our existence, or the fact that Christ shared it; indeed, it's the most profound reason to be concerned about the earthly and temporal well-being of creation as a whole and each creature in it, especially those that suffer, and among those in particular, those whose suffering is chronic and is due to the muddle or malice of another or a whole system.

Well intentioned as the origins of these two distortions may be, we need to recognize how pernicious in many circumstances they have become. These two widespread distortions have been used to manipulate believers in two corresponding ways: to accept that the unjust ordering of social relations was a matter of no concern to the Christian faith, and to suppose that their present oppression was of no significance in view of their future glory.

We need to dismantle these distortions in turn, beginning with the distinction between the personal and the political. We can distinguish two perspectives from which to tell a story. Let's imagine a journalist covering a major protest about climate change. On the one hand, her son is immersed in the demonstrations, provocative actions, disruptive gestures, and insurgent tactics of the agitators. On the other hand, she is gaining an understanding of some of the sources of information that inflame the protestors: she comes to understand the ways incendiary accusations are being released at timely intervals from one or two websites—which, on closer scrutiny, turn out to be funded by the government of a country that has a history of seeking to undermine the social fabric and consensus of its rivals. When the journalist files her story, she's drawing together the objective, bird's-eye perspective, known as the epic, with the intense, involved, committed, but inevitably partial and subjective view of her son, known as the lyric. When the epic and lyric perspectives truly intermingle, we have a form of storytelling known as the dramatic.

Jesus's ministry is consistently dramatic, in this sense, from beginning to end. Take, for example, the story of the Gerasene demoniac (Mark 5:1–20). Jesus heals a man of demon possession, and the demons go into a herd of swine that promptly hurtles off a cliff. Why would there be so many pigs, given that Jews didn't eat pork? The answer lies in the name of the demon: Legion. The pigs were kept to feed the Roman soldiers. The number cited in the story—two thousand—while on the small side, is roughly the size of a Roman legion. The story is transformative for the man from Gerasa, and a demonstration of Jesus's compassion and power; but it's also a coded statement that Israel was possessed by a demon called Rome. It's lyric and it's epic.

Take another example: Jesus's words "It is not what goes into the mouth that defiles a person, but it is what comes out of the mouth that defiles" (Matt. 15:11) are not simply about personal purity. What had come in from outside, and seemed much more significant than anything that could come out from inside, was Rome. Jesus, and the gospel writers that recorded his words, were living in a police state, surrounded by spies, and were at the mercy of the occupying power. They used metaphor where we naïvely expect to see explicit statements. The great question of Jesus's time was this: Was the Holy Land occupied because the Romans were rapacious and exploitative, or was Israel itself at fault and in need of a reformation? The politics of the time was determined by one's answer to this question. The Pharisees favored personal purity, the Sadducees political collaboration, the Zealots political rebellion. Jesus is subtly saying, "The Romans are not our biggest problem. Our biggest issue is what's inside us, personally and collectively." This is a call for personal renewal, but it's also putting clear blue water between Jesus and the three pervasive political options of the time. It's lyric and it's epic.

Take two further examples. The Roman emperor called himself the Son of God. So when we read in Mark and Matthew's Gospels that when Jesus breathed his last and the centurion said, "Truly this man was the Son of God," we behold that the man who put Jesus to death, stands at the foot of the cross and proclaims, "This dying man is my true Emperor, and I shall be loyal to him even if it costs me my loyalty to the so-called Emperor in Rome. *This* man, not the Emperor, is the real Son of God." It's a remarkable statement for a Roman commander to make. And we get a similar statement from Thomas, on the Sunday after Easter, when he meets the risen Jesus: "My Lord and my God!" (John 20:28)—in Latin, *Dominus deusque*—another title given to the Roman emperor. What Thomas sees is something the Roman emperor could never aspire to: power over death. Thomas and the centurion have a personal and a political experience: it's lyric and it's epic.

Thus, from the very beginning, Christianity is both personal and political. Personal for the healed demoniac, for those considering what to eat, for Thomas, and for the centurion; but simultaneously political for each one. Lyric and epic, in each case. The attempt to render the Christian faith personal only, and thus to eradicate its political elements, is to distort the Gospels and to misrepresent the ministry of Jesus. There is no apolitical Christianity. God is always both lyric and epic.

The reading of Christianity by which faith is about personal salvation, and political engagement is at best a distraction from personal responsibility, at worst an attempt to obscure eternal questions by concentrating on present-day ones, contradicts the Bible it claims to obey. To demonstrate this, I'm going to take a passage that's often read in such a way and show how political it really is.

> A shoot shall come out from the stock (lit. stump) of
>   Jesse,
>   and a branch shall grow out of his roots.
> The spirit of the LORD shall rest on him,
>   the spirit of wisdom and understanding,
>   the spirit of counsel and might,
>   the spirit of knowledge and the fear of the LORD.
> His delight shall be in the fear of the LORD.
>
> (Isa. 11:1–3a)

Isaiah chapter 11 begins with an uncompromising, blunt, almost brutal word: "stump." It's a horrifying word, conjuring images of amputation, loss, ugliness, finality. You look at what's left after a tree's been chopped down and you see an empty space where once there was life; a future sawn off. But if you think about a freshly felled tree, it's still got a vast network of roots underground. Those don't immediately cease to work just because there's not a lot left above the soil. And so there's always the possibility that a shoot will surface from out of the severed stump.

And that's what Isaiah describes. He's writing in troubled times. We're in the seventh century before Christ. More than half of Israel has been invaded, dismantled, and destroyed by the Assyrians. What's left is under intense threat. Yet in the midst of despair Isaiah offers a vision of a new politics. A shoot will arise from the same family that produced David, Solomon, and the great kings of Israel.

> He shall not judge by what his eyes see,
> or decide by what his ears hear;
> but with righteousness he shall judge the poor,
> and decide with equity for the meek of the earth;
> he shall strike the earth with the rod of his mouth,
> and with the breath of his lips he shall kill the wicked.
> Righteousness shall be the belt around his waist,
> and faithfulness the belt around his loins.
> (Isa. 11:3b–5)

And this will be the new kind of politics that rises from the ashes of the old. Solomon once asked God for a wise and understanding heart. This is talking about two kinds of wisdom. One's the kind that can step away, formulate ideas, and work out the theory. The other's the kind that can roll up sleeves, get in the thick of things, build alliances, and make compromises. Wisdom and understanding. Then there's another pair of virtues: counsel and might. Again, Isaiah's saying politics needs a balance of two things, in this case, careful planning and preparation, matched with vigorous execution and follow-through. Counsel and might. Like theoretical and practical wisdom, the one is useless without the other. And then there's a third pair of virtues: knowledge and fear of the Lord. On the one hand, a sense of what's possible, what works, where your limitations are, where your strengths lie; on the other hand, a sense of who God is, how small you are, how limitless are the grace and possibility and generosity and mercy of God. A rational recognition of human potential and a faithful apprehension of divine wonder: knowledge and the fear of the Lord. If the first pair echo Solomon, this last pair echo David, who in his last words speaks of just rule as that which stands in fear of God.

So out of the desperation of Israel grows a new shoot from the house of David and Solomon, and this time the lessons of those two flawed leaders have been learned. Politics is now to be characterized by theoretical and practical wisdom, by careful planning and vigorous execution, by human endeavor and divine grace. But Isaiah hasn't finished his description of what makes true politics. We now get an account of what it means to be righteous. Our culture has become skeptical about any hope of being righteous. Today we only use the word in two senses: either entirely negatively, as in the highly critical term "self-righteous," or rather condescendingly, as in the phrase "righteous indignation," with which we describe someone who's correct but has lost their temper, or at least their sense of proportion. But Isaiah also has twin understandings of the word "righteous," which we could call uprightness and faithfulness. Uprightness simply means being fair, upholding the rule of law, not making arbitrary judgments, not showing bias on account of personal favor or gain, showing dependability and consistency and keeping one's promises. But faithfulness means recognizing that life is not fair; that when the rules are enforced there are those that don't fit them and lose out through no fault of their own; that people deserve a second chance; that it's possible to be unlucky, disadvantaged, and oppressed; and that a good politics doesn't just reward those who benefit from uprightness but remains faithful to those who lose out.

You could be forgiven for thinking the new politics could stop right there. Leaders who exhibit these virtues are worthy of public support; leaders who don't are not. Isaiah promises that God will raise up a new leader who will indeed embody such qualities like no one has before. That's the politics that thinks. But Isaiah has a whole other dimension to tell us about. Isaiah wants to offer us also the politics that dreams.

> The wolf shall live with the lamb,
>   the leopard shall lie down with the kid,
> the calf and the lion and the fatling together,
>   and a little child shall lead them.

The cow and the bear shall graze,
their young shall lie down together;
and the lion shall eat straw like the ox.
The nursing child shall play over the hole of the asp,
and the weaned child shall put its hand on
the adder's den.
They will not hurt or destroy
on all my holy mountain;
for the earth will be full of the knowledge of
the LORD
as the waters cover the sea.

(Isa. 11:6–9)

Isaiah changes the focus from the politics of the city to the flourishing of the animal creation. Just imagine, he says, a life that has no danger, no insecurity, no evil. Picture being a shepherd who has no anxiety that a predator will decimate your flock. Visualize trusting your baby to linger around a snake pit, or beholding your young child train wolves, leopards, and lions. Isaiah is self-consciously revisiting the Fall narrated in Genesis 3, where a serpent took up enmity against God and humankind. This scene is a vivid depiction of what it might be like to reverse the effects of the Fall and suppose creation where life isn't defined by scarcity, envy, or antagonism, by hurt or destruction.

And then in a single sentence Isaiah stunningly brings the political and the pastoral together in a harmony of grace: the earth will be full of the knowledge of the Lord as the waters cover the sea. Everything he's said in the first part of his description can be summed up in that simple phrase, "the knowledge of the LORD": it's the best of human wisdom, knowledge, but it's the infusion of divine wisdom, the knowledge of the *Lord*. And it's as comprehensive as the waters that cover the sea. It's a sensual image of closing your eyes and lying back prostrate and feeling the warm cleansing water running over your body giving you strength and peace and healing and calm. The world will be full of the knowledge of God just like that, just like the warm cleansing water rises up over your weary, spent body. Isaiah says, "Feel the joy of that."

Here's Isaiah, in the midst of chaos, destruction, and despair, describing the resurrection of politics: a politics that thinks the way God thinks, with ideas and practicalities, planning and implementation, human effort and divine grace, upright trust and faithful compassion; but a politics that also dreams the way God dreams, with the innocence and simplicity of a child, with the withering away of animosity and hostility, with a gentle immersion in mercy and truth. What a beautiful idea. What a vision. What a dream.

But wait. We read this today not as an idle poem or a pious fantasy. It's not simply an idea, a vision, or a dream. We read it because these words became flesh. There was one who was the beautiful idea of God and the tangible reality of God, who was God's plan but saw that plan through to the very end, who knew what it meant to be human and knew what it meant to be God. There was one who was so upright he did not fight on his own behalf when he was arrested, who spent his life among the rejected and outcast of the world. There was one who sprung up from the root of Jesse and came from the line of David, who emerged from the stump of Israel, who was born in the midst of the lamb, the calf, and the kid. And there was one who came as a little child to reverse the effects of the Fall, to invade our despair and inspire us to dream again.

Isaiah's vision of the resurrection of politics turns into Jesus's embodiment of the resurrection of politics. Jesus is the idea of God made flesh, the word of wisdom and the flesh of creation, the best that humanity can do and the grace of God that meets us in our weakness. Should we ever despair about our country, our choices, or our politics, we may always go back and read Isaiah 11. Because there we discover how to walk in God's ways, there we recall how God has already walked those ways and will walk them with us all our days, and there we realize that when our spirit is spent, the Spirit of the Lord will come with the wonder of a new shoot and the simplicity of a little child and summon us into the dream of God.

This is what it means to live God's future now. Living God's future now transcends the mistaken distinction between bliss tomorrow and vale of tears today. A true politics doesn't shrug its shoulders at poverty. There is no question of a future hope being manipulated to disempower present struggle. The kingdom of God is a collective, participatory, liberating reality—not an individual reward for keeping out of trouble. This both exposes and corrects any tendency in Christians to project a future reality, to instrumentalize Jesus as the route to that future reality, and to regard hope for that future reality as a conviction detached from any practice of that reality now. There is no justification for placidity in the face of unjust social relationships today, no reason for quiescence in relation to oppression exerted on oneself, and no legitimation for inertia in response to structural or systemic wrongdoing. To attribute such attitudes to Christianity or more specifically to Jesus is no harmless error, but collusion in a conspiracy to eviscerate Christianity and replace it with an ideology of domination.

How This Story Differs from the Rival Story

The flaws the rival identifies in Christianity are real, but they invariably highlight distortions of Christianity rather than the faith itself. Christianity is a liberation movement: the exodus is about freedom from slavery and the resurrection is about deliverance from death. The power of Christianity lies in liberation from the prison of the past—the guilt about what I have done and the bitterness about what has been done to me—and from the fear of the future—that which I can anticipate, which I look to with anxiety, and that which I cannot know, which I view with blind terror. The first is dismantled by the forgiveness of sins; the second is absorbed by the life everlasting. These are the two principal fruits of resurrection.

Thus it turns out that the rival story is often Christianity in disguise. Over and again it transpires that liberation movements, even without their protagonists' knowledge, are rooted in strands of the Christian tradition. Most campaigns for justice are rooted in deep respect for the weak, the suffering, and the vulnerable, and a sense of the validity of every human life. These are profoundly Christian convictions. The elixir that unites the Me Too, Black Lives Matter, and Extinction Rebellion movements is that to be a victim can give one an extraordinary, if paradoxical, source of power. This insight is directly or indirectly derived from the portrayal of Christ hanging on the cross and Jesus's promise that the last should be first, and the first, last (Matt. 19:30; 20:16; Mark 10:31; Luke 13:30). Why is it wrong to oppress your brother or sister? Because he or she has inherent value—or, as Genesis 1:27 puts it, is made in the image of God. Why will you live to regret the subjugation you perpetrate? Because the arc of the moral universe tends toward justice, as Martin Luther King Jr. liked to say—or, in the words of Jesus in Matthew 25:40, "Just as you did it to one of the least of these who are members of my family, you did it to me." The great protest movements of our time are reminding the church of its distinctive social ideas—ideas no part of the church should ever have forgotten. One historian puts it this way: "That the great battles in America's culture war were being fought between Christians and those who had emancipated themselves from Christianity was a conceit that both sides had an interest in promoting. . . . America's culture wars were less a war against Christianity than a civil war between Christian factions."*

Yet liberation is only half of Christianity; the other half is covenant. The crossing of the Red Sea is only half of the central event in Israel's story; the other half is the giving of the law to Moses on Mount Sinai. The rival story is powerful and prophetic in that it reminds Christianity, if it should ever forget it, of its core message—but of only half

* Tom Holland, *Dominion: How the Christian Revolution Remade the World* (New York: Basic Books, 2019), 530–31.

of it. Freedom is given for a reason: that reason is relationship. The fundamental reason why God longs for people to be free is not simply that oppression is painful and burdensome, or even that freedom is creative and joyful; it is, more profoundly, that God is seeking relationship, and relationship is diminished if one party is constrained or incarcerated. That's the insight to which the contractarians come near. The rival story that the contractarians outline is one in which human flourishing rests on some notion of a contract. As I have described, I see that contract as inferior and preliminary to a fuller notion of covenant; but it is a close relation, and even in a covenant the virtues of a contract are likely to be helpful and informative.

Collective life, for Christians, is always a tension between the subversive element that, in seeking liberation, makes all institutions and structures provisional and the constructive effort that, in pursuing covenant, is always looking to lay foundations of wisdom and stability. The push for freedom frequently fails to put in place any new order worthy of the disruption that displaced the old; the desire for covenant too often settles for an inadequate contract that disgraces any covenant that aspires to anticipate heaven.

How This Story Differs from the Old, Old Story

The old, old story is one in which the Bible was largely written by beleaguered minorities, and where the early church was an oppressed minority for three centuries. The issue arises in earnest when the church comes to believe it is called to uphold those in power even when those in power perpetuate unjust social relations that shame the prospect of eternal glory; and when those in power, politically, socially, or economically, come to see the patience and hope of Christianity as qualities to be manipulated to deflect attention from the urgent need to transform structures and systems that inhibit and humiliate people.

In contrast to the first three chapters, in this case the story to live by does not change the old, old story; instead it identifies and discredits the ways the old, old story has been co-opted by interests and controls that have not had the kingdom of God as their goal. The old, old story told how liberation was obtained and given and how freedom was kept through a covenant that enabled the abundant life of creative relationship to flourish. The accusation "Drug for the poor" does not discredit or falsify this old, old story, but it does highlight that, in every generation, the church must bring forward examples, not just of the joys of the life to come, but of how those joys have been exemplified in lived communities in the present. Injustice in the world and the oppression of some by others are so widespread, and so often falsely explained or dismissed by recourse to distortions of the Christian faith, that a response is always needed. And that response can never be solely theoretical, pointing to a better version of the story: that story to live by must indeed be lived, despite the tensions between liberation and covenant, so that its living may be the example by which the world judges what the Holy Spirit can truly do.

- 5 -

INTOLERANT POISON?

OF ALL THE REASONS TO REJECT Christianity, one is perhaps held with greatest vehemence and sense of fury: the sense that the faith either intrinsically itself, or in the hands of those who use it consciously or unconsciously for nefarious ends, is no more than legitimized bigotry; bigotry that damages people, inhibits their capacity for self-love and self-acceptance, and can cause a lifetime of hurt and exclusion. This bigotry can come in a variety of guises. It has often been found in one race assuming and asserting superiority over another; it was, for many centuries, almost universally practiced in assigning men greater authority and status than women. But today it's most sharply discovered in questions of sexuality—most particularly, whether or not those who identify as lesbian, bisexual, gay, transgender, and intersex are cherished in their respective identities and recognized as precious, honored, and loved in God's sight.

The Old, Old Story and What's Wrong with It

The Standard Account

Once Israel has left slavery in Egypt, the great question of the Old Testament becomes, How is Israel going to keep the freedom God has granted it? The answer is, by adhering to the covenant God makes with Moses on Mount Sinai, at the center of which lie the Ten Commandments, which outline how God's people are to be with God and how they are to be with one another. This covenant is not a burden but a gift: it's God's gracious way of describing how Israel is to keep its freedom and to be with God. The covenant is like a wedding ring—not an indication of constraint but a joyful guarantee of faithful love. The crisis of the Old Testament is that Israel finds itself in exile, and subsequently, while having returned, dominated by foreign powers. The story gives only one explanation for this: Israel has not kept the covenant. Thus keeping the covenant is not just about personal sanctity; it's also about corporate consequences.

Jesus enhanced this precious law in four ways. First, he embodied it and, in his life, death, and resurrection, showed that the law was always fundamentally about God's utter commitment to us—a commitment that was now extended not just to Jews but also to gentiles. Second, he deepened it, for example, in his Sermon on the Mount, saying the problem was not just murder but the anger behind it, not simply adultery but the lustful thought that began it, not just swearing falsely but the duplicity that fails to stand by the words "yes" and "no." Third, he broadened it by extending it to gentiles as well as to Jews. Fourth, he made it more urgent by anticipating an imminent apocalypse, thus radicalizing discipleship so it came to mean leaving home and family and taking up a cross to follow in his steps. In these four ways Jesus turned the old covenant into a new covenant.

Paul found himself identifying both how the Jewish law now applied in largely gentile settings and how fledgling Christian communities should conduct themselves in a sometimes-hostile Roman Empire and in an often-oppressive culture. He was seeking to articulate the difference Christ makes, while reassuring those who perceive Christianity as an insurgent force that this difference is not one of seeking to unseat the secular powers. The ethic of the New Testament letters may sound socially conservative ("Wives, be subject to your husbands" [Eph. 5:22]), but in a radically new context ("Be subject to one another" [Eph. 5:21]), which consistently emphasizes not control but love ("Husbands should love their wives as they do their own bodies" [Eph. 5:28]). In a culture where the male head of the household had rights over the bodies of all within it—women, children, slaves—to do as he pleased, the early church grew rapidly among those, especially women and slaves, who found that, among Christians, they were honored and respected.

The culture in which the New Testament was written had no notion of being gay—that is, of identifying as a person for whom desire for sexual intimacy with a person of the same sex is not a choice, experiment, or indulgence, but at the core of who one is. The acts called out in the New Testament letters as contrary to the way of Christian living are ones in which a more powerful, older male exercised dominance by exploiting a younger, more vulnerable male, with no element of tenderness, mutuality, or ongoing relationship. The culture of the time had no category of abiding, cherishing same-sex relationship—only of abusive, exploitative taking of advantage.

Challenges to the Standard Account

There are three levels of challenge to this story. One is the question of whether it is ever right for Christians to seek social or political power and to use such power to advance a particular agenda. When a malign agenda is being imposed, it seems the answer to this question is no; but when a person like William Wilberforce seeks, by all means available, to sway the British Parliament against the legality of the slave trade, it seems the answer is yes. Thus the answer lies in the validity of the agenda, not in its advancement. The second level is whether the old, old story has historically been right about some of the most controversial of its stances, notably, for example, on sexuality. The third level is whether the church has acted appropriately in advancing those stances and respecting those who have held a different view.

Much of the anger generated in this area targets the first and the third levels; but the real debate lies in the second area. Of course, if the church believes profoundly in the truth and justice of its stance, it must pursue it, however unpopular, and however much, in a liberal democracy, it must respect differing views. But, more significantly, what if its stance is wrong; has always been wrong; is based on misunderstandings, misinterpretations, and distortions; and needs to be reconsidered and reframed? That's the real issue.

For the majority of Christian history, the radical and liberating character of the faith has been effaced by the need to form and sustain stable societies in which Christianity was a highly significant, but not wholly dominant, dimension of the culture. Sex and sexuality have played a prominent role in this, for a number of reasons. One is the need to ensure, yet control, reproduction, not least because of the need to restrict the dispersal of property and power. Another is to trammel the transgressive and impulsive power of sexual desire, which, if not kept within the constraints of marriage, could lead to the disintegration of the family unit, and the emergence of a large number of infants and children with no secure structure to protect and nurture them, and elderly people with no one to care for them. Thus marriage and fidelity came to sit within a triangle of reproduction, companionship, and desire, which sought to ensure that sex was a constructive, rather than a destructive, force in society. Around this structure, a culture of purity and shame proliferated, with corresponding intolerance for sex outside marriage, inconsistent standards applied to men and women, ostracism for the unwed mother, exclusion of those who would now be called LGBTI+, tolerance for intrafamilial violence, and suppression of healthy discourse around sexuality in general, with resultant hypocrisy, guilt, ignorance, and fear.

The Industrial Revolution changed the whole model of faith, work, family, and sexuality. Work became something the breadwinner left the house to do. Childhood was invented as a period when a person was too young to leave home to work. The housewife was created as a person charged with household, children, and care in a home that was no longer used for work. The nuclear family emerged as a group restricted to breadwinner, housewife, and child. Faith changed, to become something associated with the private sphere of home rather than the public sphere of work.

The last sixty years have challenged all the norms introduced by the Industrial Revolution. Women are no longer defined by the role of housewife. Parents live long after their children grow up. Employment is much more diverse. Sex doesn't invariably involve conception, and conception doesn't always require sex. The social taboos around sexual expression and divorce are not what they were. The result is that historic habits and practices around sex and sexuality are no longer underwritten by biological or social constraints that once made prudence, holiness, and conformity largely indistinguishable, at least outwardly.

Shorn of this now-outdated biological and social context, the Christian habit of patrolling sex seems at best arbitrary and unjustified, at worst pathological and perverse. It's not true to say there are now no rules around sex in popular culture, besides respectful ones about what is not considered appropriate to do in full public view. In fact, there are two: the tacit one—you shouldn't flirt with, condone approaches from, or sleep with a partner who's in a committed relationship with someone else; and the vocal one—you must not engage in or solicit sexual activity with a person who has not offered, or has indeed explicitly withheld, consent. Contemporary Western culture, particularly youth culture, has a third: you have no right to criticize or condemn another person's sexuality, and you may legitimately be ostracized for doing so.

The consequence of this new attitude is a change for which the traditional Christian approach to sex and sexuality has been completely unprepared. Historic Christian claims—that sex outside marriage is wrong, that LGBTI+ identity is "not part of God's plan," or that intimate relationships are fundamentally governed by the responsibility of rearing children and upholding social stability—once sat comfortably with a generally cautious and circumspect climate. Now they look egregious and judgmental. For centuries they needed little or no recourse to scriptural injunction or specific teaching: they were just the cultural wallpaper. Now those who defend them are pushed into either explaining why sex should be singled out as an area where specific scriptural verses are regarded as infallible in the face of enormous social change, whereas verses about war, usury, and property are not so regarded; or drawing on psychological arguments about the deleterious effects of certain behaviors on future well-being, at a time when the consensus has shifted to perceiving the suppression and condemnation of particular desires as the more harmful tendency.

In such unpropitious circumstances, why do Christian social conservatives continue to censure LGBTI+ identity or relationships (or both) so consistently, and in many cases make such censure a litmus test of Christian orthodoxy? There are three possible answers to this. One is a lack of understanding as to how socially constructed the discourse around sex, marriage, the family, and sexuality actually is, and how complex it is simply to transfer ethics from the page of the Bible to the contemporary bedroom. We've seen how sex and marriage changed before, during, and after the Industrial Revolution. But changes have taken place over many centuries: for example, the church had a relatively minor role in marriage until the eleventh century, when closer control over conjugal matters became part of Pope Gregory VII's project of strengthening the church in general and the papacy in particular.

A second explanation is a fierce defense of what is seen as the authority of Scripture, notwithstanding the fact that there are no recorded words of Jesus on LGBTI+ questions, and that, as we've seen, what the New Testament letters condemn is not what those who identify today as LGBTI+ would uphold. This concern about Scripture is especially significant in the United States, where building a political coalition of evangelicals, Catholics, and social conservatives has been crucial to Republican electoral strategy for forty years, and where wedge issues such as abortion and gay marriage have been deliberately highlighted in order to create a sense of a culture under imminent threat.

But a third answer is less historical and more antagonistic. It sees the transformation in social attitudes of the last sixty years as the long-overdue displacement of Christianity from its oppression of vulnerable populations. In this view, Christianity is patriarchal through and through, and having failed to sustain its domination over women, it has renewed its despotic efforts to constrain people of LGBTI+ identity. It's simply licensed bigotry. Christianity willingly colludes with political manipulators, because it sees itself as entitled to dictate to people how they should live, and to outlaw, judge, and condemn any who deviate from a narrow path of social conformity. It's intrinsically hypocritical, since it expends extra energies denouncing tendencies it fears (and has thus suppressed, often unsuccessfully) in itself, and projects onto others a malaise that lies within its own heart. Such a view sees Christianity as part of a general inclination of people to imagine themselves better than others: indeed, Christianity is unrecognizable outside such instrumentalization as part of a project to ostracize, pillory, and shame those it sees as inferior. The absurd attempts of the antigay lobby to maintain that society as we know it is at risk from two people being able to gain social legitimacy for loving one another simply expose what has always been true: that beneath the benign mask, Christianity is little more than an organized conspiracy of fear and control.

A Rival Story, Its Validity and Flaws

A Rival Story

In E. M. Forster's 1908 novel *A Room with a View*, a group of English visitors to Florence are driven in horse-drawn carriages to nearby Fiesole. Seeing one of the drivers canoodling with a young woman he has passed off as his sister, one of the party, a clergyman, demands the carriage be stopped and the young woman step down. But the enlightened Mr. Emerson intervenes. "'Leave them alone,' Mr. Emerson begged the chaplain, of whom he stood in no awe. 'Do we find happiness so often that we should turn it off the box when it happens to sit there? To be driven by lovers—A king might envy us, and if we part them it's more like sacrilege than anything I know.'"*

The scene epitomizes the rival story. In very few words, Mr. Emerson expresses four vital elements of a whole worldview. First, there is a fundamental law of mutual flourishing: live and let live. Tolerance respects the right of individuals to seek their own flourishing as best they may, provided they do not meanwhile inhibit the flourishing of others. "Leave them alone": we should not be in the business of making, let alone enforcing, judgments on the way other people choose to live their lives. Second, historic institutions in general, and the church in particular, offer no authoritative guidance—and of them, we should stand "in no awe." There is a deadweight of disapproval, small-mindedness, and misdirected shame, and it constitutes a millstone around the neck of a new emergent, energized, and liberated world. Third, happiness is the goal of human life, and is in short supply: if one is on the brink of happiness, it's a terrible thing to intervene and deny it to one. "Do we find happiness so often?" says the person in touch with the deepest things in life. Fourth, love is holy: it's the most sacred thing in the world, and the truest kind of happiness—as well as the most elusive. To be in the presence of love, let alone to experience it oneself, is a splendid and enviable thing: to part lovers is "more like sacrilege than anything I know."

The rival story sees itself as representing Mr. Emerson in his dispute with the censorious chaplain. We live in modern, enlightened times of freedom and equality. Discrimination is anathema. Everyone should be treated with dignity and be supported as they adopt and

* E. M. Forster, *A Room with a View* (London: Edward Arnold, 1908), chap. 6.

live into the identity they see as their own. The story assumes a contract, by which individuals hand over authority to larger institutions, in particular the state, in return for the guarantee of broader liberties, such as national security; but that these larger institutions should limit individual freedom, except in extreme circumstances such as a pandemic, is not only unjust but absurd. In recent times the rival story has made "diversity" an article of faith. By diversity it means that a kaleidoscope of experience, identity, and purpose is an unqualified asset, and a goal—and not a shortcoming, impediment, or temporary challenge. Not to subscribe to this conviction is a sure sign of arrogance, ignorance, and unacknowledged privilege: you clearly believe that only some views matter, take for granted that those views correspond with your own, and are unaware of the social conditions in your favor that make it possible to hold such a view.

In particular, sexuality is a sphere of discovery, respect, delight, and understanding—and certainly not an area for judgment, control, censure, or exclusion. While good sexual expression is one of the joys and aspirations of a healthy life, negative, punitive, and cruel treatment, psychologically as well as physically and emotionally, especially of those who are vulnerable, is among the most serious transgressions of the rival story's ethos. While there is an abiding recognition of legitimate authority in public spheres—that public officials should for example uphold selflessness, integrity, objectivity, accountability, openness, and honesty, and be prepared to set an example—there is no such standard for private life; and the distinction between public and private is explicitly drawn, although it's acknowledged that sometimes the private spills into the public, particularly for public figures.

The Validity and Flaws of the Rival Story

Three things should be said about this rival story. The first is that it contains a lot of truth. There is indeed a lot wrong with the old, old story in the way its norms and judgments have been too hastily transferred from classical times to today, have been insufficiently understood to speak to a different context with correspondingly different threats and dangers, and have too eagerly been harnessed to an agenda of imposing on vulnerable people a narrow set of values and assumptions. Christianity began as a radical social movement that had an expansive message of liberation and affirmation. It delivered people from the bitterness and guilt of the past, the oppression and meaninglessness of the present, and anxiety and despair about the future. That never meant complete license to live as one pleased, but it meant the church had a mission. Ways of life were evaluated by whether they embodied and advanced, or inhibited and discredited, that mission.

The second thing to be said, which overlaps to some extent with themes discussed in chapter 4, is that the rival story seldom acknowledges the debt it owes to the old, old story. The strongest and simplest theological argument for recognition of and delight in LGBTI+ people is that they are made in God's image like everyone else: "God made me this way because God wanted someone just like me." The case that people on the margins of society should be cherished, empowered, and liberated comes straight out of the Christian tradition that Christ's face is most explicitly encountered in the stranger, the prisoner, and the hungry. The rival story is an assemblage and repristination of some of the most foundational of all Christian principles. Many critiques of Christianity are welcome revisions arising from originally Christian sources. When the church forgets that its message is first liberation, then covenant, it needs voices now outside it, but originally inside it, to remind it of its founding principles.

But the third thing to be said is that social conservatism is not the only kind of inflexible dogmatism around. Much condemnation of people on the grounds of sexuality has been cruel, abusive, contrary to any notion of loving-kindness, and a shameful expression of power. But live and let live is not a serious ethic. It is highly appropriate to debate and discuss what it might mean to live well. The twenty-first century is a time when great diversity about love and relationships has surfaced, and when norms and expectations are in flux. It is also a time when the range of authoritative voices on such subjects has vastly expanded, and the educated, white, Western, heterosexual male is no longer regarded as the benchmark of normality. "Who are you to tell me how to live my life?" may well be a healthy beginning to a conversation, but it can't be the end of one. When you've established your convictions, you then have the even more demanding task of learning to live with people who don't share your convictions. Those who attempt to reinvent, in every era, wisdom about things that have long been part of human experience are doomed to remain perpetually adolescent. Love, it turns out, isn't all you need.

A Story to Live by, and How It Differs from Both Stories

A Story to Live By

If we fear the wrath of an angry God, we're always trying to keep our feet within the lines, to avoid trespassing into dangerous territory. We become timid, cautious, inhibited, afraid. But if we believe God has given us everything we need to follow Jesus and enter the fullness of abundant life, we're not mesmerized by avoiding pitfalls; we're inspired to live bigger lives in a bigger story.

In this bigger story we come to understand the law, as the Old Testament calls it, or the commandments, as we describe the heart of it, not as a burden to weigh us down but as a guiding star to inspire us and clarify our path. The key to that transformation lies in the word "enough."

Few people think they have enough. Not many believe they have enough money—but instead look longingly through catalogues of expensive goods and always drive a hard bargain when the sales assistant suggests there may be a little flexibility. Hardly any think they have enough time—but rather complain that life's too short. Many are attracted to goods that do things more quickly and lose their temper at the stoplight when the driver of the car in front won't drive ahead when the light turns. Few think they get enough love—but instead look enviously at couples who seem wrapped up in each other, meticulously count their birthday cards and despair at how few there are, or say, "I wonder why small furry animals prefer sitting in other people's laps to purring in mine."

If there's one anxiety most people can share, it's an anxiety about not having enough. It's just as well, because the economy depends on people thinking they need just a little bit more. If the secret got out that men could meet beautiful women without driving sleek new cars, or that families could be civil to one another without a tasty new breakfast cereal, or that it's possible to have sophisticated personal engagements without a highly sophisticated gadget on which to note them, then not only the advertising profession but half of the manufacturing industry would go under.

The Ten Commandments dismantle this nagging assumption that there's not enough. The eighth commandment, you shall not steal, invites us to investigate the psychology of stealing. This is a state of mind that says, "It doesn't matter that I fiddle my personal expenses because I work for a big institution and it won't miss it; anyway, it makes up a bit for what they don't pay me." It's an attitude that says, "I have to publish that data, even though it's someone else's research, not mine, because I need to get an academic appointment." That's stealing. Stealing is saying, "There isn't enough in the world, and if I'm going to have what I need, then someone else is bound to suffer." But God says, "You shall not steal."

The fourth commandment says, remember the Sabbath day. This invites us to explore the mind-set of working every day. "It has to be done . . . only I can do it . . . everybody is depending on me . . . there's not enough time . . . it's a competitive world out there . . . if I don't get this contract someone else will . . . if I put a bit more time in this proposal will be perfect . . . I'm not clever enough . . . I can only make up for it with hard work." Breaking the command to rest is saying, "There's only one savior in this universe; and it's me. There isn't enough time but I might just pull it off. I have to save my career, I have to save the world. I can't stop." But God says, "You shall rest."

The seventh commandment is, you shall not commit adultery. Everyone knows that adultery is more often a symptom than a cause. But the mind-set of adultery is simply that one is not enough. By contrast marriage is the great proclamation that one is plenty. All is focused on a single other—another mind, another imagination, another myriad of experiences and energies and enthusiasms and enjoyments. Could that person's depth ever be exhausted? One other person is always more than enough, when you believe that that person will listen to you until you run out of things to say, when you trust that that person will wait as long as it takes you to understand why you are the way you are, when you realize that that person will always impute the best of motives to your actions, however clumsy you feel inside. You don't need to grab the biggest piece of cake anymore, because you are one body, and her eating it is as good as you eating it. You don't have to have all the witty punch lines yourself anymore, because it's not a competition for attention that only one of you can win. You shall not commit adultery. One person is enough.

Then there's the third commandment, you shall not make wrong use of the name of God. What makes us do so? It's when the language at our disposal doesn't seem to convey the strength or depth of feeling in our hearts. We hear a ripping sound when we put on a treasured item of clothing. Our favorite sports team is losing and the weakest player on the team misses a golden opportunity. We hang on the telephone for twenty minutes and a voice says, "We value you as a customer and will be with you shortly." Somehow language seems inadequate to express the depth of our distress on these occasions. So we invoke the name of God. We make the holy into the trivial, and thus impoverish the language. Whenever we exaggerate, we do the same thing. We say the truth is somehow not enough. Don't invoke the name of God against call center operators, and don't invoke

God's name to make your life sound that little bit more eventful and interesting. You shall not make wrong use of the name of God.

And what of the second commandment, you shall not make yourself an idol? Surely the psychology of this is that God is not enough—not big enough, or at least not near enough. So I shall make a god I can relate to, a god my size—a car perhaps, a career maybe, even the scales that tell me how much I weigh. And now we're getting nearer the heart of the problem. There's an abiding anxiety that we don't have enough—not enough property, not enough time, not enough love, not enough language. But the heart of the matter is that we feel we don't have enough God.

And that's why the moment in which God speaks these words is so significant. Israel has come out of Egypt, but is already beginning to wonder if it wouldn't have been better off staying. This is the moment when God says, "I am the Lord your God, who brought you out of the land of Egypt, out of the house of slavery. I have met your deepest yearning, and have exceeded it by giving you the promise of a land to settle in. I have been with you in the darkness, listened to you in your despair, led you out of death, dispersed your enemies, guided you by my own hand. I have set you free. I am the Lord your God. The problem is not that I am not enough for you—it is that I am too much for you. Your imaginations are simply too small to comprehend me. And what you don't know is that this is just the beginning. I am the creator of heaven and earth. I have set you free. But I will also be faithful to you through unimaginable betrayal. And I will come among you myself in the form of my only child. I love every creature I have made, but I treasure each one of you as if you were the only one. I forgive you even when you have let me down seventy times seven times. Can you imagine?

"No, you can't, can you? I can see you can't. You still fall into thinking I'm not enough. You get anxious, and when you get anxious you start wanting more gods, more money, more things. I gave you manna in the desert, far more food than you needed. You still went out to collect on the Sabbath because you feared there wouldn't be enough.

I gave you water in the desert. But still your thoughts were straying back to Egypt. If only you could let your imaginations go and enter the land I am promising you, and let me set you free.

"But in the meantime, here are some rules to remind you of what matters most, that I am more than enough, that my abundance is always greater than your scarcity. Have no other gods: more of them means less of me. Have no idols: they will never be remotely enough, and will lead you to forget that I am plenty. Keep the Sabbath: I will give you all the time you need. Look after your aging parents and don't steal—I will give you everything you need. Don't kill people—they are part of the everything I am giving you. Don't misuse language—yes and no will be enough for you."

Really it comes down to the first commandment and the last. "Here are you, anxious, covetous, looking at all the fun they seem to have next door, the great parties, the great sex, the amazing children, the plentiful friends, the healthy bodies, the gorgeous golden retriever, and all the time feeling more and more impoverished, more and more deprived, more and more sorry for yourself, more and more trapped in your stunted imagination, more and more a slave. And here," says God, "am I, meticulously creating you in all your intricacy and beauty, setting you free from the darkest of prisons, forgiving you time and again even when your greatest hatred is for yourself, and coming among you to be your companion in Jesus."

Just us, and just God. Face-to-face. And that's the moment when God stretches out two hands and gives us the Ten Commandments, just like we were Moses. God says, "I have set you free. You may forget that. You may fall back into thinking or feeling that I am not enough. A lot of people do. So here are some gifts. They will help you remember your freedom. They will challenge your imagination to realize that I am a God of abundance, who gives you more than enough, far more than you could ever want or need, who created galaxies no one may ever see, who has depths of forgiveness no sinner may ever require, who gives you in Jesus more love than you could ever realize."

And we take the gift from God's hands, and we look into God's face, and we say, "May these commandments be to me always a gift and never a burden. May they always remind me that you are the one true God who has set me free. Write these words on my heart so I never forget that you are always more than enough. For now I realize that, with you, one is plenty."

But what might that mean for something the Old Testament never seriously considers—abiding, committed relationship between two partners of the same sex? The key is not to scour the Bible for a clear instruction, regardless of its logic or lack of logic, regardless of whether it coheres and coincides with the character of God as we understand it or the makeup of human character as we have come to know it; the key is to focus on the heart of the Ten Commandments, the center of the law, which lies in that word, "enough."

When a person says to another person that they want to share in a lifelong, exclusive, embodied relationship, they're saying to that person, "You are enough for me." You are enough because one person, if you really take the time to give them your serious attention, to examine their tiniest quirks and characteristics, to listen to their deepest yearnings and fears, to explore their fondest hopes and most painful wounds, and to share with them all those same things in yourself—one person is plenty. How in a lifetime could we ever exhaust the mystery, the wonder, the glory, the priceless gift of one other person?

What threatens such relationships? Not those who seek to enter them but in some traditions are barred from so doing. The threats start with these words: "You are not enough for me." You don't have enough charm to distract me from the troubles of life. You don't have enough skills to make up for all my practical shortcomings. You don't have enough money to cover my willful spending. You don't have enough patience to cope with my mood swings. You don't have enough appeal to awaken my unimaginative desires. You don't have enough energy to do your share of the household chores. You don't have enough grace to abide with my wayward recklessness. You are not enough.

The alternative threat is this: "You are too much for me." You read my mind when I'd prefer to be private. You have deep needs when I'd prefer to suit myself. You have your lively friends round when I want to be silent. Your need to flourish makes me fear I'll disappear. Your inner demons mean I can't relax. You insist on me explaining when I expect you just to know what I want and need. You want to have another child when I'm feeling overwhelmed. You spend so much money we'll never buy a house. You want to change careers yet again when we can't make ends meet as it is. You are too much.

And these two painful sentences coalesce into a third, which says, "We are not enough." We can't be grown-ups. We can't bring out the best in each other. We can't have a family. We can't hear each other. We can't trust each other. We can't deal with your mother moving in to share her declining years. We can't create such an adventure out of life that it stops us dwelling on our regrets about the past and our fears about the future. We can't hold each other without suffocating each other. We can't let go of each other without abandoning each other. We can't cope with the challenging behavior of our child. We can't find in each other a magic potion that dismantles and disperses all our other frustrations and griefs about existence. We thought we were attaining the superhuman status of lovers, but it turns out we're just two human beings. We are not enough.

When people find it hard to believe, they're saying to God, "You are not enough for me." God seems too small, too vague, too abstract, too distant, too intangible. When people are angry with God, they're saying, "You are too much for me." Too intense, too demanding, too looming, too relentless. Fundamentally they're saying, "We, even with God, are not enough." Not enough to withstand the millstone of our past or survive the threats of our future. This is the mystery: the things we find hard about our most intimate relationships are the things we find hard about God.

In the end, eternity and now are about a relationship. A relationship God has already made: with us. A relationship where God has committed everything, and so have we; although we often forget it. That relationship we could call "God with us." But it has another name. That name is Jesus. Jesus is God with us. Jesus is the marriage of heaven and earth. Eventually all human relationships end, if not by sin, then by death. But Jesus embodies the relationship that doesn't end. Jesus is the relationship that we were made for and that truly lasts forever. Jesus is God saying, gently, patiently, winsomely, lovingly, "I am enough for you."

How This Story Differs from the Rival Story

On this territory, the rival story is, quite simply, sentimental. When faced with a story that has historically been, and sometimes today continues to be, censorious, harsh, exclusionary, and self-righteous, that's a forgivable error. Our hearts may well, and rightly, be with Mr. Emerson. But it's still an error. Our heads can't be entirely with Mr. Emerson. Because all four of his assumptions are flawed. Tolerance is not an adequate ethic; you can't say "leave people alone" and at the same time say "silence is violence." Of course, it's right to leave people alone when what they're doing is harmless and trivial. But that's precisely the point: What do we regard as harmless and trivial? We are not in agreement. The story to live by is about finding God's company in the midst of complex contexts; it's not denying that there are complex contexts.

Mr. Emerson maintains that institutions, especially the church, are simply a deadweight of hidebound negativity. Some are, no question; but try living without institutions. Institutions are the way we pass on wisdom from past to future; without them we are infantilized. The story to live by is saturated with Christian Scripture, not because it lives in the past, but because it shows us a God who is enough for us, and the folly of trying to make it all up as we go along.

Moreover, in assuming that happiness is in short supply, Mr. Emerson endorses the notion of scarcity that, for the story to live by, constitutes the heart of the problem. He takes for granted that we don't have enough, whereas the story to live by argues that God is enough for us: if we focus on being with God, happiness will be among the many fruits that follow—but if we concentrate on finding happiness, we will find it too nebulous to grasp.

Finally Mr. Emerson suggests that love is the most holy thing of all. It is. But telling the difference between true, profound, enduring, forgiving love, on the one hand, and passionate desire seeking urgent fulfillment, on the other, is more of a challenge than Mr. Emerson realizes. If only the latter were always a manifestation of the former. The story to live by says our model of the former is God's love for us, embodied in Jesus. It's not an abstract, unattainable ideal, whose rare instances should be upheld and treasured accordingly; it's something that happened, for thirty-three years, most especially in agonizing death and astonishing resurrection—an incarnate event that dismantles all our sentimentality and inspires our imitation.

How This Story Differs from the Old, Old Story

I believe in this case the story to live by is entirely consistent with the old, old story. For God to say to humanity, "You are enough for me," and for humanity to respond in the same way, is the heart and goal of the covenant on which Old and New Testaments are founded. Where things get into difficulty with the old, old story is the precise details of what the law entails. This is not a new problem: the early Christians wrestled with how much of the law of Moses was now part of the new covenant in Christ, and in every generation since, issues have arisen that demand resolution of what the law means in contemporary circumstances.

It is entirely possible to say that a rule that was binding in the first century is not valid today. As we've seen, sex within a committed, lifelong, respectful, exclusive gay relationship was unknown in the first century. So what in the first century was liberating—the prohibition of gay sex, since it was almost universally exploitative and oppressive—can today seem unnecessary and unjust, since the practice is now commonplace and as often life-giving as sex between a woman and a man. By the same token, it is understandable that in some circles making this adjustment has been difficult or impossible; just as there are communities where other scriptural injunctions, such as women wearing head coverings in worship, or no one receiving communion without first making confession to a priest, are still considered mandatory. Such views aren't an intolerant poison in themselves, but they can become so if they are imposed in an egregious manner (one thinks of therapies that attempt to "cure" people of being gay), if they seek to impose such rules on people who are not members of the community, or if a particular rule is advocated out of proportion to other rules by which the community abides.

The difference between the story to live by and the old, old story is one of emphasis. The story to live by concentrates on God's purpose, to be in relationship with us, and evaluates all rules by whether they still embody and advance that purpose. There are practices that aren't specifically mentioned in the Bible, like aspects of ecological care, that could nonetheless today be elevated to the status of rules, since they so clearly express the spirit of being with God, oneself, one another, and the creation; and there are practices the Bible appears to forbid that no longer seem to inhibit being so. What's needed most of all is for the church to have the humility to recognize, when a protest movement comes into conflict with traditional practice, that sometimes it turns out the protest movement is more inspired by the Holy Spirit than the church is.

- 6 -

PERPETRATOR OF TERRIBLE HARM?

"I MIGHT BELIEVE IN THE REDEEMER if his followers looked more redeemed." Friedrich Nietzsche's stinging criticism of Christianity constitutes a powerful argument against not just the usefulness of Christianity but its truth. We can detect three kinds of problems disclosed by Nietzsche's observation. There are the pernicious features that seem endemic within Christianity—of which anti-Semitism stands out. Then there are those policies and practices Christianity has officially adopted, or with which it has actively colluded—one thinks of the Crusades and the Inquisition. Third, there is the cloak of secrecy and the looking-the-other-way in which individuals representing the church have been allowed to do terrible harm—most notably the horror of clerical abuse of children and young people. Together, this disgraceful catalogue of wrongs constitutes an almost overwhelming case that Christianity is the source of more harm than good. As Gandhi put it, "I like your Christ; I do not like your Christians. Your Christians are so unlike your Christ."

CHAPTER 6

The Old, Old Story and What's Wrong with It

The Standard Account

The church exists on broadly three levels. We could call the first level mystical. Jesus is the full presence of God to humanity and the full presence of humanity to God. After his ascension, the Holy Spirit clothed his disciples with all the gifts they needed to continue to be his body in the world. Thus "church" is the word for being utterly with God, one another, oneself, and the creation. Church is that community in which the ways of God in Israel and Christ are commemorated and practiced, and in which the final revelation of God's justice and peace in heaven is anticipated and embodied. It is the definitive (though not the only) place of encounter between God and humanity in the time between Christ and the last day. It is the place where people are regarded as God regards them, and where eternity is glimpsed in the experience of common life.

The second level we could call physical. It's the regular daily, weekly, and annual habits and practices of a community, small enough to be an association in which deep relationships are formed and restored, yet large enough to be an organization recognizable to outsiders. It is a collection of people striving together to embody the ideals of the mystical church—to act justly, love mercy, and walk humbly with God and one another. Its practices involve worship, often baptism and Eucharist, in which belonging and flourishing are expressed and renewed; Scripture reading and preaching, in which lives are shaped according to the character of God; prayer, in which together people perceive essence in the midst of existence; and encounter, in which members engage with other Christians, those of other faiths, and those of no professed faith in mutually salutary ways.

The third dimension we could call institutional. It's the whole apparatus of a human structure—perhaps the opposite of the first dimension. Decisions need to be taken; identity asserted; people employed and paid, and sometimes employment ended; discipline kept; buildings erected and maintained; statements issued; procedures followed; leaders trained, appointed, and stood down; plans made, altered, achieved or not achieved, revised, or dropped; and a cycle of activity and financial infrastructure sustained.

Each level has its respective challenges. For the first level, the question is, Is it real? It sounds wonderful, but does it have any purchase in existence? Is it too heavenly minded to be of any earthly use? For the third dimension, the issue is, is it in any tangible or visible way godly? Is it not simply an institution, like any other—and when it overreaches itself and tries to be better than or superior to other institutions, more likely to fall into arrogance, hypocrisy, or failure? For the second level, where the expectations of the first meet the realities of the third, the question is, Is it achievable? Can a forgiving, truthful, hopeful, generous community truly function—or will human weakness and limitation foil all grand plans?

Challenges to the Standard Account

Few people have any significant problem with the mystical church described above. They may doubt its existence, but for most it remains at least a fine idea. The issues arise with the physical church and the institutional church. Those issues are profound and harrowing. They cover the ground identified at the start of this chapter.

First, there are ways in which the very core of Christianity seems corrupted not just by the malign outworking of noble ideals but by its very own assertions. The most troubling example is anti-Semitism. When Pontius Pilate asks the crowd what evil Jesus had done to deserve death, we're told, "The people as a whole answered, 'His blood be on us and on our children!'" (Matt. 27:25). Perhaps no verse in any scripture has had a more damaging legacy. For centuries Christians have justified antagonism toward Jews on the claim that they killed Jesus (even though the gospel account makes clear that the Romans actually killed him). Foundational early-church theologians like mid-second-century Justin Martyr perpetuated such calumny against the Jews; early third-century Tertullian first contrasted the bellicose and wrathful Old Testament God of the wicked Jews with the gracious and compassionate God of the New Testament. In the Middle Ages, programs of ethnic cleansing excluded Jews from England in 1290, from France in 1306, and from Spain in 1492. Eventually the Jews became the scapegoat for all the ills of Christendom. The Holocaust was not itself a Christian project, but it emerged out of many centuries in which Christians had excluded, oppressed, and vilified Jews, thus creating a story in which the venom, scale, and ruthlessness of the Holocaust were conceivable. Failure to account for the Jews isn't just a populist aberration; it seems close to the heart of Christianity from the outset.

But this isn't the only inherent problem with the DNA of Christianity. When Jesus departs from his disciples, he says these words: "All authority in heaven and on earth has been given to me. Go therefore and make disciples of all nations, baptizing them in the name of the Father and of the Son and of the Holy Spirit" (Matt. 28:18–19). This, together with the dramatic coming of the Holy Spirit at Pentecost, creates Christianity's missionary impulse. One nineteenth-century Indian described Christians as "persons who travel to a distant country for the purpose of overturning the opinions of its inhabitants and introducing their own."* It has proved extraordinarily difficult to disentangle the humble, gentle ethos of Christianity from an imperial attitude of possession, control, and domination; what some contemporary theologians have called a mind-set of white supremacy and antiblackness. Is there a Christianity without proselytism and a corresponding assumption of cultural superiority? If there is, it's been a minority pursuit in the history of the church. When it comes to the truth, assertion invariably leads to coercion.

* Raja Rammohun Roy, quoted in Tom Holland, *Dominion: How the Christian Revolution Remade the World* (New York: Basic Books, 2019), 419.

Second, coercion is hardly limited to evangelism. The church has adopted methods in a host of areas that sit profoundly at odds with the ideals it claims to uphold. The Crusades are the most notorious series of events in which worship and charity morphed hideously into slaughter and pillage. Promoted by popes as piety, the Crusades, in which Europeans sought to claim the Holy Land and take it from Saracen hands, too often became genocide, ethnic cleansing, and rapacious plunder. Meanwhile there were spinoffs in Europe itself: the Albigensian crusade involved the carnage of around half a million members of a renewal movement in twelfth- and thirteenth-century southern France committed to perfection, poverty, and preaching, and known for its denial of the flesh, known as the Cathars. Not only was the twenty-year crusade from 1209 to 1229 engineered by Pope Innocent III, but the creation of the Dominican order of friars was closely linked to the whole campaign.

Then there's the phrase "witch hunt." Between 1400 and 1782, around fifty thousand people were put to death for witchcraft in German-speaking central Europe.* Protestants and Catholics, competing in some of the most contested spaces of the denominational divide, rivaled one another in presenting themselves as the most ardent defenders of the faith in the face of evil. This was not simply an outburst of local tensions and prejudices. It was an orchestrated campaign of ruthlessness. A terrifying number of casualties resulted.

The Inquisition was not dissimilar. In the fifteenth century, Pope Sixtus IV specifically ordered the king and queen of Spain to identify inquisitors who would root out Jews pretending outwardly to be Christians but in private maintaining their ancestral faith; in later years, after the expulsion of the Jews, Muslims became the target of the fanatical campaign; and during the Reformation, Protestants also.

* Gwynn Guilford, "Germany Was Once the Witch-burning Capital of the World. Here's Why," *Quartz*, January 24, 2018, https://qz.com/1183992/why-europe-was-overrun-by-witch-hunts-in-early-modern-history.

The movement grew into an alliance of throne and altar whose principal effect, besides extensive cruelty and torture, was the concentration of political power in Madrid. But it was also extended into other parts of Europe, and to the colonies in Latin America. It wasn't finally closed down until 1834.

These three examples illustrate a tendency replicated in the church's involvement in the oppression of Native Americans in the United States, particularly as the nation expanded west in the nineteenth century; in the genocide of indigenous peoples in South America during the same period; and in the treatment of aboriginal peoples in Australia much more recently. There are countless examples in other times and places. This seems to be a religion that obliterates dissenters.

Third, while the church has always claimed to be a conduit of love, joy, and peace, it has validated, housed, and hidden a host of people who have used their roles within the institution to hurt, manipulate, and oppress individuals and groups for their own purposes. While this has always been so, in our own generation the most devastating form of such activity has been the clerical sex abuse of children and the way perpetrators have found sanctuary and continued to exercise authority within the church. A report in 2018 found that bishops of the Roman Catholic Church in Pennsylvania hid evidence of child sexual abuse by three hundred priests over seventy years, meanwhile prevailing upon victims not to report the abuse and upon the police not to investigate it.* A 2009 report revealed that sexual and psychological abuse was endemic in Roman Catholic–run schools and orphanages in Ireland during the twentieth century.** The issue is global, cross-

* Laurie Goodstein and Sharon Otterman, "Catholic Priests Abused 1,000 Children in Pennsylvania, Report Says," *New York Times*, August 14, 2018, https://www.nytimes.com/2018/08/14/us/catholic-church-sex-abuse-pennsylvania.html.

** "Catholic Church Child Sexual Abuse Scandal," BBC, February 26, 2019, https://www.bbc.co.uk/news/world-44209971.

denominational, and horrifying. It has done more than anything else to destroy the credibility of Christianity in places that were once its most fervent bases of adherence. It's not hard to see why so many have concluded that the church is intrinsically hypocritical, and that the pretense of goodness is a fig leaf covering the nakedness of social, political, emotional, and sexual manipulation and control.

What defense can possibly be made of the church in the face of such a catalogue of terrible harm? And does not the indefensibility of the church on all these three levels go much of the way toward the discrediting of Christianity as a whole?

A Rival Story, Its Validity and Flaws

A Rival Story

There are two rival stories in this domain, which overlap but never entirely cohere with one another. We can call them the harsh story of order and the gentler story of understanding.

The harsh story recognizes that human beings, while they can be noble, worthy, and honorable, can also be venal, lascivious, and greedy. To avoid the triumph of selfishness requires the rule of law, dispassionately but vigorously enforced, with appropriate incentives and punishments, and healthy systems of oversight, accountability, and discipline. Any organization of people to some specific end is always liable to devolve into a mere association, that is, an assemblage of individuals with common interests, liable to exclude others and pursue narrow ends; but it may always be elevated into an institution, which embeds wisdom, seeks long-term goods, trains in virtue, and cultivates aspiration. Such a culture, accompanied by democratic habits that can remove underperforming leaders, offer routes out of disadvantage, and reward merit, is the only way to ensure a just society. Manipulative and narcissistic individuals will pursue their goals through whichever branch of society they find most permeable to their malign intentions; the church is not immune, and the cocktail of desire, devotion, and deception can prove particularly intoxicating to some. If Christianity is already in the business of misleading, distorting, and fabricating, it may provide particularly fertile soil for deceptive or coercive activity; but at heart the problem is an unwillingness to face the harsh measures needed to curtail the human propensity for evil.

The gentler story has a much more benign understanding of human nature. It sees oppression, duplicity, and the obstruction of justice as arising largely from trauma and neglect, often in childhood, and places considerable trust in the powers of therapy, understanding, and care to redeem the wayward soul. Paradoxically, it can generate a more hostile attitude to Christianity than the harsher view. This is because it is most critical of those who create misery for the young, by dogmatic, controlling forms of child rearing, or by cruel and merciless methods of discipline—both of which have often been propagated in Christian households and communities. Whereas the harsh story sees failings in everyone, and consequently perceives the need to establish systems that limit exploitation, the gentler story is more likely to identify pernicious systems of thought and practice that produce damaged and dangerous individuals; Christianity can offer numerous examples that seem to fit that story perfectly.

The Validity and Flaws of the Rival Story

The rival story is full of valid points. When it comes to harm, the church has done much, falsified extensively, facilitated much more. It resembles human institutions in many respects, and too often falls short of secular standards, let alone divine ones. It's not enough for the church to say we're all sinners, and all have fallen short of the grace of God, and that Peter the denier and Judas the betrayer were among those closest to Jesus from the start. The sins noted in this chapter are not envy, lust, gluttony, or sloth. What we're discussing here are colossal and systematic departures from any conceivable ethic of interhuman flourishing: a pathological problem with Jews, as those who would not assimilate into medieval Christendom, laying the foundations for the massacre of millions of Jews from 1941 to 1945; the use of coercion, slaughter, and torture as instruments of church policy; and the sheltering of thousands of people who had made abuse of children a way of life, suggesting that such actions were somehow legitimate or permissible. Well may the rival story say Christianity is no better, and often worse, than the world it attempts to convert.

It would be appropriate to pause here in reading to recognize the torrent of wrong that the church corporately and all Christians must in their own way recognize and confess, and for which they must make penance and seek mercy.

Once we've made such pause, no doubt a very long pause, we can identify two flaws in the rival story. One is, while the church has indeed been the perpetrator of terrible harm, it has also been the source of untold good. It's absurd to imagine an ethereal umpire totting up the good performed and the harm perpetrated and declaring a winner—especially as the harm is horrendous and no amount of good can compensate for it. The point is, any argument that Christianity is intrinsically malign—rotten to the core—has to reckon with the profound goodness of so many of its adherents—far too many to count. While Christians were among those who supported Hitler as he planned the annihilation of the Jews, Christians were also establishing the Confessing Church in Germany; issuing the Barmen Declaration, which denounced the Nazis as idolaters; and, with others, helping Jews escape once the Holocaust began. While a distorted Christian theology underwrote the apartheid regime in South Africa with the support of the Dutch Reformed Church, Christians were also at the forefront of the antiapartheid movement and the authors of the Kairos Document, which described apartheid as racist and totalitarian. That Christians have so often been in the wrong does not make Christianity itself inherently wrong.

The second flaw is that the whole structure of good and bad, right and wrong, by which the church is so often—and rightly—judged, is itself a Christian one. In other words, there is hardly a clause in the rival story, of either stripe, that is not an internal argument within Christianity itself. The whole idea that Christians should have special care for the vulnerable, a principle so egregiously transgressed in cases of clergy sex abuse of children, is based on the parable of the good Samaritan and of the last judgment, in which those most vulnerable in this world turn out to have been Jesus. The whole dispute about whether Christians should offer humanitarian kindness to the stranger, by all means convert the enemy to the faith, or destroy the enemy and in doing so deplete the work of Satan on earth, is an internal Christian debate of many centuries' duration—a debate that still surfaces, for example, in the wake of the 9/11 attacks. The language and thought patterns of Christianity have so saturated the contemporary West that this most damaging of criticisms of Christianity—that it has done so much of the opposite of what it has propounded—is invariably made in terms devised by Christianity itself. The rival story turns out to be an alternative version of the old, old story.

A Story to Live by, and How It Differs from Both Stories

A Story to Live By

The French twentieth-century philosopher Gabriel Marcel made a distinction between a problem and a mystery. A problem is something you can stand outside and walk around. It's something you can usually solve by technical skill. A broken window is a problem, but you can solve it by installing a new one. Often a problem can be solved using a technique developed by somebody else. But a mystery you can't solve. A mystery you can't stand outside. You have to enter it. A mystery is something you can't just look at. It absorbs you into it. Someone else's answer probably won't work for you. You have to discover your own.

The church is a mystery and not a problem. Some may approach it as a problem and try to offer you a solution. There are countless conferences every year offering techniques of church growth or training in family systems theory. But there isn't a simple solution that solves the church. And that's because it's a mystery. The church is the best idea anybody ever had. Dynamic unity, profound godliness, gregarious diversity, historic identity. You can't beat that. It's a fabulous combination. But it frequently becomes a monster, or a mess. It's a real mystery.

One author who describes this mess is the British novelist Rose Macaulay. She spent a lot of her life on the edge of the church, partly because of its mysteries, and partly because of her own. Her semi-autobiographical novel *The Towers of Trebizond* describes a journey around the Middle East in the 1950s. In it she tells the story of a woman named Laurie, caught between the eccentricity of the characters she meets and her own irreconcilable loves. All the while Laurie is wrestling with the absurdity of the church. Her Middle Eastern travels bring Laurie to Bethlehem, and, while in that little town of poignant beginnings, she reflects on what's so terribly wrong and yet so completely right about the church, long ago and today. Bethlehem epitomizes the contrasts and mysteries of the church she knows so well. This is what she says.

> [The church] grew so far, almost at once, from anything which can have been intended, and became so blood-stained and persecuting and cruel and war-like and made small and trivial things so important, and tried to exclude everything not done in a certain way and by certain people, and stamped out heresies with such cruelty and rage. And this failure of the Christian Church, of every branch of it in every country, is one

> of the saddest things that has happened in all the world. But it is what happens when a magnificent idea has to be worked out by human beings who do not understand much of it but interpret it in their own way and think they are guided by God, whom they have not yet grasped. And yet they had grasped something, so that the Church has always had great magnificence and much courage, and people have died for it in agony, which is supposed to balance all the other people who have had to die in agony because they did not accept it, and it has flowered up in learning and culture and beauty and art, to set against its . . . incivility and obscurantism and barbarity and nonsense, and it has produced saints and martyrs and kindness and goodness, though these have also occurred freely outside it, and it is a wonderful and most extraordinary pageant of contradictions, and I, at least, want to be inside it, though it is foolishness to most of my friends.*

This is the mystery of the church as described by someone who knows it as well as she knows herself, and loves it the way you long for something or someone unique that lingers just out of reach. What Laurie is saying is that the church has been one, but it's also been divisive. It's been holy, but it's also been sinful. It's been catholic, but it's also been narrow. It's been apostolic, but it's also been forgetful. And yet amid what she calls its "wonderful and most extraordinary pageant of contradictions" she sees a place even for her, despite all her confusions and despair.

The biggest difference between a problem and a mystery is not just that a problem can be solved while a mystery can't. It's that a problem is something you can walk away from, whereas a mystery becomes something that absorbs and engulfs you in such a way that your life

* Rose Macaulay, *The Towers of Trebizond* (New York: New York Review of Books, 1956), 195–97.

depends on it. That's what *The Towers of Trebizond* is fundamentally about. One night Laurie is troubled by a dream. In the dream she's wrestling with whether she will finally be drawn into the kingdom of God, or instead remain profoundly conflicted on the periphery. The fabled Black Sea port of Trebizond in northern Turkey becomes for her a vision of the new Jerusalem. She sees ethereal Trebizond, and she imagines herself on the doorstep of heaven. This is what she says.

> Then, between sleeping and waking, there rose before me a vision of Trebizond: not Trebizond as I had seen it, but the Trebizond of the world's dreams, of my own dreams, shining towers and domes shimmering on a far horizon, yet close at hand, luminously enspelled in the most fantastic unreality, yet the only reality, a walled and gated city, magic and mystical, standing beyond my reach yet I had to be inside, an alien wanderer yet at home, held in the magical enchantment; and at its heart, at the secret heart of the city and the legend and the glory in which I was caught and held, there was some pattern that I could not unravel, some hard core that I could not make my own, and, seeing the pattern and the hard core enshrined within the walls, I turned back from the city and stood outside it, expelled in mortal grief.*

By talking about the "pattern" that she can't "unravel" and the "hard core" that she can't make her own, Laurie seems to be echoing Gabriel Marcel's distinction between a problem and a mystery. If the church is a problem, Laurie is never going to solve it; she will remain gloomily outside it looking for the solution. Yet the church isn't a problem. The church is a mystery. And, in the power of the Holy Spirit, it's a mystery that, usually for good but sometimes for ill, can absorb a person's whole life.

* Macaulay, *The Towers of Trebizond*, 200–201.

How can we untangle the mystery a little and respond to the charges leveled in this chapter? An honest but hopeful account of the church must start with uncomplicated repentance for what the church has very often been, must then move to identifying the lessons learned, and must move on to set out a renewed vision of a humbler institution without the pretensions that have led to so much harm.

The story of young David and enormous Goliath in 1 Samuel 17 is a defining moment in perceiving Israel's identity. Goliath epitomizes the nations that surround and threaten Israel. He's ten feet tall and has so much armor he has to get someone to carry his shield for him. King Saul is also tall and has plenty of armor of his own. But Saul isn't interested. So David steps forth from obscurity. Using wit and wisdom rather than hustle and muscle, David defeats Goliath. The Philistines flee and the Israelite army is rejuvenated.

The church has always liked this story because it seems to say, stand up for the little guy. It's an attractive idea, sportingly, morally, corporately. Everyone likes to see themselves as David, with the odds stacked against them. But the truth is, the church has spent a great deal of time and energy trying hard to be Goliath. Its buildings often look like fortresses. Its leaders often dress like monarchs. Its resources often mimic those of large corporations.

The heart of the church's problem—what has led it to so many of the atrocities named in this chapter—is that it has assumed for as long as anyone can remember that it's supposed to be Goliath. It's supposed to be huge, it's supposed to be important, it's supposed to be a player on the national stage, it's supposed to be the acknowledged voice of the people. All the things Goliath was. All the things David wasn't.

There's a painful irony about what becomes of David after he puts down the slingshot. If only David had stuck with the five smooth stones, history might have turned out a little differently. Here he is, full of confidence, full of faith, full of hope, telling Saul he doesn't need the heavy armor and telling Goliath he doesn't need mighty power and bombastic big talk. David defeated Goliath. The people swung behind

David. David became king. And gradually the terrible irony began to kick in. David became Goliath. David became the inflated, bullying, beached whale he had begun his career by destroying. Just like Elvis Presley, for whom fame and fortune turned gyrating hips into bloated cheeks. David became Goliath. What a tragedy that was.

But the poignancy doesn't end there. When we read the story of David and Goliath, we don't just see the contrast with David's later life. We also think of the one whom the Gospels often call the Son of David. When we think of Jesus as Son of David, are we thinking of the David who *became* Goliath? Or are we thinking of the David who *overcame* Goliath? The tragic irony is the same as before. We know that in walking the way of the cross, Jesus was the disarmed young David who walked slowly and calmly without armor to face the Goliath of empire and death. But we constantly fall back into celebrating Jesus as if he were the kingly David of power politics and conquest—the David who became Goliath.

We say we like David but we choose Goliath. David started off with five smooth stones and a sling and ended up becoming Goliath. But Jesus didn't. We may turn Jesus into Goliath in our imaginations, in our politics, in our rhetoric—even sometimes in our worship. But Jesus never turned into Goliath. And Jesus never does. The task for the church today is not to become Goliath again. It's to become David—the David who had five smooth stones but knew exactly how to use them; the David people instantly called to mind when they encountered the disarmed, disarming figure of Jesus.

To resemble David, the church needs to embody humility and hope. Humility recognizes that Christians are not better than others—that they have often been perpetrators of or complicit in the sins and ills of history—and have much to learn from the world beyond the church. Hope nonetheless has confidence in the completeness and ultimate fulfillment of Christ's ministry and in the work of the Holy Spirit transforming individuals, neighborhoods, and nations. What together they describe is a humbler faith with a bigger God.

The twentieth-century French philosopher Michel de Certeau distinguishes between a strategy and a tactic. A strategy builds a citadel, and from its control base makes forays into the hinterland. A tactic has no home base, nowhere to store its booty, and survives by hand-to-hand encounters on the ground. Here are two familiar sentiments. "Make me a channel of your peace," says the 1967 hymn based on a prayer written in France in 1912 and widely, though mistakenly, attributed to Saint Francis. "Christ has no body now but yours. No hands, no feet on earth but yours," says the sixteenth-century Spanish mystic Teresa of Ávila. These two sentiments assume what we might call "strategy church." A strategy church makes two assumptions. The first is an unspoken sense that Jesus ascended before he'd actually finished his work, and that therefore it falls to his chosen followers to complete the work he was too busy or distracted to attend to. The second is that if one imagines an hourglass, with the top and much larger part being heaven and the bottom and smaller part being earthly existence, and Jesus being the aperture through which the angels ascend and descend between the two, then the church constitutes that aperture. The church understands itself as the principal and definitive way in which God continues to work in the world after the manner of Christ's incarnation.

We may contrast this picture with "tactic church." "Christ plays in ten thousand places," says Gerard Manley Hopkins; "Lovely in limbs, and lovely in eyes not his." Notice how this tactic language differs from the assumptions of a strategy church. Three women attended a church. The church had to shut for a few weeks for repairs. So the three women made a plan. One went to rummage sales each Sunday morning, met and talked to the regulars, formed relationships and learned much. Another went to Sunday league soccer games and had a similar experience. A third went to an Ikea store and got to know staff and customers. After a few weeks, the three women compared notes and became excited about what they were discovering and understanding. When the church reopened after the refit, they had a genuine quandary about whether to return or whether to continue in their explorations. One of them explained, "Our God is now too big to fit back into our church." What they were naming was their discovery of tactic church. Tactic church does not assume that everything God is doing comes through the church. It doesn't assume that the best example of God's ways is always the church. It rejoices to discover the surprises of what the Spirit is doing in unexpected places through unheralded people. Tactic church entails a humbler church but apprehends a bigger God.

I have acknowledged that the church has indeed in many cases been the perpetrator of terrible harm. I have sought to identify the key mistake that has led the church down the wrong path. What then matters most is to chart a better direction for the church to take. I have suggested becoming a humbler church with a bigger God. What might that entail?

It must mean building on assets. Thomas Aquinas maintains that grace perfects nature; it doesn't destroy it. God's pattern in Scripture, from Noah's flood onward, is to find ways to redeem creation, not to look for comprehensive change. Heaven is the redemption of our bodies, not their wholesale replacement. Renewal is thus first and foremost about building on assets. This is crucial for three further reasons: it embodies the conviction that God gives the church everything it needs to be faithful in each generation; it affirms those in place, such as clergy, that they have genuinely been called to good work; and it ensures that the institution remains recognizable to insider and outsider alike.

When confidence is low and good outcomes are hard to perceive, voices will always say, "We should be like industry . . . do it like the Japanese . . . make better use of social media." But the church isn't looking for a solution to a problem—one that can be imported, adapted, implanted, adopted; it's looking to grow truer to its calling in the face of challenges—and thus enter a mystery. Importing a solution rests on envy and anxiety—the desire to be like others and the loss of confidence in one's own validity. What are the church's assets? They include trust (even in places where trust has been jeopardized); a host of dedicated and faithful disciples found in almost every community across the world; the respect of key institutions of government and civil society; usually an educated and able clergy and network of lay ministries; established patterns of education, formation, training, and accreditation; and in many cases an ability to draw together diverse opinion, conviction, and practice within one body, locally and nationally.

The crucial task of a humbler church with a bigger God is to realize and release gifts. Here is the central, prophetic conviction: God gives the church everything it needs, and if the church experiences its existence as scarcity, that's largely because it has neglected the gifts God has sent it. Some of that neglect has been culpable perpetration of or participation in oppression, as we have noted. But much more has been idle or willful inattention to where the kingdom is growing. When Peter stands before the Sanhedrin, called to account for how he has enabled a crippled beggar to walk, he looks back into Israel's story, in which God had founded the kingdom not on any of Jesse's tall and powerful sons but on David, the youngest and weakest. Peter quotes Psalm 118, which describes the choosing of David, with the words "the stone that was rejected by you, the builders; it has become the cornerstone" (Acts 4:11). Peter identifies that rejected stone as Jesus. In his crucifixion Jesus was rejected by the builders—yet in his resurrection he became the cornerstone of forgiveness and eternal life. The moment of Israel's renewal was in Babylonian exile—when it too felt like the stone the builders had rejected.

Being a humbler church is not about condescendingly making welcome alienated strangers. It means seeking out the rejected precisely because they are the energy and the life force that will transform the church. The ingredients of a humbler church come from what church and society have blithely rejected. The life of the church is about constantly recognizing the sin of how much it has rejected and celebrating the grace that God gives back what it once rejected to become the cornerstone of its life. The church is founded on and comprised of stones that the builders rejected. The challenge for the church is to see Jesus in the face of the one it has rejected. And to let the Jesus it discovers in them become its cornerstone.

How This Story Differs from the Rival Story

The key to the story to live by is that it sees the church as a mystery and not a problem. There's no doubt, when the church obfuscates in the face of calls to bring abusers of children to justice, that the notion of mystery has sometimes been misused; nonetheless, the failures of the church can seldom simply be fixed by better procedures, resignation, the prosecution of "bad apples," or more rigorous training or supervision. Where failures can be so straightforwardly "fixed," they must be; but that will not eradicate all failure, because the church is not simply a human institution. The approach offered in the story to live by seeks to recognize what can be addressed by recognition and rectification, what can only be approached through repentance and reconciliation, and what requires resurrection and renewal.

That said, most of what comes to the church through the rival story, harsh and gentle, is a gift to the church, and a humbler church welcomes such a gift as a form of renewal. Humility means responsibility and true assessment of power—not abdication of power. The rival story offers a great deal of wisdom in the good exercise of power. When Jesus embodied the shape of the church the night before he died, he left the table (symbolizing heaven), took off his robe (symbolizing his divine nature), and knelt down to wash the disciples' feet (in a gesture of what it meant to take on human nature). This is the epitome of what it means to be a humbler church with a bigger God. But Jesus concluded by putting his robe back on and returning to the table. So long as

Christians see washing feet as the church's definitive way of relating to one another and the world, the pretension that tempts them to torture others, destroy cultures for the sake of a principle, or hide abusers to preserve relationship or reputation is less likely to prevail.

Paul likened the gospel to a treasure, and the church to an earthen vessel that contained the treasure. Yet the second step, besides washing feet, that can assist the church in avoiding catastrophic wrong turns is to celebrate and enjoy the manifestations of the Holy Spirit in those who would not call themselves Christians. An overdeveloped sense of its own righteousness has led the church astray in more ways than simply arrogance. A humbler church with a bigger God sees the Holy Spirit bringing the church all the gifts it needs in those it has often despised and sometimes damaged.

How This Story Differs from the Old, Old Story

In all but one respect the story to live by is a call to renewal in inhabiting the old, old story. But there is one key way in which the story to live by needs to distance itself from the way the old, old story has traditionally been told. And that is in regard to the church's understanding of and relation to the Jews.

The centuries-long and shameful Christian persecution of the Jews is the worst of all the church's terrible wrongs, because Judaism and Christianity's debt to it are so inherent in the church's whole identity. Jesus was a Jew. And, in an important sense, he still is. The first Christians were all Jews. If a large number of Jews after the resurrection never accepted Jesus, it was out of faithfulness to their Scriptures as they read them, not in brazen denial of God's covenant with them. God's rejection of Israel is simply unthinkable. God's passionate love for Israel runs throughout the Old Testament, and that love does not come to a sudden halt on Good Friday. As Paul makes clear in Romans 11, the gentiles only become part of the promise by being grafted into Israel, not by replacing Israel. The gentile Christian community is always a guest in the household of Israel. God keeps promises: If the church doesn't trust the promises of God to Israel in the Old Testament, how can it trust the promises of Jesus to the church in the New?

Without Israel the church doesn't know who Jesus is. Jesus is the embodiment of God's promise to Israel, and the embodiment of Israel's covenant with God. Fully divine, fully human. But we know very little about God that we don't find out in God's relationship with Israel. Israel isn't a ladder Christians can climb up by reading the Old Testament and then toss away when we get to Jesus. The Jews, and later others, including Nietzsche, kept asking the church a question, "Why don't you look redeemed?"—a question it couldn't answer. And so the church created a spiritualized gospel. The irony is that while the spiritualization of Jesus rendered the church practically invisible, one group through all those centuries was still visible as a distinct and recognizable body. And that was the Jews. Despite interminable persecution, the Jews are still with us. And painful and humbling as it is for Christians to realize, in many, perhaps most, respects, *they've* been a better witness to what it means to be the people of God over the last twenty centuries than has the church. The Jews are still teaching the church what salvation is.

So the sin is not so much that the Jews have failed God by not joining the church. The sin is that Christians have failed God by not exhibiting in any way convincingly to the Jews that Jesus has saved them by making them one body. What the church has to do is to say, "We thought all we needed was Jesus. But now we see we can't understand who Jesus is without understanding Israel. And when we begin to understand Israel we discover the faithfulness of God and the deep sin of the church." And once the church has said that, it's up to Christians to say to their Jewish friends, "We've been missing half the gospel for two thousand years. We can't do this without you. We want to talk to you, essentially not for your sake and salvation but for ours. We are guests in your house. God has destined us to be one body with you. Jesus has made it possible. We need you. We've horribly abused you. We'd like to start by saying sorry."

- 7 -

CAUSE OF ENDLESS CONFLICT?

IT'S OFTEN ASSERTED THAT RELIGION is the cause of all the conflict in the world. A moment's reflection identifies that an absurd exaggeration resides in the word "all": two children fighting over a broken toy are clearly in conflict, but no one suggests that the tension is due to their religious disagreements. But awareness of this exaggeration seldom reduces the vehemence, confidence, or frequency with which the argument is made. A closer examination reveals where and when this argument took hold. The Reformation of the sixteenth century triggered extensive and distressing violence and antagonism, notably the Thirty Years' War of 1618–1648. When the Enlightenment began its project of setting aside tradition and superstition, and founding knowledge on reason, the underlying motivation was to find a way to avoid repeating such carnage. From then on, the splits between Protestantism and Roman Catholicism, and between different branches of Protestantism, morphed into tensions between Christianity and Islam. Then there were conflicts between branches of Islam, and between faiths beyond Christianity, such as Islam and Hinduism in the Indian subcontinent—and the same argument reappeared; and this, despite the two world wars surfacing plenty of virulence without a significant religious quarrel between the antagonists.

CHAPTER 7

The Old, Old Story and What's Wrong with It

The Standard Account

There does seem to be rather a lot of smiting in the Old Testament. But it's not random, willful, or endemic. It's broadly of two kinds. First, the children of Israel who left Egypt and wandered in the wilderness were promised a home in Canaan; but Canaan was already settled by the Jebusites, Perizzites, Amorites, and plenty more. The stories told in the books of Joshua and Judges are about a tiny population struggling to gain a foothold and survive in a new land; over and again they see the hand of God at work as they overcome apparently impossible odds to defeat adversaries. Second, once there is a king and the nation is united, Israel continues to be vulnerable to invasion from neighboring nations. When one recalls that much of this story was written in exile centuries later, it's not hard to understand that some believed if Israel had been more ruthless with its enemies earlier it wouldn't have been overrun as it eventually was.

The New Testament brings a rather different notion of how to engage the adversary. Jesus says, "Love your enemies, do good to those who hate you, bless those who curse you, pray for those who abuse you" (Luke 6:27–28). When Jesus goes to the cross, he does so without resistance. He is grieved and sometimes angered by his differences with the religious elites—the Sadducees, Pharisees, elders, and scribes—but there's no remote question of this dispute becoming violent, at least on his side. Even his resurrection is an entirely nonviolent event, notwithstanding the language of victory and conquest subsequently associated with it. He anticipates differences of views and sets out a process for how to handle such moments gently but firmly (Matt. 18:15–22). Enemies don't stop being enemies, but there's a way to relate to enemies that doesn't seek their destruction. Paul assumes Christians are a tiny minority eking out an existence in an indifferent or hostile culture; his attitude to dissent can be lively, but there's no hint of ferocity. But the sometimes lurid language of the book of Revelation suggests that God's ways are not always ones of peace.

For the first three centuries the church was a minority community, in no position—and with no desire—to take up arms either against the regime or to quell internal disputes. But with the conversion of Emperor Constantine at the start of the fourth century, Christianity began to become a way of thinking about government and started to adopt a majoritarian mind-set. From this point on it becomes hard to discern moments when an ethic of peace and reconciliation influenced regimes in any way that marked out a Christian ethic from a non-Christian one. The ends might be somewhat different (and even that can often be disputed), but the means seem to be much the same. Conquering for Christ looks almost indistinguishable from conquering for Rome. Soon the great fourth- and fifth-century bishop and theologian Augustine distinguished between the city of God and the human city, and recognized the necessity of Christians inhabiting both; which laid the foundations for the notion of the just war. This concept, not fully articulated till a millennium later, recognized that the pacifism of the early church had, in some specific circumstances, to be set aside in order to achieve the maintenance of order and the suppression of evil.

Throughout the seventeen centuries since Constantine, there's remained a tension between two Christian approaches to the enemy without or the dissenter within. One is inspired by the parable of the good Samaritan: it approaches the stranger with compassion, understanding, and a will to coexist, and sees Christ in the face of the person of another faith as much as in the face of a fellow disciple. The other sees the words of John 14, "I am the way, and the truth, and the life," as a reason to impose conformity, not only within the faith, but upon those who have no expressed desire to share that faith. In that sense the just war is a compromise between the pacifism of the first and the crusading of the second.

It's not hard to see that the second, abrasive, and sometimes aggressive approach has drawn the criticism that religion is the cause of endless conflict. No one is especially proud of the wars that ensued from the sixteenth-century Reformation. But vestiges of those same tensions linger in, for example, the Troubles in Northern Ireland between 1969 and 1998, where a Catholic minority in the North (but majority in the whole of Ireland) sought initially civil rights and eventually independence from a Protestant majority in the North (but minority in the whole). It's arguable that the fault lines in contemporary US politics around guns and abortion have their history in Scotch-Irish immigration and an antagonism toward central authority that goes back to the battle between Catholic and Protestant in Ireland in the late seventeenth century. Meanwhile, in a country like Nigeria, the largely Christian South and the mostly Muslim North seem in perpetual tension. Catholic Croatia and Orthodox Serbia, and Catholic western Ukraine and Orthodox eastern Ukraine offer other plausible examples. The conventional defense is that conflict is an inherent part of the human condition, and that groups will attach religious labels to competition for land, resources, culture, and hegemony that would continue just as avidly with other labels.

Challenges to the Standard Account

The standard account acknowledges the propensity to violent conflict woven into the human soul and does not deny the way this tendency has surfaced in church history. Given this concession, a challenge to the standard account has to do more than point out the number of times Christianity has failed to live up to its noble ideals; it has to identify points closer to the core of the faith where Christianity is inherently flawed or hopelessly compromised on the issue of conflict.

Thus the question becomes, is there something in the DNA of Christianity that makes it incapable of abiding in tolerant, mutually respectful relations with those who don't share its first principles, or unable to make space within itself for significant diversity of conviction and practice among believers themselves? We need to take these two dimensions of the question separately.

As to addressing difference outside the faith, it's hard to avoid the conclusion that the question is really about control. The culture of medieval Europe was one of hierarchy and homogeneity. The celestial realm of God and the angels affirmed the order of monarchy and nobility, overseeing the subservience of peasant and serf. Social or theological divergence threatened the whole cosmic and terrestrial ecology. This offers an insight into persecution of the Jews: the culture couldn't tolerate a minority that stood outside this hierarchical homogeneity. Islam was an expansive, confident threat; in the context of the time, defending Christianity and defending the culture as a whole were indistinguishable. The problem, in other words, lies not in Christianity's propensity to violent conflict with outsiders; it lies in what happens when Christianity becomes the public ideology of a regime that's always at risk of losing control. The regime finds legitimation in Christianity; but more sinisterly, Christianity suspends its utter dependence on God, and instead becomes invested in its networks of worldly power. Christianity becomes aggressive when it's defending, not God, who needs no defending, but worldly power, which is always under threat. In the process Christianity loses its identity.

Moving to difference inside the faith, the Reformation dismantled the unities that characterized the medieval European world, despite its endemic conflicts, and made resistance to authority a defining principle for half of Western Christianity. It also made conflict principally an internal Christian matter, rather than an external one. The irony of Protestantism is that those who had defined themselves by their quest for religious freedom often turned out to be just as reluctant to offer it when it became theirs to grant. A story grew up that the Thirty Years' War was a war of religion, whereas in many ways it was about struggles for power that would have happened regardless of denominational labels. But the whole journey of the Enlightenment, its turning to the self rather than God as ultimate authority, and its attempt to ground truth on reason rather than revelation, arises from the longing to be free of unresolvable and bloodthirsty battles about convictions for which there seem no final arbiter. It's no exaggeration to say that these wars—or the way these wars came to be remembered—discredited Christianity such that it started to be seen by some as the curse of Europe, rather than its blessing. None of the major international and transcontinental wars since the seventeenth century have been fought on religious grounds, but the scar of the seventeenth century was so deep it still abides in the collective consciousness.

A Rival Story, Its Validity and Flaws

A Rival Story

John Lennon and Yoko Ono's song "Imagine" crystallizes the aspirations of those who maintain that religion is the cause of all the conflict in the world. Lennon and Ono suppose there isn't a heaven; and suggest if there were no countries, there'd be no reason to kill—and all would consequently live peaceably together. Beneath the simple lyrics, we can perceive three assertions that together constitute the rival story.

At the surface level, the rival story understands that conflict arises when a group of people has either an unshakeable conviction, to which it demands that everyone else conform, or a claim to property, which it is determined to seize or hold on to, regardless of consequences. Take away these pretexts—religion and property rights—so the argument goes, and you take away the factors that trigger conflict. If there's nothing to fight about, there's no fight. We might call "Imagine" the epitome of a 1960s ideal—even if it was written in the 1970s.

More substantially, given that abolishing religion and property might require rather more violent intervention and represent at least as much intolerance as the status quo, the rival story identifies the quest for absolute truth and the inability to coexist with those who differ in their notion of absolute truth as the biggest of all obstacles to mutual flourishing. The rival story argues that public efforts should prioritize creating the fairness, opportunity, education, and stability that enable a society to access all the professional and leisure avenues it could desire, and should pass no judgment and declare no interest in issues of meaning or truth—those being for individuals themselves to seek and determine in any way that does not prejudice the existence of others. In other words, the rival story creates a distinction between the public, which must have no investment in anything that could lead to endemic conflict, and the private, which may think and do as it wishes so long as that thinking and doing in no way inhibit or threaten the thinking and doing of others.

More significantly still, the rival story anticipates that policing this kind of liberal democratic society requires the development of corresponding institutions and procedures. The energy the standard account might give to propagating the gospel, the rival story devotes to establishing international forums like the United Nations and the International Criminal Court, understandings like the Universal Declaration of Human Rights and the Treaty on the Non-Proliferation of Nuclear Weapons, processes like international arbitration and causes like the advancement of democracy and encouragement of democratic institutions. To achieve Lennon and Ono's dream requires the vigilance of the peacemaker to be greater than the malevolence of the antagonist.

The Validity and Flaws of the Rival Story

For a fleeting moment, around 1990, it seemed, after forty-five years of the Cold War, that the world might be able to breathe clean air, much less tainted by ideological struggle. But the 9/11 attacks ushered in a twenty-year period, only partly curtailed by the pandemic, in which the violence of Islamist extremists once again fueled the argument that religion causes endless conflict. The rival story is more helpful in what it is for than in what it sets itself against. The huge investment in multilateral institutions that recognize the inevitability of destructive tension and frequent conflict is a wholly admirable feature of contemporary international relations. Likewise, the creation of a society in which no person's gifts are neglected, no opportunities are denied, and no discrimination is permitted is a worthy approach to dismantling the causes of conflict and the promotion of human flourishing. This is where the rival story is on strong ground. There is no good reason why any form of church should not seek to affirm and share that ground.

The rival story is on much shakier territory when it singles out religion in general and Christianity in particular as the cause of all (or most) conflict. It's just not true, whether on a trivial level or on the largest scale: the First and Second World Wars were not fought about Christianity; there were Christians on both sides. There's a parable to be found in the way, after the dismemberment of the Soviet Union, accompanied by high hopes for a rapprochement between East and West, the antagonism between Russia and the West has slowly grown to replace it. The first antipathy wasn't about religion; neither is the second. Likewise, the simmering tension between China and the West is not a religious tension: China persecutes some Christians, but some Muslims even more.

Nor, more seriously, does the rival story succeed when it maintains that Christianity in particular and religion in general are inherently conflictual and violent. I have acknowledged the lamentable history of how the church has often colluded in or campaigned for the state's forceful eradication of enemies or competitors. But this has never been the only way in which Christianity addresses tension within or without. And there is no legitimate way a religion that focuses on the horrifying execution of an unarmed man who never took up the sword can be described as inherently or intrinsically violent.

More subtly, the rival story habitually asserts that the only way to foster tolerance, avoid damaging conflict, and achieve a peaceable public life is to banish discourse about ultimate purposes and meanings to the margins of the private and personal. As we have seen, societies that have discouraged or outlawed public expression of transcendent aspirations have still found plenty of things to fight about. The path to peace does not lie in closing down the most significant of all human pursuits—the quest to discover, reflect, embody, and promote the eternal quality of existence. In return, Christianity has to prove that it can hold to a conviction about truth that does not require all to share that conviction, and demonstrate that both the holding of such profound convictions and the outworking of those convictions in social relations are a blessing for the whole society to enjoy, not a burden for some to endure.

A Story to Live by, and How It Differs from Both Stories

A Story to Live By

I

Rather than imagine a world that has no conflict, or idealize the church as a community beyond tension, it's better to understand what Christianity is really saying about difference and disagreement, however poorly it has historically reflected those commitments in its ministry and mission.

We should first distinguish between five key terms. The first is "difference." Difference is not, in itself, a problem. It's written into the character of creation. It's life-giving and life-creating. The creation story in Genesis 1 is not a quasi-scientific account of how the universe came to be: it's a repeated refrain emphasizing that difference is created, purposed, and good. Difference is not the cause of conflict and violence, although difference is often a common feature in conflict and violence. Conflict and violence often indicate a failure to harness the positive energy of difference.

The second term is "tension." Tension is what arises when difference triggers distress or competition. Why might this be? Sometimes a party finds change demanding. In other cases an individual or group has been used to unquestioned possession or authority, and is unused to challenge. There are times that a process of adaptation is rushed, and the new or emerging presence or procedure appears before the necessary understanding and habituation are fully in place. Very often, there is already a climate of insecurity, suspicion, or panic, and difference becomes the bearer of these well-developed anxieties. But there are also cases where more conscious forces of manipulation are looking to undermine a relationship, and they seize on difference as a way to exploit vulnerability.

The third word is "conflict." Tension crosses the threshold into conflict when conventional respect and courtesy are set aside, the wider context of understanding and appropriate dialogue is dropped, and the need to be victorious, the desire to vanquish, and the impulse to assert one's own perspective take over. The simmering pot boils over and the lava of anger pours out. All the positive features of tension are jettisoned, and all thought for consequences, civility, and dignity is extinguished: confrontation is all.

The fourth word is "war." In war, the relatively limited extent and duration of conflict are abandoned, and nothing is immune from the all-consuming conflagration; there can be no exemption or any neutrality: everything is funneled into the binary perspective of with me or against me. War is a virus that infects everything it comes near. It revalues all qualities, instrumentalizes all relationships, commandeers all assets.

The fifth key term is "violence." It's often possible to pursue conflict without violence, but almost never to pursue war without violence. War is the physical or structural attempt to dominate and subjugate the other, arising from meticulous planning or spontaneous rage.

Once these five terms are articulated and understood, we can begin to recognize that Christianity, at its heart, offers a way of cherishing difference and taking the positive energy of tension so as to transcend conflict while also, at the same time, presenting a pattern for dismantling conflict, war, and violence and finding peace beyond them. Christianity is all about finding ways to make diversity fruitful and generative rather than damaging and conflictual.

The tendency within Christianity is to make one of two mistaken assumptions. The first is that if all were being faithful, all would agree; and therefore one or the other party in a quarrel must be wrong, which means the party in the wrong must be persuaded, implored, or coerced to come to the correct opinion or left behind to languish in ignorance and wrongheadedness, at best, or sin and malice, at worst. The second is that there are many pressing and urgent matters for Christians to attend to, from the advance of the faith to the extirpation of injustice, and that pausing, delaying, or straying off track to be reconciled with a recalcitrant neighbor simply takes too much time away from more propitious enterprises. These twin convictions, frequently jointly held, ironically make Christians more prone to conflict, war, and violence than others: because these two convictions are precisely ones that allow benign tension to turn into malign conflict.

What do they both miss? They miss the heart of Christianity: that reconciliation is the gospel. It's not a wearisome detour, to address conflict that should never have arisen. It's not an indulgence of time and energy, when there are much better places to invest one's focus. It's what the gospel is all about.

To grasp this means to return to the five key terms introduced above. Difference is a source of extraordinary energy: perhaps the greatest source of energy. The creation story is a careful delineation of difference, tracing how things were ordered toward harmonious interaction—or what I'm calling creative tension. It is a description of peace. Everything is ordered, not to passivity or flaccid inactivity, but to creative tension and energized difference. Peace is not static: it refers to the dynamic way difference evokes flourishing life. This is how things are supposed to be.

Things are, of course, often not like that. Difference sometimes provokes destructive tension, which issues in conflict. While conflict can simmer for a long time without becoming visible, it can easily turn into violence and war. While Christianity is in the first instance about the peace that comes through creative tension, it is secondarily and most commonly about how to manage and recover from destructive tension, violence, and war. Here there are two kinds of processes: what we might call the human sequence of how to stop war, and what we might call the divine pattern of how to find peace. I shall explore each in turn.

As to the human sequence of how to stop war, we may delineate six initial steps. The first is to become resolved. This means to recognize that one's whole identity has become enveloped in conflict, which has turned into something like an addiction—and that one's life has been profoundly diminished as a result. It's a decision to cease to let this conflict dominate one's whole existence: to accept the truth of a friend's counsel, "You're bigger than this." The second step is to cease to fight. This means acknowledging that what is going on is indeed war. It can't wait until the sense of injustice and hurt has been reduced. It means saying, "Nothing good can start until this stops." It's a recognition that war is not the route to the good things one so earnestly seeks. The third step is to tell a truthful story. This means going back before, often long before, the commencement of hostilities, to unearth the resentments, bitterness, and hurt that fostered a climate of animosity. It means revealing the power differentials that make reactive violence a different matter from the imposition of injustice that preceded it. A truthful story includes the elucidation of the knowledge of what happened, the understanding of the motivations and circumstances of those who perpetrated atrocities, and the legacy of seeking that such activity may be less likely to happen again.

The fourth step is to say sorry. An apology is almost impossible until a truthful story is narrated. An apology is a form of words that expresses both acknowledgment of responsibility, without resort to mitigating excuse, and genuine sorrow, not simply for the significant hurt and the irreplaceable damage but also for the wrong intention that brought about such hurt and damage. Many things that look like an apology in fact aren't, since they avoid or misconstrue part of this definition. The fifth step is to make penance. This is the other half of an apology. When something is wrong there is hurt, which can usually be overcome in the course of time; but there's also damage, which can't be restored: the dead child, the lost dreams, the shattered sculpture. Penance is a gesture that indicates an understanding of the weight of that damage and the impossibility of full restitution, but also of the need to show oneself willing at least to make steps in the right direction. The sixth step is to form an agreement—in other words, an understanding of how things will be from now on; identifying the circumstances and behaviors that triggered the conflict, and seeking to diminish the first and alter the second. An agreement isn't a fantasy that there will be no more destructive tension—it's a resolution of how that tension will be addressed in better ways.

Turning to the divine pattern of how to find peace, we come to the seventh step, which is to reach repentance. This involves admitting that an apology is insufficient. Apology suggests a mistake, an aberration, a detour from an otherwise worthy path. Repentance is the excruciating acknowledgment that instead this is an addiction—I am captivated by the idea that I can find peace by annihilating my enemies. As in a twelve-step program, I need to accept that my life is out of control. The eighth step is the active half of repentance: to seek mercy. It is a genuine attempt to enter the victim's consciousness and see events from their point of view—thereby recognizing culpability and expressing explicit remorse. It's the first of the steps to move from ceasing to make things worse to beginning to make things better. The ninth step is forgiveness. Forgiveness is a decision by one or more parties not to be defined by resentment or antagonism, to seek a bigger life than one constantly overshadowed by this painful story, and to allow one's perception of the harm received no longer to stand in highlighted isolation but to blend slowly into the myriad of wrongs and griefs to which the world has been subject across time. It is both a gift of the Holy Spirit and a positive act of will—to cease letting resentment dominate one's life.

The tenth step is to be reconciled. Reconciliation means seeking a future in active relationship with the one who has perpetrated so much harm, believing and discovering that the former enemy holds part of the key to one's own flourishing, and that, without that key, one will remain in some sense still in the prison of hatred. Reconciliation means turning difference and tension from threats into possibilities, from dangers into life forces. It's the turning of the most profound energy in the universe from destruction to glory. The eleventh step is being healed. Healing is not about reversing the hurt or damage but about realizing that one's life is no longer dominated by enmity, and perceiving in this benighted period a source of compassion, dignity, and hope. It's the restoration of the broken and despoiled as a gift. Finally, step twelve is being raised. Only at this point does it become clear that salvation and this process of peace are the same thing. Resurrection is the ultimate word for restoring relationship between God and creation. Peace, salvation, and resurrection are more or less identical. Christianity is a peace process—of being reconciled with God, oneself, the neighbor, and creation.

Returning to why we might want to avoid the demanding and apparently distracting business of reconciliation, it's now easier to see what's wrong with both conventional reasons. The idea that if we were living well we wouldn't face tension is wrong because creative tension is precisely a feature of living well. The point is to develop the skills and dispositions to turn creative tension into flourishing existence, and not to let it become destructive and the pretext for conflict and violence. Living without tension is not really living at all. Abolishing difference is abolishing life. The idea that we haven't got time for reconciliation because we have more important things to do is likewise wrong because there are no things to do that aren't in some degree forms of reconciliation. Every activity involves some kind of relationship, and every engagement in relationship is either enhancing it, in the face of the many things that might deplete it, or restoring it, in response to those things that damage it. To say one has more important things to do is simply to say "I'm tired of this grueling context of peacemaking, and I'm going to turn to a different one that seems more achievable." There is no third option.

II

Here is a story that illustrates almost all the stages of reconciliation. Clarence Smoyer was nineteen. It was March 6, 1945. Blond, curly-haired Clarence, from Armstrong County, Pennsylvania, was in a Pershing tank, rumbling toward a crossroads through the desolate bombed-out cityscape of Cologne. "Gentlemen, I give you Cologne," his commander shouted down the radio. "Let's knock the hell out of it!" Clarence had already lost a cousin and a brother-in-law in battle. He said, "Amen to that." He exchanged fire with a German tank, which quickly slipped behind a row of houses. Then suddenly a colleague in his tank shouted, "Staff car," and Clarence saw a vehicle crossing the debris-strewn terrain of the crossroads. Immediately he unleashed a string of bullets. The car crashed into the sidewalk, and out flung the body of a young, unarmed, civilian wavy-brown-haired woman.

Clarence's guts emptied and he tried to look away. But war doesn't stop for tragedy. His tank was facing a German Panther, whose gun was so powerful that its shells could splice one American tank and plunge through it into the next. Clarence destroyed that fearsome tank and became a hero for doing so. But he never celebrated. The face of the woman in that car haunted his dreams for decades after the war. Finally, fifty years later, he was sent a videotape of the battle. It showed everything—his tank, the German adversary, the car, and the wavy hair of the dead woman.

In his seventies, Clarence started having nightmares. He'd wake up fighting, punching the bedclothes, afraid he'd hit his wife. Medication couldn't calm him down. He couldn't function. He saw the woman before him, day and night. He had one desperate thought. Maybe he wasn't the only one who shot that woman. Could gunfire have come from the German tank too? And then he did a remarkable thing. He thought, "I wonder if the German tank gunner is still alive. Maybe I could meet him, and ask him."

In March 2013, sixty-eight years after their tank guns had been poised to destroy each other in the very same city of Cologne, Clarence Smoyer met Gustav Schaefer, all five feet of him—the gunner in the tank Clarence had destroyed that afternoon. Clarence was terrified at what Gustav would say—but Gustav extended a hand, and, in a gentle voice, said, "The war is over. We can be friends now." The two men walked to the scene of the battle, the crossroads of their lives.

Clarence explained, "I saw a film of it—"

Gustav interrupted. "So did I." He'd seen the same footage on TV ten years earlier.

Clarence pointed to a lamppost. "There was a woman," he stuttered. "She fell out of the car, riddled with bullets. This is where I see her in my dreams. I still have nightmares about it."

"So do I."

Dumbfounded, Clarence said, "There wasn't time to study the car. I was told to shoot anything that moved. So I shot it. I shot her," he confessed.

Then Gustav said the words that transformed Clarence's life forever. Slowly, methodically, Gustav replied, "That's why I shot it too."

Clarence was stunned. The guilt that he'd carried for sixty-eight years, the memories that had chewed up his life for the last fifteen of those years, he didn't bear alone. Both men had shot at that car. Both men had killed that woman. Once deadly enemies, they each found that the only person who could lift their burden of horror, guilt, and trauma, was one another.

But that's not the end of the story. They found out who the woman was. Kathi Esser was twenty-six. Her three sisters had all lost their husbands in the war. She worked as a clerk in a grocery shop. It seemed one day she and her boss both snapped, got in the car and tried to escape the carnage of Cologne. Unfortunately for them, they drove into the crossroads between Clarence's and Gustav's tanks. Kathi was buried in a mass grave two hundred yards away. Sixty-eight years after her death, Clarence and Gustav each placed a yellow rose on her grave. Then they had tea with Kathi's family. One of Kathi's nieces said, "You didn't kill Kathi. The people who started this war are the ones who killed Kathi." Clarence's journey of atonement was over. He and Gustav kept in close touch until Gustav's death in 2017. Clarence sent a bouquet to the funeral, with the inscription, "I will never forget you. Your brother in arms, Clarence."

Clarence never stopped dreaming about Kathi. "I don't wake up flailing any more, and I can sleep a full night," he said in 2018, a year before he died, aged ninety-eight. "I still see her in my dreams. I think I always will. I don't think she haunts me. It's different. It's not a nightmare anymore."*

The First and Second World Wars were different from almost every previous and subsequent modern war, because they largely involved not professional soldiers but conscripted young men—many of them no more than teenagers. The tank is a fitting image of what it means to be a conscript—trapped in a situation that's not of your making, choosing, or wanting. These people were scooped up out of their regular lives. Gustav's had been a simple existence. He was a farm boy from northern Germany. His family didn't have electricity, or a radio, or more than a few books. His big adventure was cycling to the railway line to watch the trains whistle by. He had no investment

* John Blake, "A World War II Hero Returns to Germany to Solve a Mystery—and Meet an Enemy," CNN, November 11, 2018, https://edition.cnn.com/2018/11/10/us/ww2-reunion-us-german-veterans/index.html, and also Adam Makos, *Spearhead: An American Tank Gunner, His Enemy, and a Collision of Lives in World War II* (New York: Ballantine, 2019).

in the war. He had no grudge against Jews. He had no animosity toward America. The crime of war is that it takes two peaceable young men, Clarence and Gustav, with no reason to meet—and makes them deadly enemies. It's true that the intensity of war gave each of their lives an urgency, an importance, and a sense of solidarity with their comrades that they probably never came close to matching thereafter. It's also true that Clarence was celebrated as a hero for his achievements and courage that March day in Cologne.

But Clarence was having none of it. All he could think of was Kathi, that young woman who could take no more grief, no more suffering, and no more fear, and who was tragically plunged into the center of the battle, there to die at the hands of ally and enemy alike. And Clarence, despite his nightmares and despair, did comparatively well. By contrast, his commander, Captain Mason Salisbury, returned home from the war, graduated from law school, and become a lawyer at a big New York firm. One winter weekend, he stayed at his parents' mansion on Long Island, played tennis, and dined with his family. The next morning his father found him slumped in a car in the garage. Mason Salisbury had taken his own life at age thirty. Losing so many friends in battle was too much for him to bear. Who wants to be a hero, if that's what a hero's inner life is really like?

Here we have four people—Clarence, Gustav, Kathi, and Mason. Their stories show us what Christianity and redemption mean in the face of the horror and devastation of war. Mason shows us what redemption doesn't mean. It doesn't mean victory, triumph, and celebration, if those things are masks for inner turmoil, profound dislocation, emotional trauma, and a conscience like a bomb crater.

Kathi shows us who Christ is. Christ is the one who goes into the place of enmity, carnage, and horror, and who loses his life because of a battle he had no part in causing or continuing. Yet through his life and death, not straightaway, but finally, comes a reconciliation with mortality, guilt, bitterness, and one another, by which the nightmare of war is over and the dream of new life emerges. Without Kathi, none of the good and beautiful parts of Clarence and Gustav's story would have come about. But for seventy years, neither Gustav nor Clarence knew who Kathi was. So with Christ: the fact that we don't know him or acknowledge him doesn't mean that, long after his death, he is not making beautiful the bombed-out cityscape of our lives.

Meanwhile Clarence and Gustav show us the almost invisible work of the Holy Spirit. The Holy Spirit was working in that camera crew whose footage Gustav and Clarence both saw fifty years after it was shot. The Holy Spirit was working in the circumstances that led to both men seeing the film. The Holy Spirit was working in the grace that led Clarence to track down Gustav, and in the words of reconciliation and solidarity that bonded them together. The Holy Spirit was working in the generous hearts of Kathi's family that forgave the two guilty men and bonded the three households together in a moment of healing unimaginable seventy years before.

Kathi's death, and the guilt and horror that accompanied it, filled Clarence's and Gustav's dreams for the rest of their lives. After their meeting with each other, and the solidarity they found, and their joint act of honoring Kathi, and the forgiveness they received from Kathi's family, those dreams didn't end—but they were no longer nightmares. That's perhaps the best we can hope for from the legacy of war. Two brave men, each trapped by the tank of their human predicament, each killed an innocent, noncombatant woman and spent the rest of their lives scarred by the horror of what they'd done. No one wanted to know. Half the world wanted to call them heroes. Half wanted them just to forget about it. Until they met each other, and in each other found solidarity, respect, understanding, peace.

Kathi's broken body became a blessing that brought reconciliation and overcame the dividing wall of hostility. That's how Christianity works. We can call the meeting of Clarence and Gustav and Kathi's family beautiful, tender, generous, forgiving, hopeful, reconciling, life-giving. But we have a word that means all those things and brings what these people went through to the heart of our lives and the throne of grace. That word is "communion."

How This Story Differs from the Rival Story

The challenge of the rival story leaves Christianity needing to do three things. First, it needs to show that it is not inherently violent. Second, it needs to demonstrate that it is possible to hold convictions deeply and sincerely, and to maintain the rectitude of those convictions, without that leading to violent conflict with those who believe differently. Third, it needs to exhibit a constructive willingness to participate in forming practices and building institutions that foster conditions that prevent wars from beginning, that bring violent conflict to a swift conclusion, and that reconcile parties in the aftermath of conflict.

By arguing that Christianity is inherently a peace process, both personally and collectively, privately and publicly, I've sought to address these three tasks. Taking the first task, Christianity at its heart is the opposite and contradiction of violence. It is about the formation, enjoyment, and restoration of relationship. It establishes ways to dismantle obstacles to relationship, reduce threats to relationship, and restore relationship when it has been threatened or damaged. Any version of Christianity that thinks it can do that by pursuing violence is claiming to head to a destination by setting out in the opposite direction. Any pursuit of violence is a vote of no confidence not only in the twelve-step process outlined above but also in the way Christ went to the cross rather than destroy his enemies.

The second task, the respectful negotiation of difference—of identity, experience, story, or conviction—is likewise at the heart of Christianity. God is utterly different from creation; God makes a creation in which creatures are profoundly different from one another; every human being is significantly different from every other human being. Such is a source of energy, creativity, dynamism; a pretext for dialogue, trade, discovery; a stimulus to relationship, partnership, understanding. There is no inherent reason why it should lead to destructive tension and conflict—although it often does. Difference is fundamentally a gift, not a threat. It abides in heaven: it's integral to life.

As to the third task, the rival story puts its faith in processes and institutions that foster peace. And it's right to do so. But here there's a subtle difference between the rival story and the story to live by. The rival story always suspects that difference cannot be ignored indefinitely—or imagined away; indeed, that difference is, in the end, a destructive and divisive quality, which must be carefully monitored and managed. By contrast, the story to live by believes existence began and will end in harmonious difference: even God's essence includes difference, the three persons of the Trinity in perfect accord. For the story to live by, peace is normal, hostility an aberration; for the rival story, institutions and processes have been created to avoid the chaos that would otherwise ensue. So Christians and others should invest with equal vigor in social commitments that build up civic life and the rule of law, but for slightly different reasons, since Christians trust that peace will inevitably finally prevail, whether we live in accord with it or not; and all that hinders peace will pass away, however much it seems currently to hold sway.

How This Story Differs from the Old, Old Story

Two temptations surface repeatedly in the old, old story. The first is that God is synonymous with victory, and thus that all feats of conquest and extension of power, sometimes including forcible conversions, are appropriate ways to honor God. Put this together with an unquestioned confidence in the rightness of one's convictions, and the inability of such truth to cohabit with untruth, and you have a cocktail that comes close to justifying all critics' complaints about the bellicose nature of religion. The second temptation is to fear, explicitly or implicitly, that God's kingdom will not prevail, in the short or the long term, and thus be persuaded that force is needed to ensure that it does. The first problem with this view is the tendency to confuse God's kingdom with other kingdoms, often egregiously worldly; the second, even more serious problem is the fact that if God is God, that is, that which lasts forever, God's kingdom will inevitably prevail and doesn't need protecting by means that bear no correspondence to God's ends. What jeopardizes God's kingdom is not the fact that it has enemies, even enemies armed to the teeth—but the evidence that even its most ardent proponents don't truly believe it can survive without actions that portray it in a grisly light.

In the end, the difference between the story to live by and the old, old story on this issue comes down to interpretations of Christ's cross. The old, old story tends to regard the cross as an event that, though it looks like a defeat, is in fact a victory: a victory over sin and evil, a satisfaction of a debt, the expunging of guilt, or the defeat of death. Because of that victory, Christians claim the right of victory in all subsequent conflicts. By contrast, for the story to live by, the cross is indeed a defeat—the inevitable result of utter goodness encountering the reality of human folly, and the epitome of the inability to see difference as created and good. But in that defeat the cross shows us Christ's commitment never to cease to be with us, whatever the cost or consequences. That allows Christians to be defeated, time and again, knowing that in such defeats, through the Holy Spirit, Christ will never let them go. A win in mortal conflict would be a poor witness to such faith.

- 8 -

ONE PATH AMONG MANY?

OUR EIGHTH QUESTION IS DIFFERENT from the other nine. It doesn't ridicule, express disappointment, or reel away in hurt or horror. It simply takes a sociological study of the world's population. It notes that 15 percent claim no religion. A rather larger 85 percent do: Christianity accounts for 31 percent, Islam 23 percent, Hinduism 15 percent, Buddhism 7 percent, and Judaism 0.2 percent. There are of course plenty of others, including Sikhism, Baha'ism, Jainism, and African traditional religions. On this evidence, it makes two challenges: either all these religions are manifestations of the same, basic human and transcendent phenomena, or they are making genuinely distinct claims to truth—and can't all be right. Either way, a conventional portrayal of Christianity as *the* way, *the* truth, and *the* life isn't sustainable.

The Old, Old Story and What's Wrong with It

The Standard Account

Christianity begins with a unique event: the resurrection of Jesus of Nazareth after his crucifixion by the Roman force occupying Palestine at the time. As its early exponents grew in number around the

Mediterranean, they perceived two dimensions to its message. On the one hand, the story begins with Abraham and continues through a particular people who received a covenant under Moses. On the other hand, there's a sense arising in the Babylonian exile that this particular story is that of the whole world, and the earlier accounts of Adam and Eve and Noah reflect that global dimension. Jesus fuses the two aspects, and the early church told a particular story with universal significance, as Paul shows in the early chapters of his letter to the Romans. What happened when Christianity became the religion of the Roman Empire three centuries later was that the Christian faith and classical civilization came to converge significantly.

Thus, as that classical unity began to disintegrate from the fifth century onward, and started to be recovered in the eleventh and twelfth centuries, it became difficult for many to disentangle the particular story of the Jews, the universal significance of that story anticipated in parts of the Old Testament but confirmed by Christ and by Paul's gospel, and the culture of classical antiquity that eventually came to embrace the Christian story.

From the first there were two areas of tension. One was with the Jews: the particularity of Jewish tradition was seen as irrational and obstinate in the face of the widespread practice of Christianity. The other was with the Roman gods: here the narrative was that old-fashioned superstition had been superseded by universal truth. Then Islam, when it arose in the seventh century, posed a very different question. This was a faith that assumed political control; indeed, it made no distinction between what already, by the Middle Ages, Christendom had come to regard as church and state. Whatever its claims to truth, what most occupied the church about Islam was its march across North Africa and the Middle East and into southwestern and southeastern Europe.

From the late fifteenth century onward, Christianity's encounter with other faith traditions came to be overshadowed by the church's largely unquestioning alliance with the desire to bring commerce and civilization to territories beyond the Mediterranean and the North Sea. The religious practices that were met were generally treated as local superstitions, and sometimes regarded with horror. Conversion to Christianity went alongside the introduction of Western education, health care, infrastructure, and governance. Christianity was most often the religion of the colonial power, and it was sometimes hard to disentangle from that assumption of dominance. Nonetheless, gradually it became clear that some traditions, such as Hinduism and Buddhism, had extraordinarily deep roots, and those who spent time in serious dialogue with their proponents came to have profound respect and admiration for their practices and convictions.

Now Christianity had a choice to make. Did it (1) regard itself as the indisputable purveyor of truth, and thus perceive all other traditions as either superstitions or inadequate quests for truth, fulfilled and superseded by Christianity? Did it (2) see itself as a noble and profound tradition but also acknowledge that there are other noble and profound traditions, and seek to abide alongside them, without seeking converts, and together reach for an ultimate truth within each tradition and yet beyond any of them? Or was there (3) another path, which combined respect for others with assertion of Christianity's own claims?

Until fifty years ago, the overwhelming majority of Christians belonged to churches that had difficulty recognizing the validity of Christian denominations other than their own, let alone the value of other faiths. It was invariably pointed out that Jesus said, "I am the way, and the truth, and the life. No one comes to the Father except through me" (John 14:6), and Peter said, "There is salvation in no one else, for there is no other name under heaven given among mortals by which we must be saved" (Acts 4:12)

Challenges to the Standard Account

It's not always clear whether the proliferation of faith traditions is a reason to suppose that none of them can be right or to assume that all of them must be on to something, so either all of them have some part of a general truth or one of them may indeed be right and the others are pale imitations of it. The same evidence can be argued perhaps equally well in any of three ways. But the first two are each, in their contrasting manners, challenges to the standard account, which favors the third interpretation. We may take those two challenges in turn.

Here's the starkest challenge. Christianity claims to have the whole truth about everything, everywhere, and always, but there are other claims to truth, some of which also claim to own the whole truth, everywhere, and always: so they are all evidently wrong. This is a difficult argument to sustain, for two reasons. The first is that many who hold such a view would be very comfortable with scientific accounts of key features of the world and our life experience. But once it is acknowledged that all claims to truth assume certain starting points—every assertion has to begin somewhere—then it is hard to explain why science isn't a tradition alongside these other traditions. But if you have begun with the argument that all traditions that have competing claims to truth are wrong, then you've automatically denied the truth of the tradition in which you stand. The second reason is closely related. If you are claiming that all faith traditions are wrong, you are presumably supposing that you are standing on neutral ground, from which you can get an objective perspective on all faith traditions. But is there such neutral ground? Isn't every perspective shaped by unconscious assumptions and guided by unacknowledged biases?

The milder challenge isn't a complete rejection of the truth of Christianity but asks questions of the idea that a particular tradition can contain the whole truth about everything. On the surface it seems eminently reasonable. If you live in a diverse cultural environment, and see your Muslim neighbor head out early to pray at the mosque, your Christian neighbor head to early mass, and your Hindu, Buddhist, and Jewish neighbors each pursue their respective devotions, you're bound to wonder what's the truth behind or beyond all this.

But the argument depends on a core assumption—that you're comparing like with like. It tends to be a basic, unquestioned assumption. But finding a definition that incorporates every faith tradition without impoverishing most or all of them or leaving unique features out is extraordinarily difficult.

A challenge that's more specific to Christianity, and that arises out of the narrative set out in the standard account above, is that Christianity is a false universal. It's just a particularity imposed on the majority for a long period that is now fading away at different speeds in different cultures around the world. Other religions are also fading after periods in which they were imposed. Any uniqueness or superiority of Christianity is thus both absurd and arrogant. This challenge highlights the way, for several centuries, Christianity both harnessed the whole of the heritage of classical antiquity and claimed cultural homogeneity in Europe, thus making it seem to be the default conviction of all rational human beings. Such an assumption was maintained when Christian-influenced colonialists imposed a corresponding order on the rest of the world. But as that colonial dominance faded and social patterns diversified, Christianity, shorn of its universalist and rational pretensions and forced to stand alone without the favor of ruling elites, became exposed as a curious historical relic with no purchase on emerging cultures. While this argument has rhetorical power, it has to reckon with the fact that while there were 600 million Christians worldwide in 1910, there were 2.3 billion in 2011. Christianity isn't dying out any time soon.

A Rival Story, Its Validity and Flaws

A Rival Story

At the risk of sounding flippant, the rival story points out that there are a lot of rival stories. From this observation, two versions of a rival story emerge.

The first says there's something called religion, and there's something called fact, and the first one may have some personal and cultural value, so long as you don't get it mixed up with the second one, and so long as you closely monitor its practices to prevent manipulation or exploitation and refrain from letting it have any kind of political power. When it comes to religion, the rival story perceives some common features. Religions grow out of people's inadequacies, fears, and longings. People search for meaning; dread death; speculate about life beyond death; seek connection with ancestors; feel guilt; nurture anger; want certainty; search for permanence; try to influence events; aspire to power. Religion explains, harnesses, congregates, and shapes; it reassures, promises, comforts, and inspires; it evokes belonging, purpose, hope, and kindness. There are few people who don't feel such things or want such things. But, the rival story maintains, just because one may feel or want such things, that doesn't make the conventional ways of finding them true. There can be wisdom to be found: one example is the way Buddhist practices have been adapted and repackaged and are today known as mindfulness. But one shouldn't take the truth claims too seriously. The best way to approach religion is to take the best parts from each one: the generous love of Christianity, the loyal obedience of Islam, the meditative practices of Buddhism, and so on.

When a person calls themselves spiritual but not religious, they're saying they're glad to adapt the practices of world faiths, and add some more of their own, but they're less drawn to the institutional and communal expressions of those faith traditions. The designation implies that the practices are meaningful and helpful, but the truth claims involved are unreliable and the institutional entities are unattractive. It's a recognition that religion has a public, accountable, visible character, and a decision not to participate in that dimension, but to customize an eclectic range of practices for an internalized understanding of validity and value.

From this perspective, the whole notion of story is unreliable. A story is one person's arrangement of information in a plausible sequence. It may bear little or no relation to history, science, or truth. This version of the rival story is content to rest with dispersed information alone, even when it can't be construed as part of a meaningful story: life may ultimately prove to be one great cosmic joke, but there's no necessity for a cosmic performer to be telling that joke; we all have to apprehend parts of that joke for ourselves. Religions are all part of a doomed quest to make coherent what will never finally fit neatly together.

The second version of the rival story has a different attitude to stories. It accepts that even the story that there is no story is itself a story. It recognizes that the scientific account is also a story—in fact, many stories, for the idea that "science" represents a single story is itself a fantasy. Nonetheless, this view is not simply cautious about religion; it's suspicious and even hostile. It doesn't take an eclectic approach, choosing the best features of many traditions—in fact, it tends to elide differences between faith traditions. It's inclined to see religion as a unit and to regard it as a flawed, even pernicious attempt to manipulate people by distorting truth. While recognizing the many stories contained in the term "science," it nonetheless asserts a "story of everything" that seeks to eliminate all features of what it perceives as religion and to limit its arguments to those derived from repeatable phenomena, extensive experimentation, and widely attested observation.

The Validity and Flaws of the Rival Story

In many ways the credibility of the rival story rests upon one's estimation of the status of the word "ancient." The five great traditions of Judaism, Buddhism, Hinduism, Christianity, and Islam are all more than 1,400 years old. Is this an indication of their validity, or of their obsolescence? The rival story has more than one form, but common to almost all versions of the rival story is a sense that we now know better. The words "ancient" and "wisdom" don't belong together. The more aggressive version of the rival story accuses religion of overreaching itself; yet the rival story can't genuinely number humility among its own particular virtues, either.

But the real question is about the key term whose self-evident nature is often assumed, particularly by challengers to the standard account but often by its advocates also: the word "religion." The letter of James says, "Religion that is pure and undefiled before God, the Father, is this: to care for orphans and widows in their distress, and to keep oneself unstained by the world" (James 1:27). James is assuming that his readers are Jews who have become believers in Christ; for him, the term "religion" means putting these convictions into practice; indeed, it so deeply embodies one's faith that the terms "theory" and "practice" cease to be in tension but become one seamless whole. That was how "religion" was understood until the Reformation. But the Reformation created a problem: rival denominations whose practice looked, in most respects, the same but whose convictions differed in certain hotly contested areas. From then on, religion gradually became a generic term for an aspect of human behavior with certain characteristics, such as awareness of transcendence, ritual devotional actions, and anticipation of life after death. From there it's a short step to assuming that all religions are basically the same, because once you've established a set of criteria that a variety of traditions meet, the differences seem merely circumstantial.

The irony behind the more aggressive versions of the rival story is that they assert very strongly the merits of empirical research, quantitative evaluation, and close observation. But they fail to apply those disciplines in their treatment of what they call religion. It's true to say there are many claims on the soul of human beings, and many assertions of truth, beauty, and goodness. It's even true to say that some features of faith traditions look similar, and that those who oppose each other, sometimes violently, might do better to seek learning and discovery across historic and cultural divides and to take the risk of open discourse about matters of depth where identity and conviction are at stake. But it's not true to say that all religions are the same, unless you've first configured the definition of religion in such a way that it is automatically both homogeneous and irrelevant.

Where the rival story has merit is to the extent that it identifies where Christianity has gone wrong. Christianity getting entangled in domination and empire obscured key features of Christianity. It's not at its best "chairing the meeting" of faiths, assuming it epitomizes the goals of "all people of good will," and evaluating other traditions by the extent to which they resemble a broad outline of Christianity. Christians have made a major misstep in too often assuming that the key question is whether sincere adherents of other faiths are "saved." It's not for Christians to decide or claim to know the eternal destiny of anybody. Making Christianity simply or primarily a vehicle for attaining eternal life impoverishes Christianity and misconstrues other faiths. It's a vain project to attempt a comparison of world faiths and imagine that Christians are "better" than others.

Christianity isn't a "religion" in the way the term is generally used. It has no stake in the defense of the term "religion," if religion means of ancient origin, involving a charismatic founder, engaged in ritual activities, and concerned about life after death. Such a definition doesn't do justice to its depth, practices, and ethos. And trying to fit other traditions into such a straitjacket pays no serious respect to their integrity, diversity, or identity either. Definitions of this kind are a form of resistance to the true claims of Christianity—an attempt to keep it at arm's length, where it can be discussed objectively; as if it were not making demands that can only be responded to subjectively. Religion is only a single, unified, coherent concept in the eyes of those who seek to reduce all religions to harmless human aberrations or infantile comfort blankets.

In the light of the failures of Christianity, the inclination to be spiritual but not religious is understandable. But from the point of view of Christianity, it's an absurdity. Christianity is about a new community; what Christians call the "body of Christ" is a collective entity, by which a diverse assortment of people are bestowed with the Holy Spirit and become a tangible presence of Christ in the world today. It's not so much about their state of mind or heart, it's about their common commitment to embody the way of the cross together. For them "religion" means not abstruse institutions or obscure rituals or hypocritical leaders, but the daily practice of finding the forgiveness, perseverance, and hope to be a sustainable community. To seek a state of mind or heart detached from that practice is to withdraw from the principal project of being a Christian disciple.

A Story to Live by, and How It Differs from Both Stories

A Story to Live By

The heart of this debate lies with Jesus's famous words "I am the way, and the truth, and the life" (John 14:6). The issue doesn't lie with the words "way," "truth," or "life." It lies with the word "the." If Jesus had said "*a* way, *a* truth, and *a* life," he would have fulfilled all the criteria the rival story is looking for; that is, he'd have offered himself as one option (or three) among an eclectic pick-and-mix potpourri of spiritual wisdom and ethical example. But it's the "the" that rankles in the contemporary conscience. No one gets to say "the." Rather than avoid these famous words, I'm going to suggest that reading them correctly is the key to recalibrating Christianity's relationship with other faiths, and rather than saying it's the other faiths that have to "get with the program," I suggest what needs to change is the conventional understanding of Christianity. If Christians are to understand the words "way, truth, and life" today, they need to repent, be transformed, and hear them as if for the first time.

Why do I say repent? Here I want to cite a very important distinction first made by Augustine in AD 397. Augustine said there are things we use, which last for a limited time, and things we enjoy, which last forever. The things we use are a means to an end, like a ladder that we employ to get us from the ground onto the roof. The things we enjoy are an end in themselves; "use" is the wrong language for them. There's nothing beyond those things that we would want or need to attain by means of them. Instead, we rejoice in them for their own sake. In God's case, we worship. Worship is a kind of enjoyment—it's a way of relishing, cherishing, celebrating, appreciating, being thankful for the object and allowing it to fill all our dispositions and sensibilities.

I say we need to repent because Christians should have regarded Jesus as someone to be enjoyed but instead they've treated him as someone to be used. "That's unfair!" many might say. "That's not true—surely we worship Jesus." But see how Christians use Jesus. Christians have a project. That project is most simply to get out of life alive. People don't talk about death because they fear it might be infectious; but everyone knows about death. We know that having children and building institutions and leaving legacies and seeking celebrity and owning many mansions are all ultimately futile, even though we invest huge efforts in seeking such things. They can't transcend death. But Jesus—he offers eternal life. That's his unique selling point. And eternal life solves the death problem pretty effectively, and more reliably than cryogenics.

See how this instrumentalizes Jesus. We cease to enjoy Jesus, attend to his character, rejoice in his particular qualities, rest on his words. Instead we turn him into a ladder for getting up to the roof—the roof being, in this case, heaven. If a better or more reliable way of getting onto the roof became available, we'd be off after it like a shot. This is the attitude for which Christians need to repent. It treats God as a means to an end. Peace, harmony, blessing, and communion in this transitory life, and an entry ticket to the next, everlasting one. It looks like very good value.

That instrumentalization has dominated the way "the way, and the truth, and the life" is read. People quote, "I am the way, and the truth, and the life," but in practice only get as far as "the way." We then go down two side tracks. Side Track One is, "Do you get to heaven if you don't acknowledge Jesus as your Lord and Savior?" See how this question is fixated on the ladder analogy. We take for granted that we're all using Jesus as our ladder, and we want some plaudits for having chosen the best ladder, and we're eager to tell anyone who's on any other ladder that they're a fool and not as wise and worthy as us. So we cite these words, "I am the way," and we say, "Told you—our ladder's the best and your ladder's rubbish. I can see the dry rot from here."

Side Track Two is, "How do people of other faiths get to heaven if they don't recognize Jesus?" This question is equally fixated on the ladder analogy. Not only do we assume that the point of Jesus is to get us onto the roof, but we take for granted members of all other faiths are as committed to the roof project as we are, and we regard their traditions through the impoverishing lens of being inadequate ladders. This raises an intriguing but absurd specter: Jesus, sitting at the Last Supper, giving his disciples a quick guide to the inadequacies of other faiths in achieving such a project. The notion is ludicrous. This shows what ridiculous gymnastics we're led into by our commitment to instrumentalize Jesus.

The way to repent of this tendency is to focus on how Jesus begins this celebrated sentence: "I am." Those two words are the most important words in John's Gospel. Jesus prefaces his seven self-declarations with them. "I am the true vine," "I am the resurrection and the life," "I am the good shepherd," etc. "I am" is the Greek translation of the Hebrew word for the name of God, usually spelt YHWH and pronounced Yahweh or Jehovah, although it's so holy that Jews don't pronounce it at all, often substituting the word "Adonai" or "Lord." It's sometimes said that Jesus's words in John 14, "Whoever has seen me has seen the Father" and "I am in the Father and the Father is in me," are radical statements of Christ's divinity, but in truth it's already all here in these two little words, "I am." Jesus is cut from the same cloth as the Father. Everything that the Father is in the Old Testament is now embodied here in Jesus.

Which takes us back to what "everything" really is. Rather than get hung up on the first word, "way," we need to begin with the second word, "truth." This is the truth the Old Testament is proclaiming. Israel is in exile. It had land, king, and temple, and was a significant presence in the Near Eastern world—the whole of the then-known world. But it lost it all. In exile Israel wrote down its story. It recalled that it found its identity in a covenant. That covenant was made with the source, destiny, and ground of all being, Yahweh, the essence that caused, sustained, and purposed all existence. In order to make such a covenant Yahweh had delivered Israel from slavery, having previously saved it from famine. To keep that covenant Yahweh had given Israel a law, a way of maintaining its freedom. But what had Israel done? It had allowed that covenant to lapse into a contract, losing the bond of love and reducing it to a transactional process by which Yahweh gave an entitled Israel blessings. In other words, Israel had turned from enjoying God to using God, and had instrumentalized God as a ladder to attain prosperity and security. In exile Israel repented. And in exile Israel saw a new face of God, a God who was with Israel rather than for Israel, a God of covenant, not contract, a God who longed to be enjoyed, not used.

This is what Jesus means by the word "truth." I am this truth. I am the God who is covenantally with you, not the instrumental god who is contractually for you. Truth means everything that isn't instrumental and is instead final. By final I mean everything that's an end, indeed *the* end, the very purpose of creation and the raison d'être of the whole universe. The purpose of creation is that God and humanity be companions forever. The utter embodiment of God, and the perfect representative of humanity, are found in the same person: Jesus. Jesus is therefore the raison d'être of everything. Which is why he says, "I am the truth." Not "the one who speaks the truth" or "the representative of the truth" but—the truth. "I am" is the truth—and the truth is "I am."

See how small-minded is the attempt to turn Jesus into a ladder to get us to heaven. There *is* no heaven that's not utter relationship with

God and restored relationship with one another, ourselves, and the renewed creation. The absurd idea that we could somehow use God to get out of life alive and let everyone and everything else go hang is precisely the kind of sin that put Israel in exile and jeopardizes our own destiny. We only experience that utter relationship with God in Jesus if we let go of any desire other than the desire for that relationship. If we seek God because we want heaven, we don't deserve heaven. If we want God because we want to avoid hell, we're headed for hell. But if we desire God because we want nothing other than to be in utter relationship with the source, origin, and purpose of the universe, the essence of all things, and if we trust that the God who came in flesh as Jesus and died emptied of all but love and rose because in the end love is stronger than death will ultimately never be separated from us—if that's what it's all about for us, all about forever for us—then God will give us that relationship forever. And no virus or terrorist or tragedy or horror will ever change that.

Where does that leave the "way" and the "life"? The life is simply living in that truth. The life is that unambiguous, uninhibited, unconstrained relationship with God, ourselves, one another, and the renewed creation that we call heaven. For a host of reasons, some of our own making, some due to the limitations of our creaturehood, some due to the faults of others, we currently don't experience that future in all its fullness. But that's where the "way" comes in. The way is living God's future now. The way is to live abundant life. The way is to enjoy the green pastures, still waters, and right pathways that populate the kingdom of God. The way is any moment we transcend the envy, anger, bitterness, and malice of existence and glimpse God's essence, embody true relationship, turn "for" into "with" and live God's future now. The second-century theologian Irenaeus of Lyons put it succinctly: "The glory of God is a human being fully alive." When are we fully alive? In heaven—when we're utterly in the presence of the truth. Who alone has been fully alive among us? Jesus, who represents to us life and embodies truth and thus is the way. If and only if we enjoy Jesus as the truth and stop using him as a ladder to eternal life will we finally have found our way.

In the biographical film *Rocketman,* Elton John blazes a trail through youth and adulthood to riches and fame. But he never finds true relationship. Instead, all his encounters become a series of exploitative liaisons in which talent and sex are instrumentalized in a fruitless search for affirmation. Eventually in therapy he sees his child self and is asked what that child needs. Having cast aside the grandiose clothes of his extravagant display, he walks slowly toward his childhood self and gives that child the hug and the love he desperately yearned for all along. He couldn't find how to make true relationship, so he commodified everything to find alternatives and ended up on a path of self-destruction. Only then was he ready to meet someone who loved him for himself alone, who had no desire to use him—only to enjoy him.

We're all Elton John. We're all rocket women and men trying to propel ourselves to heaven and failing in greater or lesser degrees of humiliation and shame. Jesus isn't doing a deal with us. This isn't a bargain. He's not a ladder we toss away once we're on the roof. He's saying, "Make me your truth. Don't use me to get what will turn out to be a false security. Enjoy me so deeply that you find a life that never runs out. Only then will you find your way."

How This Differs from the Rival Story and the Old, Old Story

What has the foregoing to do with interfaith understanding? It points out that the eternal life question is a red herring. Truth is not a competition in which the most plausible route to eternal life is declared the winner. Faith is not a quest to prove everyone else wrong. Truth is enjoying God for no other purpose than recognizing that God is God. Faith is the pattern of convictions and practices that deepens trust and amplifies relationship. Jesus is the heart of Christianity not because he provides a pathway to eternal life but because he embodies God's desire to be with us. Other faiths are not rivals to be out-argued and outdone to demonstrate Christianity's superiority; they are a gift to Christians to understand better who God is and how to live a life in relationship with God.

What then does it mean for Christianity to abide in a world in which there are other paths that in some respects look similar but make assertions incompatible with Christian claims? We need at the outset to distinguish three categories of "other faith." In the first place there is Judaism. Judaism is not an "other faith." It is Christianity's parent. It does not dwell elsewhere. Christians are living in a house that Jews built and had been living in for a long time before Christians moved in. Christians often make the mistake of thinking Jewish thought and faith development ceased at the end of what Christians call the Old Testament. This is far from the case: the Talmud refers to the host of authoritative writings that constitute subsequent commentary and reflection. Nonetheless, Christianity was cradled in Judaism's manger, and Jesus was a Jew. Christianity is inextricable from Judaism and can never see it as "other."

Then there is Islam. If Judaism is a parent, Islam is a cousin. Christianity and Islam have many ideas, figures, and stories in common. The term "Abrahamic" is used to describe the three faiths that all arise from a single source. There are profound differences: most obviously, the Christian doctrine of the Trinity is anathema to Jews and Muslims. But the three traditions have huge amounts in common and bear strong family resemblances.

Thereafter there are a variety of traditions, most obviously Hinduism and Buddhism, but many more besides, which have much less of a family resemblance and in some cases differ in significant ways from the generalizations often made about religions—such as belief in a divine being and the promise of life after death.

Dialogue among these traditions may be based on the notion of a common core that they all share. That core may go under the name of religion, or it may be more broadly described as humanity, civilization, or consciousness. This view supposes that the more the traditions talk with one another, the closer they get to the one thing they are all searching for. But this view diminishes all traditions by assuming that there is such a "one thing." A second view is that faiths must talk to one another or they will all end up killing each other. This is a modest aspiration, but in humility a reasonable one. But the real reason for conversation across faiths is to be profoundly enriched by the gifts that come from the stranger. Christians believe they depend first of all on God and secondarily on the community of faith, but also on the stranger.

Israel's life in the Old Testament is littered by occasions when the stranger is a saving gift. Melchizedek brings out bread and wine and blesses Abraham. Pharaoh's "fat cows" sustain Jacob's family in times of hardship. Balaam blesses Israel in the sight of her enemy Balak. Ruth demonstrates the faithfulness and imagination that Israel will need under her descendant David. Achish of Gath gives a safe home to David and his followers when they are pursued by Saul. The Queen of Sheba applauds the wisdom and prosperity of Solomon. Perhaps most significantly, Cyrus opens the way for the Jews to return from exile. Israel depends on these strangers. Strangers are not simply a threat. They are not all characterized by the hostility of Moses's pharaoh, of Goliath of Gath, of Sennacherib of Assyria and Nebuchadnezzar of Babylon. Time and again strangers are the hands and feet of God, rescuing, restoring, and reminding Israel of the provision and grace of God.

In the same way, Jesus and the early church discover faith and mercy among strangers. On meeting the centurion whose servant he is asked to heal, Jesus says, "In no one in Israel have I found such faith." The Samaritan leper is the only one of the ten healed that turns back to praise God and thank Jesus. Finding the resilience and devotion of the Canaanite woman who seeks healing for her daughter, Jesus similarly says, "Woman, great is your faith!" Cornelius's visit from an angel pushes the church into revising its understanding of gentile faith. The Samaritan is the one Jesus upholds as the model of a good neighbor.

The stranger is a gift to the church, not a burden, rival, or threat. As all the scriptural examples demonstrate, the stranger represents the hand of God, becoming present in the church to rescue, restore, and remind. The stranger is not the harbinger of scarcity but the sacrament of abundance—not the drainer of resources but the bringer of gifts. Caring for and conversing with the stranger, sharing food and offering friendship, is not a matter of altruism; it is done in the simple trust that this person has something precious that will sustain or build up the life of the community, even if that gift is slow to be revealed or hard to receive. This is the stone that the builders rejected, but it is destined to become the cornerstone. This is the crucified one, but it will be the one gloriously resurrected.

One spiritual leader said, "You may be at a time in your spiritual life where your faith in God or sense of closeness to God's ways is thin and dry. If so, go and find someone for whom faith is alive and full of joy, and spend some time living and being alongside them: and as likely as not you will find that person is from a more socially disadvantaged part of your community." The reason for that is perhaps because such a person has established less insulation between themselves and the grace of God—insulation like insurance policies, forms of accreditation, influential friends, and access to elaborate health care. These are words of humility that should shape the Christian approach to other faith traditions. There are seasons when a Christian's sense of clarity or joy about their respective faith is weak and troublesome, and when their sense of hope for the interfaith enterprise is thin and dry. At such times, Christians need to spend time alongside those for whom faith in general and faith in interfaith dialogue in particular are lively and overflowing. And as likely as not, those people will not be where one would expect to find such conversations, in a religion department of a university, for example; as likely as not, they will be among the most socially disadvantaged people of their neighborhood.

It's appropriate for Christians to be agnostic about whether there's an overarching phenomenon called "religion" that every member of a faith tradition has in common. It's not something Christians really need to know. What Christians do need is a conviction that they have a great deal to learn from members of other faith traditions. Christians are more likely to learn from people of other traditions if they make it clear that they are persons in need. They would like to learn how better to pray, how to live a disciplined life, how to fast, how to meditate, how to be a gracious presence in the life of their neighbors. For they represent a tradition that needs to learn how to bring people of different races together, how to hold diverse opinion within one body, how to break an addiction to violence, how to use power to set people free. Christians approach those of other traditions not first of all with the words "This is what you must do to be saved" but with the words "I believe God shows me things through people like you." That way the existence of other traditions is not proof of the falsehood of Christianity but evidence of the generosity of God.

- 9 -

ARROGANT NARCISSISM?

IT'S NOT UNUSUAL TO HEAR the claim "Science has disproved religion." This resolves into four kinds of contentions. There's a claim about creation—that the big bang disproves Christian ideas about how all things began. There's the question of providence—that evolution discredits Christian perceptions about how life developed and humankind came to be. There's a question of method—that science demonstrates Christian claims in general to be weak and unsubstantiated. And there's a rather different allegation: that Christianity has promoted a sense of domination over the earth that has led eventually to the ecological crisis, a crisis that proves the inadequacy or culpability of Christianity.

The Old, Old Story and What's Wrong with It

The Standard Account

The creation accounts in the book of Genesis portray cosmic order, the power and purpose of God, and the place of humanity in relation to God, the other animals, and the rest of what today would conventionally be called nature. They do not allow for development, or progress: they depict a static world, in which God arranges creatures and the firmament in their right stations.

For both the Jews in exile, and subsequently under foreign domination in the last six centuries before Christ, and the early church, a beleaguered minority in the centuries before the conversion of Constantine, this cosmology offered an inspiring sense that, however lowly their state and however desultory their prospects, God was above and beyond, and God was not just their tribal god but the maker of all things who would restore order in due course. Once minority status was replaced, for Christians, by a sense that God had ordered earthly, or at least political, affairs in tune with this heavenly theater, then the accounts took on a rather different character. No longer were they subversive texts, affirming the legitimacy of otherwise oppressed communities; now they sounded suspiciously like government propaganda, dragooning God onto the side of order and the status quo.

Which illustrates the perennial issue about knowledge and discovery: To what extent do they underwrite, and to what extent do they undermine, the existing social and political hierarchy? For the period of Christendom, when Christianity was the unquestioned faith of the European rulers and those under their influence, the creation story underwrote the way society was ordered. When Copernicus showed that the earth circled round the sun, when Galileo highlighted the tensions between astronomy and the teaching of the Roman Catholic Church, and when Darwin proposed the theory of evolution through natural selection, the threat was not just to the scientific establishment or to ancient cosmology; it was to the whole assumption that God ordered people in hierarchies and ordained society accordingly.

This assumption was not just about social conservatism or powerful elites protecting their privilege. For example, the perception of a godly cosmos was one in which everything had its nature, and everything could be perfected by grace. Thus wheat had its nature, as did a vine; that nature was fulfilled as they came to be turned, through a combination of divine and human agency, into bread and wine, respectively. Then through grace—the action of the Holy Spirit, working through the church—they would be changed again into the body and blood of Christ. Just as male and female, rich and poor, earth and heaven found their true unity as Joseph and Mary, Magi and shepherd, humanity and the angelic host gathered around the manger, so all beings were called to appropriate forms of service and each of those dimensions could be transcended by participation in the story of God.

So resistance to the "progress" of science was never simply obscurantism or the privileged clinging to status and power. It was in significant part suspicion that science would disenchant the world, impoverish existence, and dispel the ways ordinary existence could attain divine significance. Nonetheless, if people are looking for an adversarial science versus religion narrative, the reaction of senior church figures to threshold moments in the history of science, and to Galileo especially, who remained under house arrest for the last twenty-five years of his life, provides plenty of ammunition.

But it's mistaken both to portray the relationship between Christianity and science as between two opposing worldviews and to depict it as a debate external to Christianity. On the latter point, reason and revelation have been in healthy tension from the beginning of the church. Take two examples. In the account in Matthew 2:1–11 of the incarnation, the focus is significantly on the visit of the Magi. Matthew portrays "science," as we may call it, in the wise men searching the heavens and seeing a star. He depicts revelation in the chief priests and the scribes searching the Scriptures and finding reference to the birth of a ruler in Bethlehem. The story displays science taking the Magi to Jerusalem, very close to where Jesus is born; but only revelation can take them to Bethlehem—that last vital link in the journey. Meanwhile John's Gospel describes the incarnation in these terms: "The Word became flesh and lived among us" (John 1:14). This is an argument that reason became revelation—that the logic of the universe became a person. A second example is the story in Exodus 14 of the parting of the Red Sea. The narrative blends two accounts. In one version "the Israelites walked on dry ground through the sea, the waters forming a wall for them on their right and on their left" (Exod. 14:29). In the other version, "The LORD . . . threw the Egyptian army into panic. He clogged their chariot wheels so that they turned with difficulty . . . [and] tossed the Egyptians into the sea" (Exod. 14:24–25, 27). The first account is a supernatural miracle; the second account is a theological rendering of the Israelites crossing much more successfully than the Egyptians. The point is that reason and revelation didn't begin to clash in the sixteenth century: they've been in creative tension with one another since the Old Testament was written down.

Challenges to the Standard Account

The nub of the argument about science and faith isn't whether some Christians have reacted very defensively in the face of scientific discoveries and challenges, and so distorted the faith as reactionary and wooden; neither is it that some scientists have exaggerated the tension, or evidenced an antipathy toward religion so profound and abrasive that it seemed to go beyond a dispassionate argument and become a crusade. Instead, the dispute lies largely in the answers to three far-reaching questions.

First, is Christianity intrinsically founded on certain purportedly historical events that simply cannot have happened? This is not simply the creation of the world, but also the Israelites' crossing of the Red Sea during the exodus from Egypt, the virginal conception by which Jesus came to be born fully human and fully God, and his resurrection from the dead on the third day after his crucifixion. These are all events that sit uncomfortably with the findings of modern science, in which the world is a single planet among a universe that comprises a hundred million galaxies, each of which contains a hundred million stars; and in which waters of a sea do not spontaneously part, virgins do not conceive, and dead bodies, after decomposing for three days, do not come back to life. Critics point out that such things cannot be part of a contemporary worldview, and that Christianity is empty without them. Christians respond that these are unique events, which science, committed as it is to the study of repeatable phenomena, cannot comprehend; and that if there is a God, a concept too enormous for science to encompass, such things are not beyond the power of the one who makes all things.

Second, and more broadly, is the whole mind-set of faith a flawed form of thinking, in which evidence is not properly evaluated and too much weight is given to culture, inherited values, and mythical stories, where an objective appraisal would rule out such arbitrary elements? In Rudolf Bultmann's words, "We cannot use electric lights and radios and, in the event of illness, avail ourselves of modern medical and clinical means and at the same time believe in the spirit and wonder world of the New Testament."* This question isn't just about particular events that have been given ultimate significance. It's about the assigning of significance to anything besides those phenomena that have been carefully assessed and objectively quantified so that their quality is beyond doubt. No events from antiquity can meet those criteria. In fact, one might almost suggest that no events at all can meet such criteria—because the very criteria themselves rule out unique events. Science is all about evidence, and faith is thin on evidence. In that regard, faith lacks the basic conditions of being taken seriously. Science also begins with the assumption that nothing exists unless it can be proved to exist: so there needs to be some kind of convincing evidence that would persuade any clear-thinking person to accept God. In other words, it rules faith out of the picture; science simply offers a better set of hypotheses to explain the same set of phenomena for which religion used to offer the only available explanation. Science proceeds by replacing each best explanation with its

* Rudolf Bultmann, *The New Testament and Mythology and Other Basic Writings* (1941), selected, edited, and translated by Shubert M. Ogden (Philadelphia: Augsburg Fortress, 1984), 4.

successor, and religion, along with magic and astrology, needs to take its seat among the series of now-obsolete debunked explanations.

In particular, it is often maintained that the big bang and the theory of evolution through natural selection constitute not just a refutation of the authority of the Bible but an insuperable challenge to a whole Christian way of thinking. They both exchange design and purpose for less transparent forms of development. The earth wasn't created—it just came to be. Humankind was not placed on earth by the tender hand of a loving God; it simply emerged from a strand of apes. It could have been otherwise, and could one day be otherwise again, since the chain of evolution has not reached its climax. Chance and contingency appear to demolish the whole scriptural narrative of a God in intimate relationship with humanity, who comes in incarnate presence to be with humankind and ensure its eternal well-being.

Third, does the legacy of Christianity, particularly its claim that God has given humanity dominion over nature, constitute an arrogant narcissism that has led inexorably to the ecological crisis? This is a different kind of challenge, and a more recent one. The issue focuses on the words of Genesis 1:26–28: "Then God said, 'Let us make humankind in our image, according to our likeness; and let them have dominion over the fish of the sea, and . . . over every creeping thing that creeps upon the earth.' . . . And God said to them, 'Be fruitful and multiply, and fill the earth and subdue it; and have dominion over the fish of the sea and . . . over every living thing that moves upon the earth.'" This has been taken, some argue, as the pretext for humankind to perceive itself as set apart from nature (rather than being one with nature) and as charged with exploiting nature without reserve. Some would draw a direct line from this text to the technological destruction of the planet—a line that goes straight through the incarnation, because the incarnation is the affirmation that humankind is made in God's image, and through the resurrection, because Jesus's resurrection is the assertion that for the flourishing of humanity, all laws of nature may be suspended.

CHAPTER 9

A Rival Story, Its Validity and Flaws

A Rival Story

While William of Occam was a fourteenth-century Franciscan friar, and thus hardly a poster child for debunking Christianity, the rival story is inspired by his assertion that the simplest explanation is always the best. The rival story's simple explanation goes like this. The universe began with a big bang. It took a few billion years for things to settle down. The real bang-crash was still going on zillions of light years away, but by a strange, yet rational, collection of circumstances, one planet in a minor galaxy developed the conditions for life to begin. A principle emerged called the survival of the fittest, and in a ruthless and brutal pattern of visceral contests, those forms of life gradually became more sophisticated until they started to develop self-consciousness. Once they'd done that, they started to plan, refine, reflect, and make meaning. But such meaning as they made had no larger purchase. It was simply their attempt to recognize and value those features of their existence that rose above their raw animal condition, in which shelter, food, clothing, company, reproduction, and death set the template for life.

Unsatisfied with the mundanity of things, and overwhelmed by the paradox that while individual life ends, life in general continues, these self-conscious beings started to put their existence in the context of something greater, richer, deeper, and more enduring. They talked of a life force that lay above and beyond the earth and their existence. They sought ways to communicate with this life force and discern its purpose. But these were, in the end, sad, doomed, and tragic ways of failing to come to terms with their accidental, purposeless lives. In truth, the only value these people reliably found in the years that came between birth and death was their sense of achievement in asserting themselves over one another, and the sense of belonging they felt when they knew they were appreciated, desired, or understood. Everything else in life was a conspiracy of busyness, designed to keep hearts and minds so preoccupied with small battles, easy comforts, and manageable projects that they would never reflect in despair at the pointlessness or meaninglessness of it all.

Consider how the covid-19 pandemic illustrates this rival story. The virus was devastating for those who became very ill, terrifying for all who were most at risk, and disastrous for the many whose livelihoods were ripped away from them almost overnight. But what was most deeply troubling about the pandemic was that it laid bare the rival story in the rawness of its struggle for survival and the emptiness of its attempts to rise above the melee and make meaning and purpose. The busyness and urgency and all the paraphernalia of a full and active life were stripped away, and there was no shield from the uncompromising necessities of survival and the unrelenting approach of death. When people panicked, felt the weight of anxiety closing in, sensed despair or depression in their bones, the realities of the rival story were all too apparent. That was not the pathology of a few; that was a regular reality for everyone.

The rival story has a particular reason to invest in ecology. It supposes that, in one of two ways, humankind is poised for a significant new chapter in its history. Either artificial intelligence will develop to the point that most conventional jobs will be done by nonhuman intelligences, leaving humans free to experience unprecedented leisure and comfort; or death will cease to be inevitable, and life will come to be extended indefinitely; or both. It would be a terrible irony if, just as humankind was about to embark on this remarkable new part of its earthly story, its own failure to tend its living environment would disrupt or halt its inexorable march of progress. Success in relation to the planet lies not in conquering or subduing it, but in so living in relation to it that it provides everything humanity needs. The rival story's regard for ecology is not, finally, a devoted respect for the biological conditions that gave humankind birth; instead, it's a sophisticated form of self-regard—a desire to sustain circumstances that can enable humanity to flourish and that offer forms of enjoyment beyond humanity's capacity to manufacture. Eventually, whatever happens, humanity will inevitably die out and be superseded in due course by a superior species, as humanity replaced what went before it; unless humanity can relocate to another planet. But eventually, even then.

The Validity and Flaws of the Rival Story

The curse of the Christianity-science debate is that, too often (and particularly in the United States), what is portrayed is a caricature of science and, even more, a caricature of Christianity. In truth, the great majority of Christians, and in particular the many Christians to be found in the upper reaches of the scientific research community, have long ago integrated the key insights of Copernicus, Galileo, Darwin, and their successors into their understanding of the world. Meanwhile the great majority of advanced scientists, whether or not they are people of faith, exhibit a humility in respect of scientific claims to truth, and toward the great faith traditions, that does not dismiss the latter as simply inadequate and disingenuous forms of science.

Thus there is much validity in the rival story. The achievements and discoveries of science have been extraordinary. They are best understood as a form of love—close attention to the object of love, detailed study of its ways, absorbed observation and recording of its characteristics and patterns. Research is the disciplined practice of this form of love: the collective willingness to subject findings to the scrutiny of peers, such that any outcome is a truly collective effort, not testimony to the brilliance of a lone explorer. In such ways, science represents the best qualities of human endeavor. It is the spirit of science to regard arguments like the big bang and natural selection through the survival of the fittest as themselves best-yet explanations, rather than definitive givens. That's not to suggest the findings of future research won't continue in the same trajectory; it's simply to recognize that science deals with most-plausible hypotheses, and faith in science is about commitment to method, rather than to the inevitably incomplete outcomes that method yields. It wouldn't be science if it maintained it had supplied the last word on any subject. In that sense the rival story is both a recognition that it is itself a story and a best guess about the appropriateness of the shape of its own story. Its objection to Christianity, if it has one, should be about the apparent certainty of some Christians' assertions—rather than a desire to replace one unquestioned certainty with another.

Moving to details, the big bang is not in itself an insuperable challenge to Christian faith. Once one has acknowledged that the creation stories in Genesis are not claiming to be eyewitness accounts of historical events but portrayals of the truth about human nature and God's relationship to creation, the specifics of how the universe came into being should be a point of wonder and awe rather than occasion for antagonism and distrust. More complex is the slowness and apparent self-perpetuating nature of the coming-to-be of Earth as a planet conducive to the emergence of life. This is more challenging, because of the Christian emphasis on God as relational, and the suggestion in the rival story that any kind of relationship could only emerge after 14 billion years of inanimate existence. Yet what no one knows, even theorists of the big crunch (by which it's imagined the universe will eventually collapse in on itself), is whether we should regard 14 billion years as a long time. It's obviously a long time for us; but is it a long time for God? In the light of eternity, evidently not. Meanwhile the existence of such a stupendous number of other solar systems and galaxies is bewildering to any attempt to grasp the extent of reality; but it's as much a reason to grow in awe as a cause to deepen skepticism. If life were to be found elsewhere in the universe, and that life had a consciousness and self-awareness corresponding to humankind's, it would create in Christians an expectation of finding that God had in some way become incarnate among such creatures also: it would change humanity's notion of its own uniqueness, but it need not alter Christians' notion of God's characteristic purpose.

The most challenging of all scientific arguments for Christians are the twin assertions of Darwin: that humankind is not specially created but is descended from less sophisticated mammals, and that the process of survival of the fittest is written into the nature of life. The first assertion raises the whole question of how the Holy Spirit acts in the world. Does it "intervene"—that is, positively bring about events that otherwise would not have happened, to achieve a desired purpose? Does it "shape"—that is, constantly foster conditions for outcomes that suit its benign purpose? Or does it improvise—that is, largely allow "nature to take its course," relying on what seem like luck, surprise, and accident, and not having a specific design toward which everything tends? The notion of incarnation—that God purposed to be with us in Christ from before the foundation of the universe—transforms this debate. It exposes the language of "intervention" as rooted in a Deist assumption that God made all things and then retired to a lofty vantage point. Incarnation asserts that God is utterly invested in creation, not just at the start but all along, and is present through the Holy Spirit in ways that can be recognized by their resemblance to Christ's life and ministry. Improvisation is a notion that comes closest to the convictions of science and the trust of Christianity.

Which leaves natural selection. This is a process so much at odds with the ways of God as revealed in Jesus—who said, "Love your enemies, do good to those who hate you. . . . If anyone strikes you on the cheek, offer the other also. . . . Do to others as you would have them do to you" (Luke 6:27–31) and also "Are not two sparrows sold for a penny? Yet not one of them will fall to the ground apart from your Father" (Matt. 10:29). The contrast is not just about the primal competitiveness but about its mechanistic character. The simplest way for Christians to come to terms with these contrasts is to regard natural selection as a result of the Fall. But that assumes that the Fall is an adequate explanation. More satisfactory is to perceive that in every context, throughout sensate life (and insensate—even trees and plants) and especially among humans, there is an option toward narrow self-interest and an opportunity for collaboration, understanding, and tenderness; and the world we have is a result of the extent to which such choices have historically been made, and the adaptations in species that have resulted. This is an approach that acknowledges the power of the theory of natural selection but does not yield to the mechanistic vision to which the theory can too easily give rise.

One way in which science should truly refine Christianity is in relation to the creation. Whereas Jesus's commands to "love the Lord your God with all your heart, and with all your soul, and with all your mind, and with all your strength" and "love your neighbor as yourself" point to three objects of love—God, neighbor, and self—today most Christians would assume a fourth—creation, as an extension of the last two and an expression of the first. A reappraisal of humankind's relationship with the rest of the planet was long overdue and began a generation or two ago. It has implications not only for survival but for renewal of humanity and its surroundings. It is however to the church's shame that for the most part Christians have been led to this discovery by scientists rather than vice versa, and that much of that interest remains motivated by enlightened self-interest rather than genuine reverence for creation. Nonetheless, the idea that Christians fulfill their calling by dominating the earth and subduing it is fast being displaced by a richer notion that humanity is called to be the priest of creation, bringing all things to their true purpose, the worship and celebration of God.

And that recognition, that all things are here for a purpose, marks the only fundamental point of difference between Christianity and science—and a subtle but persistent flaw in the rival story. Christianity believes in purpose: that all things are here for a reason, a reason not limited to the compilation of causes of how they came to exist, tracing back to the big bang: there is a *why* that goes beyond that. All things are created to participate in the glory of God by being in relationship with God, a relationship embodied definitively in Jesus

Christ, fully human and fully God. Science makes no such assumption: it either actively rejects such logic, or it rules it as speculation and therefore beyond its domain. When it does the former, it sets itself up as a rival, even an antagonist, to Christianity; when it does the latter, it creates the conditions where it may be a creative, and sometimes critical, friend. It has become fashionable to regard the story that there is no purpose as the default against which Christianity must assert its claims. But that's highly problematic when placed in ecological context. For if the survival of the fittest were to be our compass in the face of the ecological crisis, it's hard to see how a constructive ethic could emerge.

A Story to Live by, and How It Differs from Both Stories

A Story to Live By

A different way of telling the story starts in a different place and finishes in a different place. The story to live by goes like this.

There's something called essence. It's outside, beyond, and largely incomprehensible to existence. It's made up of three persons in utter, devoted, and dynamic relation to one another. It dwells in forever, eternity, beyond time and space. It chose to create time, space, matter, shape, life, energy, consciousness—what together we call existence. It did so not as an experiment, a game, a challenge, or a breeze—but for one reason only: because it desired to be in relationship with something, someone, outside itself. It created the universe, from one explosive start, and waited until all the constituents for life had come into focus: since it's outside time, the odd 14 billion years were as a day. Once human beings had taken shape, relationship began to take on a different dimension. The Trinity, as we call the three persons, began to interact with human consciousness. Eventually it settled upon one people, Israel, with whom to be in covenant relationship.

But the whole purpose of the story was that the Trinity could become known and be in relationship with humanity and the creation in person. In the fullness of time this happened. Honoring the covenant, one person of the Trinity took human flesh as a member of the people of Israel. This fulfilled all the hopes of Israel, and the whole design of the Trinity. That person brought the entirety of humanity face-to-face with God and the entirety of God face-to-face with humanity. Yet the virus that had beset humanity from the beginning, the fatal flaw that poisoned existence, dismantling trust and distorting love, got to this relationship too: humanity rejected the utter human, utter God, and killed him in the most gruesome manner imaginable—the way it disposed of recalcitrant slaves—as a fearsome example to others who might rebel.

And this is the crucial moment in the story. At this point the Trinity might have abandoned the relationship. Humanity was flawed; its allergic reaction had rejected the purpose of its existence. It had chosen the rival story. Despite all its despair, depression, and denial in the face of the rival story, when offered a story to live by it had turned it down as comprehensively as possible. And see: if the Trinity had left it there, there would be nothing, nothing at all to stand against those who said that speculation and exploration of transcendence and meaning were just a tragic failure to come to terms with the limitations of existence, and in the end sadder than the cynicism of mechanistic determinism.

But the Trinity didn't leave it there. The Trinity kept the story going—kept the relationship going. The Trinity not only restored the second person to existence, but when that second person, Jesus, had restored relationships with those who'd panicked and fled, the third person, whom we call the Spirit, came to shape all people in the ways Jesus had offered. And when existence finally comes to an end, not just for each one of us but for all things, Jesus will be there again at the threshold of time and eternity, when our consciousness will be suffused by essence, and, with the Trinity, we will finally be taken into the wonder of forever.

That's the story to live by. See how Jesus's resurrection is so crucial in this story. Jesus's birth is fundamental, but that was in the DNA of existence from its very inception. There could be no existence without essence, and essence resolved to be with us in Jesus, so there's no existence without Jesus. But his resurrection is different. It comes at the moment that the whole Story of Everything could be lost. It reveals God's utter commitment to be with us, however determined we are to reject the offer of love, the source of life, and the purpose of all things. Those who are convinced there's no reason to think beyond or outside the rival story would be perfectly justified if it weren't for the resurrection, for, without the resurrection, God would be like a beautiful sail on a ship that was nonetheless headed for the rocks. It's Easter, not the coronavirus, that changes everything. It's Easter that shows God will never give up on us. It's Easter that demonstrates that this relationship, for which God created the universe and because of which Jesus died, is finally, ultimately, eternally unbreakable.

The covid-19 pandemic was a terrible thing, which killed some, damaged many, and impoverished the great majority. But most of all what it did was to lay bare the difference between the rival story and the story to live by. For the rival story, the virus was an intense, bleak, and almost unbearable demonstration of what's finally true for us all—that we live short, troubled, and incomplete lives with no abiding value or purpose. For the story to live by, the virus was a truly scary example of what life could feel like if the story to live by were not true. When, in the Easter story, Mary Magdalene turns round from the tomb to the risen Lord, she turns from death to life, from grief to restored relationship, from despair to the one who will finally never let us go (John 20:11–18). She turns from the rival story to the story to live by. She invites us to do the same.

Where then do science and ecology fit into the story to live by? Science is principally in assumed tension with the notion of revelation—that is, how God communicates to us. To think of revelation we need to reflect on the ordinary and the extraordinary, the oblique and the direct, the general and the personal: we need to find ways of talking about the disclosure of God's person and purpose that do justice to God and to our ability to understand.

There are broadly five kinds of revelation. The first one we could call awe. It's something so fabulous it makes you stand and exclaim, grab someone's attention, take a photo and share, or simply stop still in silence. You could be beside the ocean and behold the sun changing from yellow, through orange, to red, before disappearing under the horizon. You could be beside a huge waterfall and see tons of water cascade over and plummet to the ground. You could have just become a parent and witness a tiny hand with even more minuscule fingers, all alive and ready to begin living. This kind of revelation is about wonder: it can be immensity or minuteness, breadth or detail. Most importantly, it's about something any human being can behold, and any person can experience. It's not about me; it's about the world, the universe, in all its complexity and enormity.

The second kind of revelation really is about me. Whereas the first we could call awe, the second we could call intimacy. It's about an astonishing coincidence—too absurd to be an accident. It's about a quiet voice in your ear, whispering to you that it's time to set down your period of grief and mourning and begin to live again. It's about an amazing deliverance—that terrible risk you took that turned out well, that reckless action that astonishingly had no negative consequences, those words of wisdom that somehow came back to you at your hour of greatest need. These are secrets: only you know them, and yet at such moments it feels like something greater than you must know them too—and must be taking them up into some greater narrative that you're not creating alone. Anyone could experience such things, and maybe everyone does—but only you experience precisely these things in this way, and they stand apart from the other events of your life, making you shudder with relief or collapse with wordless gratitude.

Both these kinds of revelation have disadvantages. It's interesting that both are at least as much alive and well as ever and have relatively little relation to churchgoing Christianity. The awe one, for example, has no obvious connection to Jesus, nor any discernible relation to any ethic—it's something you see, not a way you live, or a form of interacting with other people. The intimacy one keys in to an idea that we're at the center of the universe and any spirituality is largely about enhancing our experience and well-being.

These first two kinds of revelation describe profound experiences that aren't always straightforward for people to connect with the personal God of Jesus Christ. The next two kinds address that problem. The first of these two, or third in all, we could call word: it's simply the Bible. The way the Bible is often read in worship models how Christians anticipate God speaking: the gospel (in most cases the words of Jesus) is read in the context of the rest of the New Testament and of the Old Testament—in other words, Jesus is encountered through the story of Israel and the early church. The Bible itself is largely made up of the first two kinds of revelation—awe and intimacy—digested over the centuries and recorded as authoritative by a community. Jesus did unprecedented things, but just as important, he embodied the character of God revealed in the Old Testament. Christians believe that when the Bible is read in this way, the Holy Spirit speaks today.

The fourth kind we could call action. When Christians do certain things, they can expect the Holy Spirit to communicate with them in certain ways. Reading the Bible in the context of worship is among those ways. Sharing in the sacraments, notably Holy Communion and baptism, are two particular ways. Holy Communion is a social process by which people gather, confess, hear, proclaim, intercede, make peace, recall their story, share food, and are sent out renewed in mission. It's an enactment of the church's core convictions, and Christians expect God to communicate with them at some stage in this process. There's a further sacrament that's described in Matthew 25:31–46: it's the sacrament of encounter with the bereft—those bereft of food, drink, security, shelter, health, and liberty. When Christians see people who are so profoundly bereft and relate to them in humane and respectful ways, they expect to meet God. The same is true of when Christians keep silence in contemplation and order their being around devotion of God.

Having appreciated the third and fourth kinds of revelation, it's important not to belittle awesome discovery or personal experience. Word and action give meaning and purpose to awe and intimacy. Revelations one and two could stand alone, and never be integrated into a dedicated life, if they could never be interpreted through the lens of revelations three and four.

Marvelous as the third and fourth kinds, word and action, are, there abides a danger that revelation can become a private language spoken between God and select individuals, from which others are excluded. Which is why the fifth kind of revelation matters so much. We could call it surprise. This kind of revelation disarms the church by unveiling the action of the Holy Spirit in the regular or instantaneous action of a person or community that makes no claim to Christian faith—yet nonetheless renders activity that imitates the life of Christ. When a person lays down their life for another, speaks truth in the face of intimidation, or forgives despite huge loss, the Holy Spirit is revealing the wonder of God in generosity of heart, wherever it may be found. And there's no question the occurrence of such moments is infinitely greater than the capacity of the church to celebrate them.

Each of these five kinds of revelation has its detractors. The first kind, the "sunset" version, certainly points to the wonder of the natural world; but if you hold that the world came to be this way through a chain of facts attributable to physics, chemistry, and biology dating back to the big bang, there seems no need to suppose a god behind it all—and in any case, such an assumption would have to account for nature's ghastliness, and not just its glory. The second kind, the religious experience, could quite evidently be psychologically generated. Everyone has known coincidence: everyone has put two and two together and made five, only later to realize the truth was four all along. Things attributed to supernatural causes have often turned out to have natural explanations. The third kind, the Bible, has a number of drawbacks, which we explored in chapter 3; in short, it's not reliable in the way we would demand a twenty-first-century source to be. The fourth kind is perfectly explicable, as people across time search for meaning in their lives and depth in existence through ritual and habitual action. The fact that they seek it doesn't mean they find it, and the fact that they believe they've found it doesn't mean there's a substantial truth at the heart of it. It could just be seen as a worthy but ultimately fruitless search for purpose. The fifth kind could simply be overinterpreted coincidence: luck, chance, or accident.

Yet this survey of five kinds of revelation—awe, intimacy, word, action, and surprise—while not together constituting the kind of proof scientists seek, nonetheless gives us a way of conceiving Christianity's relationship to natural and social science. Natural science calibrates the quality of awesome encounter—the wonder of creation. Social science quantifies the depth of intimate discernment—the personal experience. But neither can account for the authority of Scripture or the vitality of dynamic action found in the third and fourth kinds of revelation. And both science and faith are humbled by the surprises found in the fifth dimension. At the same time, perceiving the created order as fundamentally a form of revelation—and thus an insight into the character of God and an invitation to worship—is the beginning of a much more fruitful theological understanding of ecology.

And that brings us again to the Magi. The story of the Magi is the definitive revelation story for Christians, because it brings together all five kinds I've just described. It starts in the East, with the first kind, awe and wonder at the star. In Jerusalem the wise men experience the third kind—they hear, from the chief priests and scribes of the people, the story, about the babe being born, not in Jerusalem, but in Bethlehem. In Bethlehem the wise men find the fourth kind of revelation—they encounter Jesus through service—the giving of gold, frankincense, and myrrh. And before returning they have the second kind, the personal discovery—the dream that tells them to go home another way. And the whole story is an example of the fifth kind—the way the truth of the incarnation was more apparent to distant stargazers than to almost anyone among God's chosen people.

How This Story Differs from the Rival Story and the Old, Old Story

There's no question the old, old story has sometimes overreached itself—has sometimes sought to fill not just theology books but science textbooks, has turned stories about the nature and purpose of all things into quasi data for research and investigation. The story to live by is more easily reconciled with the world of science, research, and objective inquiry. It sees science not as a threat but as a partner. It does not boast about theology being the queen of sciences, but humbly suggests that something like the quality of a substance to be found on the moon or the nature of reproduction for the praying mantis is best expressed in scientific terms, while the purpose of existence or the nature of love is better articulated in theological language. The two realms are complementary, and codependent. It is useless to expend energy trying to get one to quash the other. It would be like asking the sky to destroy the sea.

The suggestion that "science has explained all that away" has both an unnuanced notion of the word "explain" and a very limited conception of what is intended by "that." True science increases wonder, rather than setting out to dismantle it. Science means knowledge, and those who grow in knowledge only become more aware of what they don't know, or more in awe of what they do know—but could never replicate or reproduce. The term "explain" is in entirely the wrong frame of reference. Earlier, in describing the church, I cited Gabriel Marcel's distinction between a problem and a mystery. The distinction is equally helpful here. A problem can be a mathematical puzzle or a logistical challenge; it can be a dilemma or an obstacle.

Whichever it is, the key is to establish a regular procedure by which it may be fixed. The person who finds the solution will most likely be using an approach or formula developed in many comparable situations and applicable to many future scenarios. The emphasis is always on finding a quick solution and moving on to further endeavors.

By contrast, a mystery cannot be the subject of generalization: it is unique, has never been encountered in exactly this way before and never will again. It covers matters more profound than a simple problem. The joy lies not in solving it—it can seldom be "fixed"—but in entering it, relishing it, allowing it to evoke wonder and amazement. It should be obvious that theology is about mysteries and not problems; it may be less obvious that science is too. It is an impoverished notion of science that perceives it as solving one problem after another. While science can often do that, science as a whole is better understood as entering a mystery. It doesn't just engage the hand in technique; it demands the heart and soul in discernment and discovery. A notion of science that regards it simply as a "better explanation" of things than theology doesn't just misunderstand theology; it undersells science. To regard science as the identification of explanations reduces science—which is better understood as establishing how the different constituents of existence subsist and relate to one another.

The five kinds of revelation outlined in the story to live by establish a healthy relation between science and faith. Science takes its place as the first of the five kinds, and social science has a place in the second. But it is neither possible nor necessary to live by only those two kinds: the sociologist will point out that pretty much everyone has their own version of the third and fourth kinds, whether Christian, of another faith, or of no professed faith; and most people, willingly or otherwise, cannot finally avoid acknowledging the wisdom of surprise—the fifth kind of revelation, which comes from outside one's acknowledged sphere of authority. Because the story to live by has a more expansive notion of revelation than the old, old story, it has a greater capacity for healthy dialogue with science (and other kinds of and claims to truth) and less tendency to compete for dominance.

In the end, science presents itself as a method of acquiring knowledge that accumulates and arranges facts in such a way as to create indubitable fact. Christianity presents itself as a way of understanding relationship and existence in such a way as to establish profound trust. There is no way to live by facts alone, but neither can those who live by trust live in contradiction to fact. Why would they want to? But both appearances exaggerate the contrast. Both science and Christianity seek after fact, but both realize that there can be no fact without an infrastructure of trust. If science is wrong to speak of fact without recognizing the significance of trust, Christianity is wrong to speak of trust if that means neglecting or overriding fact. Hence the relationship between Christianity and science should be one of mutual appreciation and gratitude. Which might require rather greater humility from both parties. Maybe the ecological crisis will hasten such humility.

- 10 -

CRUEL FANTASY?

FAITH IS A MIXTURE of belief and trust. Belief means conviction that certain things happened; other things, though not visible or tangible, are nonetheless true; and further things will come to pass, even if prospects for them currently seem unpropitious. Trust allows conviction to develop into relationship; it means resting security, prospects, future, and identity on that relationship, such that if the trust is let down the result is bereavement, humiliation, heartbreak, and betrayal. The Nicene Creed, which begins "We believe in God . . . ," is an assertion of belief. The statement made by Stephen as he is stoned to death in Acts 7:59–60, "Lord Jesus, receive my spirit. . . . Do not hold this sin against them," is a declaration of trust. This final chapter moves from conviction to relationship—from belief to trust. It considers the accusation that Christianity is not just untrue but is a cruel fantasy, because it promises a relationship that never materializes, and thus encourages people to place their trust in an unworthy object.

The Old, Old Story and What's Wrong with It

The Standard Account

The most inspiring dimensions of Christianity are those in which promises are made and kept. Jesus pledges to his followers, "Ask, and it will be given you; search, and you will find; knock, and the door will be opened for you" (Matt. 7:7). It's a simple relationship of trust and provision. In a similar vein, Jesus reassures his disciples (Matt. 6:25–33) that they should not worry about what they will eat or drink or wear—for God knows their needs and will provide for them; instead they should strive for God's kingdom, and all these other things will follow. They should look after the things of God—and God will attend to their practical needs. The best example of this is in Exodus 16, when the people of Israel are in the wilderness after crossing the Red Sea and God showers down manna for them to eat. Meanwhile, Paul promises that God is faithful and will not let us be tested beyond our strength; and when we are tested, God will provide a way out so that we may be able to endure it (1 Cor. 10:13). The most vivid illustration of that conviction appears in Genesis 22, when God calls Abraham to sacrifice his son Isaac but, the moment before the boy is to die, provides a ram caught in a thicket to take the boy's place and become the sacrifice instead.

God's provision is detailed and extensive. Isaiah (65:17–25) envisages God preparing a new order of flourishing life, in which Jerusalem will be a joy, and its people a delight. There will be no weeping or distress, no infant mortality, and people will live well beyond one hundred years. They shall build and inhabit houses, plant and enjoy vineyards. And their relationship with God will go beyond even the naming of and response to need: for "Before they call I will answer, while they are yet speaking I will hear." Eventually, foresees the book of Revelation, God will create a new heaven and a new earth, will abide with people forever, and will do away with death, mourning, crying, and pain. The holy city will be a place of extraordinary beauty, and it will need no temple, because God will pervade its streets (Rev. 21).

This portrayal of sustained relationship, abundant provision, and a flourishing future all rests on an understanding of God that is faithful, true, and good. While there are many accounts of God's anger and negative judgment, these are in almost every case presented as the flip side of a God who seeks righteousness and justice even at ultimate cost, as

Christ's crucifixion demonstrates. God is frequently described as slow to anger and abounding in steadfast love (Exod. 34:6; Num. 14:18; Pss. 86:15; 103:8; 145:8; Jon. 4:2). Moses assures his successor Joshua, "It is the LORD who goes before you. He will be with you; he will not fail you or forsake you. Do not fear or be dismayed" (Deut. 31:8). Hosea portrays the pining of a God who loves Israel like a gentle parent:

> I led them with cords of human kindness,
> with bands of love.
> I was to them like those
> who lift infants to their cheeks.
> I bent down to them and fed them. . . .
> How can I give you up? . . .
> My heart recoils within me;
> my compassion grows warm and tender.
> (Hos. 11:4–8)

This long-suffering goodness finds its climax in the cross, where Jesus faces the most profound rejection by disciples and authorities yet stays true to his commitment to humankind to the end.

The promises, provision, and character of God converge most poignantly when believers face hardship, adversity, hostility, or danger. In the Twenty-Third Psalm, we are shown a God who shepherds us in right pathways, by still waters, in green pastures, and through the valley of the shadow of death. This is a God who is enduring and personal, hears our prayers, abides with us and is trustworthy, and never lets us down. Likewise in the prophet Isaiah we are promised (43:1–7) that we should not fear, because we have already been redeemed; that we are called by name; that when we pass through waters we will not be overwhelmed but God will be with us; that when we walk through fire we shall not be burned; because in God's sight we are precious, honored, and loved, and because we were created for

God's glory. Perhaps most famously, Paul assures his Roman correspondents (Rom. 8:38–39) that nothing will separate them from the love of God in Jesus—"neither death, nor life, nor angels, nor rulers, nor things present, nor things to come, nor powers, nor height, nor depth, nor anything else in all creation." Even such painful moments can become gateways to a deeper trust in God.

Challenges to the Standard Account

Perhaps the most ironic scene in the Old Testament comes in 1 Kings 18, when the prophet Elijah challenges the prophets of Baal to a contest. It's the ultimate showdown between the monotheism of Israel's God Yahweh and the tribal gods of the Canaanite peoples. Elijah prepares a bull for himself and another for the 450 prophets. But when the prophets call down fire, Elijah teases them, saying, "Surely he is a god; either he is meditating, or he has wandered away, or he is on a journey, or perhaps he is asleep and must be awakened." Then Elijah calls on God and God vindicates him. The irony is that the mocking Elijah directs at the prophets of Baal resembles the derision pointed at Christians today.

Elijah's options, now directed back at Christianity, resolve into three possibilities. God doesn't exist; God is weak; or God is malign. The first was explored in chapter 1. The second and third were discussed in chapter 2. The theme that unites all three, and forms the allegation central to this chapter, is that God is unreliable. The God presented in the Bible contradicts this theme; of him it is said,

> The steadfast love of the LORD never ceases,
> his mercies never come to an end;
> they are new every morning;
> great is your faithfulness.
>
> (Lam. 3:22–23)

But the facts are everywhere before us: prayers seem to fall on deaf ears, that is, if there are any ears to hear them; the righteous suffer, the wicked prosper; God fails to honor our petitions, and we don't feel God close to our senses; life is often miserable, and its mysteries defy explanation.

The point here is not, as elsewhere, about the existence or nonexistence of God. The point is that God seems unworthy of trust: unreliable. The history of the church should, ideally, tell of the spreading glory of those who wait upon the Lord, and renew their strength, mount up with wings like eagles, run and don't weary, walk and don't faint, as promised in Isaiah 40:31. But a bitter account of church history would trace how it progressively invested more and more security in places of trust that would prevail even if God were not faithful. Emmanuel Cardinal Suhard described a witness as one who engages not in propaganda, or in stirring people up, but in being a living mystery. "It means to live in such a way that one's life would not make sense if God did not exist," he said. The prophetic church of Suhard's vision would always be fragile and never secure in a worldly sense, because it depended on the resurrection and the guiding hand of the Holy Spirit, not on a healthy bank balance and influential friends. In this sense, a bitter account points to the way the church has been precisely the opposite. It has developed centers of power—power of knowledge and procedure, power of offering and withholding forgiveness, power of political influence, power of extensive control over health care and education—and what is power if not the cultivation of choice, authority, and control, capabilities that enable a person or institution to retain initiative even when trust is lost? The worst kind of faith is surely that which asserts, imposes, or assumes belief all the harder in the absence of trust; the kind that says, "If you don't trust my truth, respect my power."

This is a very different critique from that provided by history or science. The latter two approaches, when hostile, maintain that Christianity is simply untrue—based on events that did not take place or phenomena that don't exist. But this approach is agnostic on whether Christian beliefs are grounded on things that did not happen or could not be. Instead, it maintains that God is an unreliable relationship partner. The Bible constantly argues that humankind is an untrustworthy partner in God's covenant, while, in the words of Psalm 119:90, God's faithfulness endures to all generations—for God has established the earth, and it stands fast. But this criticism points out that such faithfulness is patchy, at best. Some prayers appear to be answered—albeit often not in the way that the intercessor anticipated. God does sometimes turn out to have worked all things for good for those who have been faithful, and even for those who have not. God even seems to work through those hostile to and subversive of the kingdom, such that, like Joseph in Genesis 50:20, one can sometimes look back and say they meant it for evil but God meant it for good. But not often enough. It seems too often, the child with the life-threatening condition dies; the terrible accident, causing untold damage and death, does indeed happen; the kindly grandparent, who embodies gentle faith, descends into agonizing dementia; the vulnerable teenager is yet trafficked into virtual slavery: and no new-every-morning God pops up to do anything about it.

In the words of Isaiah 64:1, the cry of this criticism is that God would just "tear open the heavens and come down." The old, old story maintains that God has, most of all in Christ. The challenger replies that a God who does so intermittently, unreliably, and fitfully is just playing with us.

A Rival Story, Its Validity and Flaws

A Rival Story

The rival story begins with a sober assessment of existence. Life can be harsh; it contains no guarantees of reward for good behavior; it can contain bad luck as much as good. Trust is necessary, because there will always be things beyond our control, and some of those things are the best things of all—love, care, respect, dignity, honor. There is no secure relationship on which to rest our trust; and when we place our trust elsewhere—on technology, for example—we put ourselves at the mercy of those who create or manipulate those things to which we entrust ourselves. We are infuriated when our computer crashes or our phone fails to function; because we had placed on these gadgets the trust we feared to rest on our human relationships. There's no way to avoid trust, and there's no way to guarantee the object of our trust won't let us down.

That said, we do well to build in security where we can. We can't rely on anyone; there's no point in looking to a fantasy protector. Nonetheless, in the continuing trade-off between freedom and safety, some lessons emerge: develop skills, cultivate adaptability, earn qualifications to demonstrate your capacities to the skeptical, don't fall into debt, nurture health and fitness, read the fine print, remember anything written on the Web can't be erased: such guides to life can prevent one getting out of one's depth. More constructively, recognize that pleasure, experience, enjoyment, and meaning are commodities in short supply: grow in self-knowledge, don't let others seduce you into where they think pleasure and enjoyment are to be found, but make your own judgments, and be sure to let experience be your best teacher. Don't allow others to dictate meaning to you—for celebrity and attention are fickle friends, and such truth as life yields is hard-earned and largely derived from mistakes carefully evaluated. Thus we learn to rely on ourselves alone, and turn the self into our god.

Often for very good reasons, the rival story struggles with the notion of trust. In many ways the rival story is an attempt to construct a world that doesn't depend precipitously upon trust. If your parents haven't given you an experience of safety or security; if your key relationships have been ended prematurely by death or desertion; if your formative experiences have been ones of antagonism, exploitation, violence, or neglect; or if no one around you has given you reason to perceive your own worth or value your own talents, there may be every good reason why you wish to spend your mature years establishing mechanisms that ensure you never need to trust. Moreover, if you have for a long period been caught in a tangled web of another's addiction, deception, or repeated betrayal, you may feel you have no more than a choice between replicating such destructive patterns of relationship and avoiding any relationship that could trample you down again.

For such reasons and many others, life can appear, to many, a foraging exercise—gleaning items of fleeting pleasure, consoling distraction, or unreliable depth, and from them trying to construct enough stability and resilience to endure the next disappointment or disaster. The idea that any person—let alone divine being—could provide sustained companionship and abiding faithfulness that might transcend the flawed and fragile quality of trust is dubious or dangerous; and the divine relationship might appear little more than an imaginary friend to overcome the desultoriness of earthly ones. Much better to establish, piecemeal, a citadel that, if not eternal, will remain impregnable for some time to come.

The Validity and Flaws of the Rival Story

The rival story provides an apt ethic for a life without a transcendent dimension. The seventeenth-century philosopher Thomas Hobbes famously described existence in the state of nature as solitary, poor, nasty, brutish, and short. His solution was a deal by which people gave away a significant part of their freedom for a healthy dose of security. The rival story offers an emotional version of Hobbes's state of nature. It describes a state of distrust where confidence in one another is limited and hard-earned, relationships are fragile and often exploitative, few teachers prove reliable besides one's own experience, security means planning for the worst, and safety means reducing nature and other people's opportunity to hurt you. Such a conclusion is a sober antidote to any notion that Christian faith is a panacea that turns sadness to joy and sorrow into dancing.

However, the rival story simply doesn't do justice to the splendor, texture, and potential of life. It's true that things are often hard, sometimes unfair, and seldom simple or transparent. Conviction, in the sense of what the White Queen in Lewis Carroll's *Through the Looking-Glass* calls believing "as many as six impossible things before breakfast," may appear to be simply an escape from the unreliability of relationships and circumstances. But belief of this kind is always a balance between understanding and obedience. Understanding means appreciating that the notion of God as Trinity, for example, or the description of Jesus as fully human and fully divine, is the best approximation of Christian experience and testimony available. Obedience means recognizing that the moment comes when further inquiry is futile, or simply prevarication, and it's time to live one's convictions rather than just adhere to them. Obedience without understanding may resemble "blind faith"—a loss of individual autonomy that contemporary culture finds troubling and an offense to the human spirit. By contrast, understanding without obedience is more in tune with the contemporary mood: it's the habit of evaluating the distance to be jumped, the depth of the pond, the swing of the rope, the impact of entering cold water . . . but still not leaping from the rock; as if one could remain there forever.

But belief is only one half of faith, and perhaps the less important half. Belief is integral to human existence because belief means accepting as authoritative, and thus as the basis of making other judgments, convictions that are not entirely verifiable by empirical observation but are nonetheless worthy of commitment: what a skeptic might call useful fictions. A secular example might be human rights. People believe in human rights, work for them, fight for them, die for them; but their existence isn't provable—one can't point to a place where they live, or a barometer that tells when they are present in an intense way. They are useful fictions, to which many people who are skeptical about Christian belief are nonetheless sacrificially committed; and criticism of such conviction is largely frowned upon. Such belief illustrates that it's hard to live a life beyond narrow (and inevitably doomed) self-preservation without convictions of this or a comparable kind. Thus the rival story, though sober, is seldom fully accurate, because it is so hard to live in such a desiccated way.

The other half of faith is trust. It's true that trust leaves one subject to disappointment, hurt, and betrayal, and that it can involve making promises that are hard to keep. But it's also true that one cannot live without trust: not only because that would mean reducing one's capacity to those actions one could oneself perform—only to eat food made by oneself, use transport made by oneself from one's own raw materials, never become a parent, and so on—but also because one couldn't always and indefinitely perform those actions. Most obviously, when one is an infant and young child, one can perform hardly any actions, and one's whole life requires trust—trust one is unaware of bestowing. The question therefore is not how to construct a life that doesn't require trust but how to make a circle of relationships, indeed a society, that fosters a culture of trust.

Trust is built by small, retractable steps. You lend a small sum of money; it's returned with interest in a timely manner. You then lend a larger sum of money; it doesn't return on time, so you revert to a smaller sum, before entrusting a larger sum. Likewise, courtship is the period of time between two people finding mutual attraction, desire, and companionship, and those same people establishing a depth of trust on which to build commitment. Trust is a combination of experience and projection. Experience looks back to examine whether, when tested, these commitments have been honored, and whether, when not honored, a healthy and genuine process of transparency, apology, reconciliation, and resolve to act differently has ensued. Projection looks forward, to assess the likelihood of past performance indicating future outcomes; this is a judgment not just of word but of character—not simply of will but of resilience. An alcoholic may be full of remorse and commitment when sober, but those undertakings may count for nothing when temptation arises; and we are all addicts, in some way.

So Christian faith is not absurd simply by dint of being faith, since faith, in both its senses—cerebral belief and cordial trust—is indispensable to and ineradicable from life. The point is, given that trust is so tender and belief invariably a risk, how to ensure that the object of faith is a worthy one. That is the business of finding a story to live by.

A Story to Live by, and How It Differs from Both Stories

A Story to Live By

I

In this chapter the story to live by becomes two stories—because faith means belief, and faith more fundamentally means trust. So while they are ultimately inextricable from one another, I shall consider belief first and trust second.

It's about the oldest joke in the book. In a pantomime it's called "He's behind you." The point is, the audience can see something the character on stage can't see. The thing is, it never stops being funny. In the classic *Fawlty Towers* version, Basil Fawlty is horrified to find a dead body in his hotel and refuses to admit it, even when the poor man's relatives come looking for him. In the drastic climax, Basil is standing with his back to the coat stand, propping up the dead man's corpse behind him. One of the man's relatives attempts to reach past Basil and claim his hat. "You can't," shouts Basil, realizing that helping the man to his hat will disclose the presence of the dead body.

"But I'm leaving," remonstrates the relative, only inches from the object of his request, "and I need my hat."

Basil summarily replies, "We'll have it sent on," and survives to fight another day.

What we're talking about is irony. Irony is where one party can see something the other party can't see, and the first party can see all the confusion the second party gets into by missing that one single piece of information.

The story of Thomas in John 20:26–29 is a classic piece of irony. The story concludes the original manuscript of John's Gospel for a reason: it is the definitive account of how a person who can't make the leap of faith comes nonetheless to believe. The disciples know that Jesus has risen from the dead; he appeared to them on Easter evening and showed them his hands and side. The readers know that Jesus rose from the dead, because they've read that part of the story. Jesus obviously knows he's risen from the dead. The only one who doesn't know is Thomas. And what a fool he makes of himself. All the disciples tell him the wonders they have seen, but he's having none of it.

The first time I played Jenga, I was in a circle of about thirty people, and the host arranged things as if he was about to do a magic trick. Everyone seemed to know what to do, and pulled out blocks from apparently impossible angles. I had no idea what to do. So I just pulled a block out at random. Everyone laughed at my foolishness. Then the game began again, from the beginning. Again everyone pulled out blocks from impossible places. And again, I assumed I should just do the same. But once again the tower came tumbling down. I felt two inches high. Like Thomas must have felt on that second Sunday night.

It's common today to read the story of Thomas a different way. Thomas had a point. All this resurrection stuff is a bit far-fetched, and Thomas was the plain man just speaking up for common sense and honest doubt. Thomas becomes the hero of the story, not because he believed but because he didn't. Somehow Thomas becomes the modern human being who stands in for all our misgivings about faith. This resurrection malarkey is all very well, says Thomas, but what about the fact that the universe is massive beyond imagining—how could God have singled out just this tiny planet on the edge of beyond? It's all very well, but what about all the suffering in the world? It's all very well, but what about all the other faiths? It's all very well, but what about all the evil done in the name of religion? It's all very well, but where do we actually go when we die? In all these ways we reverse the shape of the story, and Thomas becomes this massive question mark, and it's Jesus and the disciples that look stupid and Thomas is the righteous one, who stands up for all the ambiguity and inconclusivity of modern life. No longer is the joke on Thomas. The joke's on the disciples for being so credulous and unsophisticated and just plain old.

But remember how irony works. In irony, the person who's caught out thinks they're the clever one. They think they can see the vital thing, whereas in fact they're missing the vital thing. In this case, we think we're the clever ones. We assume we're the center of the universe. We take for granted that our judgments about things are the best informed such judgments have ever been, that our doubts are more intelligent than the faith of our ignorant forebears, and that we have the perfect vantage point from which to assess eternal truth.

But pause a minute. We just said we occupy a small planet at the corner of an unimaginably colossal universe. We did not make this planet. We think we're clever because we can trace a largely plausible pattern of evolution. But we didn't start that evolution off, or set its terms or pace. We think suffering is a blot on the curriculum vitae of an almighty creator, as if we have the blueprint for a perfect planet and we could implement it at any time, complete with eternal life and our favorite team winning the league every season. We think there's a bunch of world religions, and we take one look at a few of the others and decide they're obviously all the same, even though the things that really matter about Christianity are things that no other faith upholds. We decry the evil done in the name of religion, quietly turning our gaze away from the evil done in the name of pretty much every profound human tradition and rather idealizing a world in which no one held any conviction dear or sought ever to arrange society around any constructive social vision. We think the fact that we have no sense experience of people who have died must mean those people have ceased in any way to exist, because of course we, who live at most for fourscore years and ten, obviously have privileged access to the ultimate destiny of where beings dwell forever.

Thus the story of Thomas is telling us the exact opposite of the way it's so often read in modernity. The story isn't saying the joke's on the naïve, uneducated, deluded disciples. The joke's on us—we, who think we're so wise, so measured, so sanguine in our skepticism, our reluctance to believe, our shrewd detachment from the enthusiasm of following the risen one. We're the objects of the irony. Great is the mystery of faith.

Yes, we are on the edge of the universe, and yes, God is infinitely different from us, not just in encompassing the universe but in being beyond the universe. Who do we think we are to be skeptical and mistrustful of this God of utter wonder and glory? And behold, here we are, life, human life on this tiny insignificant planet. Why? Because that other and utterly distant God wanted to be in relationship with a creature who could respond, could reciprocate, could return joy, laughter, depth, love. And just seeking relationship was not enough. That God, in the fathomless mystery of love, wanted to become one like us, to be in true and eternal peace with us, to communicate as one of us with us. And when, by the astonishing and perverse allergy of our nature, we hurled this wondrous gift from our presence, even death could not prevent God from finding a way to restore that relationship and disarm our violent rejection.

And the disciples realize all of this on that first Easter evening. But Thomas is having none of it. Maybe in hurt, maybe in crushing disappointment, maybe in grief, he places his own misgivings way out above God's gracious hand of reconciliation. But the grace of God in Christ finds a way into the heart of even the great skeptic himself, and just as in the famous prologue of John's Gospel, so in this great climax, grace and truth are united again.

See what that means for all our doubts. We think suffering is God's great fail, the great letter F in the heavenly exam results. But see how God takes that suffering into the divine life, demonstrating how all suffering will finally be not expunged but like the cross transformed into a dimension of glory. We think other faiths show that everything's relative. But here we see God become one like us, be touched and wounded and handled and manhandled and pierced: Where else is such wondrous love as this? We think faith is discredited by its worst exponents, when there aren't any worse examples than Jesus's first disciples who denied and betrayed the one who was emptied of all but love. Those first disciples gathered that night in the upper room—they knew better than anyone that Jesus came for sinners who desperately needed his redemption, not for saints who knew no wrong. We think we have no knowledge of where we go when we die; but isn't this precisely why Jesus came back to his disciples in flesh and blood, so that as this very story tells us, the church may believe what it hasn't seen on the strength of what it has seen? And on the strength of what we have seen, we trust that God wills not just to join us in our temporary existence but to draw us into the glory of divine eternity—being with the Holy Trinity together forever.

That's the power of this story. We identify with Thomas. His skepticism is fair game. We think the joke's on the disciples. But we're wrong. Layer by layer Jesus's incarnation and resurrection dismantle all our temerity in supposing that we have the vantage point from which to cast our critical gaze on the paltry action of God. Jesus doesn't humiliate us by exposing our faulty logic and fragile self-importance. He just says, "Look for yourself: death couldn't hold me; neither can your misgivings. Don't dig yourself into the grave of doubt; come out into the joyful light of faith. Do not doubt, but believe."

One modern novelist said, "If you're a believer you'll fight a believer over a shade of difference. If you're a doubter, you doubt only with yourself." Come to the party, Thomas. You'll love it. We've been waiting for you.

II

And so to trust. Ballet is a form of performance dance whose roots are in fourteenth-century Italy. Over the centuries it has become globally recognized and has formed the foundations of many other kinds of dance. It became shaped by French terminology and technique after Catherine de' Medici became queen of France in 1547. The heart of ballet and the center of every dancer's training lies in the five positions in which it is standard to place one's feet on the floor. First position means pointing the feet flat, touching and turned out; second position is the same, with the feet twelve inches apart; in third position the feet are placed adjacent but in opposite directions with the toe of each touching the arch of the other; fourth position is the same, with one foot twelve inches in front of the other; and fifth position, which is the really difficult one, is similar to third position, but with the two feet entirely overlapping one another. If you can do all five positions, you're well on the way to being trained in ballet. The point, of course, is not to know what the positions are but to reproduce them as second nature.

When you first come into contact with Christianity, it can feel a lot like ballet. Not because its practitioners are lithe, talented, and disciplined, or because the result is melodious and beautiful, but because there's a lot of technical jargon, much of it in a foreign language; because people seem to be passionate about it and have never got time or vocabulary to explain why; and because it hits you somewhere so deep and so visceral that quite quickly it starts to shape the way you think, and move, and live.

When you read the absorbing roll call of people of faith in Hebrews chapter 11, it's like being inducted into a hall of fame—a catalogue of the great ballet dancers since 1400. It makes faith exotic, because it involves conquering kingdoms, shutting the mouths of lions, quenching raging fire, escaping the edge of the sword, being stoned to death, and being sawn in two. But it can give the misleading impression that faith is for superheroes. In fact, the opposite is the case. Like a ballet teacher, I want to walk through the five steps of faith, to explore what it means to join what we could call God's dance.

First position is, there's a reality that's deeper, truer, and more permanent than this one. Before about three hundred years ago, this was a largely uncontroversial assumption. So much of life was unexplained, everyone took for granted that it was controlled by unseen forces. But in recent centuries the chain of cause and effect has linked so much of the known universe that it's become tempting to think it can gobble up everything. When we use the phrase "people of faith," this sense of a beyond is pretty much the only thing all such people can agree on. Of course, a lot of people don't share this conviction. It's pretty much impossible to prove or disprove. But even ardent atheists in practice often operate out of an aspiration to see beyond appearances, take life further than face value, and live in the light of eternity rather than simply the realm of the five senses. This is the appeal of profound music, love, beauty, poetry: it reaches something beyond mere life. When it's considered an end in itself, it tends these days to take the name "spiritual but not religious."

Second position is, that deeper reality is a personal being who has a single overarching purpose—to be in relationship with us. This is a large step from the first one, and quickly dismantles the rather fanciful idea that people of faith all fundamentally believe the same thing. For Christians, first position doesn't count for much: true faith begins here. Here lies the reason for creation, the sense of a story with advances and setbacks, and a possible ending, when that relationship is completed, celebrated, and enjoyed forever. Here also, more poignantly, emerges a context for love. After all, you can't love a deeper reality; you can only love one with whom it's possible for you to be in relationship. This is a vision you can shape your life around.

Third position goes a step further again. That personal being, who constitutes that deeper reality and has that single purpose, is fundamentally shaped to be with us in human form in Jesus of Nazareth, a first-century Jew who dwelt among us, showed forth his glory, died as an outcast, and rose again. This may seem to many a breathtaking leap. Interestingly the Gospels, which you'd think would have an interest in taking us gently through first and second position and breaking the news when we were in the right mood to hear it, actually skip first and second position and come right in here. The first words of Mark's Gospel are "The beginning of the good news of Jesus Christ, the Son of God." No messing around there. The resurrection isn't an optional epilogue to the Gospels: the Gospels are accounts, written for those who know about and trust in the resurrection, of who this person was and how he came to be crucified. The resurrection is the central moment when our past is redeemed and our future made eternal.

Fourth position maintains that in Jesus we can see the foundation of a new community with God, with one another and with the new creation. The resurrection and the sending of the Holy Spirit are a declaration of God's faith in the world, because if we were worthless, God wouldn't have given us this opportunity. This means God really intended the church—as an experiment in hope that people could embody and share the resurrected life of freedom, justice, peace, and joy—but God also set forth the kingdom, surprising and redeeming the church by letting glory also spring up elsewhere.

And fifth position is that there's a place in this story that only you can fill, and it is waiting for you to step into it. All these previous steps remain perfectly valid in their own right, but they only take effect for you if you're open to this fifth step. Think about the litany of the faithful in Hebrews chapter 11. The writer gathers this cloud of witnesses in order to say, here are those who took up the mantle, stepped into their destiny, and entered the story, with remarkable results. There would have been a story without them—God would still have found a way—but how glorious to be one of those who answered the call and fulfilled the purpose of your creation.

Each of us is different and, like ballet dancers with their own respective stomach muscles, legs, ankles, and feet, each of us is challenged by a different one of these five positions. I don't think there are many people who move logically through the five positions like a deductive problem solver. Instead, we wonder what our life is for and want it to make a difference, so we go straight in at number five and perhaps work our way back from there. Or we're captivated by the person of Jesus and move back and forth from position three. Or maybe we believe from experience and conviction that humans are social animals, and thus that there needs to be something more or less like the church—and we start working out the rest from position four. And over the course of our lives, which position we're most drawn to, and which we find a stumbling block, may change. When people lament that fewer people go to church in the West than fifty years ago, what they're seeing is that in our generation people seem to find fourth position more problematic than they used to; those people are not necessarily much differently aligned in relation to the other four positions. Perhaps a more general trend is that increasing numbers of people want to keep the first and fifth positions while bypassing the middle three.

The truth is, none of the five positions make a whole lot of sense on their own. How can you want your life to make a difference if you don't have any notion of the story of which you think you are a part? What's the point in believing there's a reality deeper than this one if it makes no difference to anything else you think or do? The phrase "blind faith" is often used as a criticism, but it could be a description for holding tightly to one of these five positions while losing contact with the others. By contrast, the term "simple faith" is usually used as a compliment, but it could be a way of saying that you really connect with one of these positions and you're happy to let the other four coalesce around you.

The amazing thing about the constellation of the faithful in Hebrews 11 is that even they didn't uphold all five positions. They all predated Jesus, so they didn't have number three or, arguably, number four. But they still went ahead and shut the mouths of lions, quenched raging fire, escaped the edge of the sword, were stoned to death, and sawn in two. And that shows us what really matters about faith. Faith is fundamentally trust in God's faith in and faithfulness to us. There's a truth deeper than our being, a love truer than our knowing, a life beyond our comprehending, a community more significant than our experiencing, a purpose more wondrous than our discovering.

Hardly anyone has perfect posture when it comes to all five positions. You'd doubt whether it was genuine if they did. But that's not the point. Faith isn't about adhering to certain doctrines, any more than ballet's about keeping balanced and still. We weren't made to be sure and right and certain: we were made to dance—to dance with God. And God doesn't want us to wait like a wallflower until we're confident of all five positions. God says, "Bring what you've got onto the dance floor—and I'll do the rest." Faith isn't, in the end, about taking a great leap into the darkness. It's about allowing yourself to be drawn into a dance.

How This Story Differs from the Rival Story and the Old, Old Story

The rival story presents many reasons not to believe and not to trust. However, it doesn't sufficiently acknowledge that we can't live without a significant degree of both belief and trust. The story to live by presents an account of Christian faith that highlights which aspects of belief are largely part of being human, and where specific claims of Christianity need to be identified, assessed, and either rejected (if a better account comes along) or accepted, albeit provisionally, at least initially. The same is true of trust: the story to live by offers an account of trust that perceives trust in God as an extension of the trust inherent in human life, and focuses on Jesus as the trustworthy face of God who remains the same yesterday, today, and forever.

Yet the story to live by does not deny the force of the rival story's skepticism. The rival story is not an arrogant account that aspires to an independent existence, which never has to place its trust in anyone or anything. The story to live by regards the rival story as a narrative based on fear, or at least suspicion—a sentiment understandable if life experience has dealt debilitating blows to a person's capacity or inclination to trust. So the story to live by doesn't impose an alternative story but rather gently points out the impossibility of living without a story—without belief or trust—and encourages incremental development of trust from small beginnings. The only abrasive element in the story to live by is its confidence that its story is in no degree less plausible than the other stories widely available.

A significant difference between the story to live by and the standard account is that the latter assumes a number of social conventions and assumptions that together render Christianity, if not true, then plausible, credible, and respectable. Among these bulwarks are the preponderance of believers among the general population, the degree to which the church exerts influence corporately, the degree to which publicly recognized and esteemed individuals confess Christian faith and make it the subject of their public reasoning, and the extent to which Christian imagery is familiar and public life revolves around Christian traditions and festivals. Take this superstructure away, and the standard account could feel naked, and short of the public validation it tends to take for granted. The story to live by intentionally seeks to dwell outside this superstructure and makes a virtue of doing so by thereby identifying itself more explicitly with the contexts in which the Bible was written—the New Testament by the small and sometimes persecuted early church, the Old largely by exiles in Babylon, five hundred miles from home.

The story to live by accepts many of the challenges to the standard account. Simply repeating salutary promises found in the Bible does not dissipate the fightings within and fears without that constitute the struggle for faith. The story to live by accepts that much of belief and trust is maintained in the minor key of lament: many questions, reproaches, and griefs remain unanswered. One story that epitomizes the ethos of the story to live by is that of Jesus and the disciples at the end of John 6

(vv. 66–69). A number of Jesus's followers start to drift away, finding his path hard to tread. Jesus turns to the Twelve and asks them, "Do you also wish to go away?" Peter answers, "Lord, to whom can we go? You have the words of eternal life. We have come to believe and know that you are the Holy One of God." In these words lie both belief and trust, but also a sadness born of recognition that this is not an easy path; neither is it one that settles every question. Nonetheless, the disciple says, rather like Martin Luther, "Here I stand: I can do no other."

In the end, however, trust is not something one can demand or prescribe. Trust comes as a response to the one who proves trustworthy. You can't just say, "To whom else can we turn?" You actually have to turn. Not once, but repeatedly: when confused, or tempted otherwise. The only inducement is not logic, argument, or rhetoric—but joy: the joy seen most evidently in the life of another person who has already turned, and now turns to you, stretching out a hand that you may join the dance.

A FAITH TO LIVE BY

I trust in perfect relationship, utter with, true essence, forever,
so distinct that we say Trinity, so together that we say God.

I trust that this Trinity willed to enjoy us as a companion,
and so initiated existence, flung forth the universe, fostered the world,
and drew us out of evolving life, so as to come among us
    in Jesus Christ.
In Jesus, born of Mary, fully human, fully divine,
we behold God with us, forever now,
guiding us to be with God, ourselves, one another, and all creation.
In his death we see God's pledge to be with us whatever happens;
in his resurrection we behold nothing can separate us from God;
in his ascension we discover God's will finally to draw us
into eternal essence, utter with, forever.

I trust in the Holy Spirit, active since the dawn of time,
at work in every living being from when its life begins.
The Spirit dismantles every barrier to our being with one another,
making us present to Christ and Christ present to us.
The Spirit dwells in the covenant between God and Moses,
and gives the church everything it needs.
The Spirit prepares every heart to be with God

and cultivates the kingdom in believer,
those of other faiths, and unbeliever alike.

I trust in the one whom Jesus called Father,
who sends Jesus and the Holy Spirit,
who through them shares our prayers,
and is in communion with us
through baptism, Eucharist, Scripture,
and encounter with the rejected and isolated.
Together the Trinity heals our past through forgiveness
and bestows our future in everlasting relationship,
that all creation be finally fulfilled in God's glory. Amen.

STUDY GUIDE

THIS GUIDE IS SET OUT as an eleven-week course; it would work equally well for solo reflection. The weeks correspond to the chapters of the book; the final week focuses on the faith to live by but is also a capstone session. The emphasis, as with the book, is not just on belief but on trust—not just finding a faith but on that being a faith to live by. Each week has two kinds of prompts: "tell about," which invites participants to share experiences in the past, and "wonderings," which invite participants to share the fruits of their imagination or their speculation about the future. Some wonderings are appropriate for every session:

- I wonder which part of the chapter was most troubling for you.
- I wonder which part was the most inspiring for you.
- I wonder what the heart of this issue is for you.
- I wonder which part of the story to live by you think you could live by.
- I wonder whether this chapter leaves you feeling angry, disillusioned, humble, hopeful, or joyful.

If the prompts for each week don't prove helpful, it may be best just to stick to the same five each time. Note that the prompts aren't questions. They don't have a right or wrong answer. They are genuine invitations for participants to share experience and imagination. Some of them may lead participants into deep personal territory. It's perfectly normal and acceptable for people not to choose to share: the session may be equally valuable for things sparked in the group but not shared there.

Week One

Tell about a time when it felt like the universe had no heart.
Tell about when it felt like God was a delusion.
Tell about when it felt like it all made sense.
I wonder if every form of knowledge is a story.
I wonder whether there is a story you live by without having proof it's true.
I wonder whether truth is personal.

Week Two

Tell about something terrible that happened to someone else, and whether it was mischance, muddle, malice, or martyrdom.
Tell about something sad that happened to you, and whether it was mischance, muddle, malice, or martyrdom.
Tell about what the difference between a God of *for* and a God of *with* means to you.
I wonder whether there was an actual, historical Fall.
I wonder if sin and evil are completely different from limitation and weakness, or on a continuum.
I wonder what difference it would make if God were with us in our suffering.

Week Three

Tell about what you find most infuriating about the Bible.
Tell about what you find most important about the Bible.
Tell about what most makes you doubt the truthfulness of the Bible.

I wonder if you feel the stories in the Bible describe people like you.
I wonder what you would like the Bible to say that it doesn't.
I wonder what the notion of improvisation means to you.

Week Four

Tell about a time you were told to shut up when you wish you'd spoken up.
Tell about something that was radical that you were persuaded to treat as tame.
Tell about a time when you felt the church backed the wrong side of an argument.
I wonder whether your sense of justice is formed by or countered by your understanding of Christianity.
I wonder how much you feel Christianity has been hijacked by people with their own agenda.
I wonder what it feels like to discover that the rival story is often Christianity in disguise.

Week Five

Tell about an issue on which you've changed your mind in the last ten or twenty years.
Tell about a person close to you who takes a view on an issue you find hard to respect.
Tell about something that seemed unusual or strange but is now true of your own family.
I wonder whether there are some things that the church today legitimately sees differently from how the church in the first century saw them.
I wonder whether the ideal is not everyone being the same but everyone appreciating difference.
I wonder whether there are some differences one can never appreciate.

Week Six

Tell about something terrible the church did.

Tell about a time you felt the church had no credibility at all.

Tell about something really good that you've seen used for really bad purposes.

I wonder if it's possible for a really wonderful person to do really terrible things.

I wonder if it's possible to love the church even though you know many of its faults.

I wonder what change you'd make to the church to make it better.

Week Seven

Tell about a conflict you've had and what it was really about.

Tell about a quarrel that seemed like it was about religion but turned out to be about a lot else as well.

Tell about a time you've made peace, or helped another person do so.

I wonder whether it's true to say all of life is reconciliation, or avoiding reconciliation.

I wonder whether Christianity is fundamentally a method of making peace.

I wonder whether war is ever inevitable.

Week Eight

Tell about a person you know of another faith and what you've learned from them.

Tell about something you admire about another faith.

Tell about something that makes you nervous about another faith.

I wonder whether there's a thing called religion that Christianity is one version of.

I wonder whether Christianity has been turned into a mechanism for overcoming death.

I wonder whether your faith more closely resembles a contract or a covenant.

Week Nine

Tell about a scientific fact that seems to be irreconcilable with Christianity.

Tell about what the climate crisis means to you.

Tell about a time you've felt life was a struggle for meaning and significance in the face of mechanistic determinism.

I wonder whether love and trust are in the end more than biochemical functions.

I wonder whether science and faith are competing over the same territory, or different territory.

I wonder whether Christianity helps or hinders the response to the climate emergency.

Week Ten

Tell about a person you thought you trusted who turned out not to be trustworthy.

Tell about learning something like ballet, where you gradually built one dimension on top of another.

Tell about a time you trusted but didn't believe, or believed but didn't trust.

I wonder whether you're fundamentally looking for belief or for trust.

I wonder which you're closer to finding.

I wonder what it would mean for you to join the dance.

Week Eleven

Tell about the part of a story to live by you like the best.
Tell about the part that's the most important.
I wonder what you think is missing from the story to live by.
Tell about the part of this course/book you've liked the best.
I wonder what you think has been missing from this course/book.
I wonder how your life will be different now.

31901067968257